TWAYNE'S WORLD AUTHORS SERIES

A Survey of the World's Literature

FRANCE

Maxwell A. Smith, Guerry Professor of French, Emeritus
The University of Chattanooga
Former Visiting Professor in Modern Languages
The Florida State University

EDITOR

Valery Larbaud

TWAS 597

Valery Larbaud

VALERY LARBAUD

By JOHN L. BROWN

The Catholic University of America

TWAYNE PUBLISHERS
A DIVISION OF G. K. HALL & CO., BOSTON

Copyright © 1981 by G. K. Hall & Co.

Published in 1981 by Twayne Publishers,
A Division of G. K. Hall & Co.
All Rights Reserved

Printed on permanent/durable acid-free paper and bound
in the United States of America

First Printing

Library of Congress Cataloging in Publication Data

Brown, John Lackey, 1914–
Valery Larbaud.

(Twayne's world authors series ; TWAS 597 : France)
Bibliography: p. 205–11
Includes index.
1. Larbaud, Valéry, 1881–1957. 2. Authors, French–
20th century—Biography.
PQ2623.A65Z673   848'.91209 [B]   80–19174
ISBN 0–8057–6439–9

To the Memory of

Justin O'Brien

Contents

About the Author

In his varied career John L. Brown has been a European editor for Houghton-Mifflin Co., a Paris Correspondent for the New York *Times*, Sunday edition, and a Cultural attaché for American Embassies in Paris, Brussels, Rome, and Mexico City. He is currently a professor of Comparative Literature, Graduate School, at Catholic University in Washington, D.C. Professor Brown has written some ten books, among them, *Panorama de la littérature contemporaine aux EE-UU.* (Gallimard, Paris) which was awarded Le Grand Prix de la Critique and translated into German, Spanish, Portuguese, etc.

Preface

Valery Larbaud's distinctive and firmly established position in the French literature of this century has been recognized from the time of the First World War and before by critics and by that minority of discriminating readers to whom he always very consciously addressed himself. There exists, however, no overall treatment of his work, designed for the general cultivated public, either in French or in English. Many specialized articles, of course, as well as a number of doctoral dissertations have appeared both here and abroad, but they are of primary interest to the student. Moreover, with the exception of *A. O. Barnabooth, His Diary*, translated by Gilbert Canaan (London: Dent, 1924), *Poems of a Multimillionaire*, translated by William Jay Smith (New York: Bonacio and Saul, 1955), and the essay on Saint Jerome, "Le Patron des traducteurs" from *Sous l'invocation de Saint Jérôme*, translated by William Arrowsmith (*Arion*, NS, vol. 2, no. 3, pp. 314–57), Larbaud's most important works are not available in English.

The present volume attempts to fill an evident need. It provides a detailed chronology, since much of Larbaud's writing, as we shall observe, was derived from his own personal experiences—his travels, his friends, his sentimental adventures, his literary discoveries. The text itself deals with the complete range of his production—from his youthful poetry through his final essays—a body of work which, as he himself insisted, did not lend itself to formal classification. From the beginning of his career, he had embarked upon a long and innovative quest for " 'l'oeuvre totale,' which would go beyond conventional genre distinctions, which would 'get it all in.' " In a very contemporary fashion, he aspired to compose simultaneously the text and the antitext, to advance in several directions at once, to throw the light from a number of angles. And, of course, the very fluidity of his art may prove disconcerting to critics and readers who are bent on categorizing, on affixing labels, on putting things in their place once and for all.

As background, we have introduced this study with a "psychological profile" of the writer in order to explore the origins of the themes which absorb him throughout his lifetime and which have a direct connection with his own early childhood and adolescence as the only son of a masterful, widowed, and wealthy mother, the incarnation of all those bourgeois virtues that he early came to detest. Subsequent chapters describe and analyze his activity as a poet, as a writer of fiction (which, considering its considerable autobiographical content, constantly verges on "semifiction"), as a critic, essayist, and translator. The conclusion attempts an assessment of his importance, not only in his own country, but also within a large, international context as a "cosmopolitan man of letters," as "the European representative of French literature," as a humanist profoundly imbued with the tradition of the past, yet prophetically attuned to trends and techniques of the future. In the iridescent, ever-mobile, literary universe which he created, it is not only the formal shape of the texts which is being continually transformed. Their "meaning," too, is difficult to pin down neatly, for they are as multi-layered, as "divers et ondoyants," as the personality of their author. They share the ambiguity of much significant contemporary writing and are "about" a number of things at once. One thing, however, is quite evident. For the attentive reader they procure something of the pleasure that Larbaud certainly felt in composing them, the pleasure that comes from the *dégustation* of a fine wine, when it is savored slowly and (to use one of the author's favorite words) with *volupté*.

Many persons have contributed directly or indirectly to the composition of this essay, but I wish to thank particularly Melle Monique Küntz, Director of the Municipal Library of Vichy, which houses the extraordinarily rich Fonds Valery Larbaud. In the course of the past years, this High Priestess of Larbaud studies, admirably seconded by her staff, has opened to me the treasures of the collection, which includes Larbaud's personal library, some forty-five volumes of manuscripts, and thousands of letters, and has guided me in my use of them. Always encouraged by her interest and good counsel, it was a privilege to have been able to write much of this text seated at Larbaud's own desk, surrounded by his books, his pictures, his lead soldiers, and various images of his tutelary hippopotamus, and under the agreeable impression, not of "doing research," but of engaging in a wide-ranging conversation with the creator of Barnabooth himself.

JOHN L. BROWN

The Catholic University of America

Acknowledgments

I am grateful to Editions Gallimard for permission to quote or paraphrase brief passages from Valery Larbaud's works and to the Fonds Valery Larbaud of the Municipal Library in Vichy to quote or paraphrase manuscript material in its collections. All translations into English are my own.

Chronology

1881   August 29. Birth of Valery Nicolas Larbaud in Vichy. Only son of Nicolas Larbaud, owner of the "Source Saint-Yorre," and of Isabelle Bureaux des Etivaux. The father, free-thinker and Provençal; the mother, Protestant and *Berri-chonne*, the daughter of a Republican politician forced into exile by Napoléon III.

1889   Death of Nicolas Larbaud, leaving one of the most considerable fortunes in Vichy. The son is brought up by his mother and maiden aunt, spoiled, protected, and tyrannized.

1891   Larbaud sent to the Catholic *collège* of Sainte-Barbe-des-Champs, near Paris. The three happy years spent in this cosmopolitan school left a lasting impression.

1895   Transferred to the Lycée Henri IV in Paris.

1896   Publishes (at his mother's expense) a small *plaquette* of verse, *Les Portiques*. Transferred to Lycée Banville, in Moulins.

1898   Long trip to Spain with his mother. Passes first part of his "bac." As a reward, under the chaperonage of the family's business advisor, he is permitted to take a long European tour, including Russia and Turkey.

1899   On his eighteenth birthday, longing to cut the apron strings, he demands his "émancipation légale." His mother refuses. Enters the Lycée Louis-le-Grand. Discovers Whitman. Is expelled for insubordination at the end of the term.

1900   Publishes (at his own expense) *Les Archontes ou la liberté religieuse*.

1901   Publishes a translation of "The Rime of the Ancient Mariner." Travels with Marcel Ray to Berlin, where he works on an essay on Whitman.

1902   Continues preparation at the Sorbonne for a *licence* in English and German. On his twenty-first birthday, demands full control of his inheritance. His mother, claiming he is incompetent, refuses. Bitter disputes between mother and son during this period, which Larbaud called "l'année infernale."

1903 Trip to Italy with "Isabelle," his mistress of the moment, an adventure almost literally transcribed in the *nouvelle*, "Mon plus secret conseil."

1904 Lives in Toulouse, writing and studying.

1905 Travels in North Africa to visit distributors of the mineral water from the Source Saint-Yorre. Trip to Scandinavia and to Spain, with his new mistress ("Inga" of "Amants, heureux amants...").

1906 In Montpellier, preparing his *licence*.

1907 Passes his *licence* in English.

1908 Publishes (anonymously) *Poèmes par un riche amateur*. Excused from military service for reasons of health.

1909 Living in Warwickshire and working on a series of impressions of the region, published posthumously as *Le Coeur de l'Angleterre*.

1910 Return to Paris. *La Nouvelle Revue Française* publishes *Fermina Márquez*. Friendship with Gide and especially with the poet, Léon-Paul Fargue. Received into the Catholic Church on December 24.

1911 Friendship with Claudel, Francis Jammes, Alexis Léger (Saint-John Perse). Trip to England, where he settles down in Chelsea, to be used as the setting of the *nouvelle* "Beauté, mon beau souci."

1912 In Florence, doing research on Walter Savage Landor's residence there.

1913 Publication of *A. O. Barnabooth: Ses Oeuvres complètes*.

1914 Contributes a series of weekly "Letters from Paris" written directly in English, to the *New English Weekly* of London. Volunteers for military service. Refused for reasons of health.

1915 Volunteer medical orderly in the military hospital of Vichy.

1916 In Spain. Settles down in Alicante, where he remains for the next four years, working principally on his translations of Samuel Butler.

1920 Return to Paris. Meets James Joyce in Sylvia Beach's book shop, Shakespeare and Co.

Chronology

1921 A year marked by absorption in the work of Joyce. Publishes the *nouvelle* "Amants, heureux amants..." in *La Nouvelle Revue Française*. It is dedicated to Joyce. Gives a lecture on Joyce in Adrienne Monnier's bookshop.

1922 In Genoa, encounters Mme Maria-Angela Nebbia, who will be his lifelong companion. Begins to contribute literary chronicles (written directly in Spanish) to *La Nación* of Buenos Aires.

1923 Publication of *Amants, heureux amants...*, a collection of three *nouvelles*: "Beauté, mon beau souci," "Mon plus secret conseil," and the title story.

1924 Member of editorial committee of Princess Caetani's review, *Commerce*, during the entire life of the publication, 1924–1932.

1925 Publishes *Ce Vice impuni, la lecture. Domaine anglais.* Spends summer and early autumn in Italy.

1926 Trip to Portugal.

1927 Publication of essays, *Jaune Bleu Blanc.*

1929 Publication of the French translation of *Ulysses*, "entirely revised by Valery Larbaud." Spends several months in Rome.

1930 Death of Mme Larbaud.

1931– Travels in Italy with Mme Nebbia. Continues to work
1933 principally on his translations and on critical articles.

1934 Travels in England.

1935 Visits his friend Marcel Ray in Albania. On his return to Paris in August, he suffers a crippling stroke.

1936 Larbaud will remain an invalid until his death, unable to walk or to speak coherently.

1941 Publication of *Ce Vice impuni, la lecture. Domaine français.*

1946 Publication of *Sous l'Invocation de Saint Jérôme.*

1950 Gallimard begins the publication of the complete works of Valery Larbaud.

1952 Receives the Prix national des lettres.

1953 Named *commandeur* of the *Légion d'honneur.*

1957 Dies in Vichy, on February 2. Chosen to figure among the ten contemporary writers representing French literature at the Brussels International Exposition of 1958.

Abbreviations

Pl.

Valery Larbaud. *Oeuvres*. Coll. Bibliothèque de la Pléiade, ed. G. Jean-Aubry and Robert Mallet. Paris: Gallimard, 1957.

FVL

Fonds Valery Larbaud in the Municipal Library of Vichy.

Cahiers

Cahiers des amis de Valery Larbaud. Vichy: Municipal Library of Vichy.

St. J.

Valery Larbaud. *Sous l'invocation de Saint Jérôme*. Paris: Gallimard, 1946.

N.R.F.

Nouvelle Revue Française.

Hommage

Special number of the *Nouvelle Revue Française*, *Hommage à Valery Larbaud*, September 1, 1957, 5e année, no. 57.

Aubry

G. Jean-Aubry. *Valery Larbaud, Sa Vie et son oeuvre. La Jeunesse (1881–1920)*. Monaco: Editions du Rocher, 1949.

Colloque, '72

Colloque Valery Larbaud tenu à Vichy du 17 au 20 juillet, 1972. Discours, Textes consacrés à Valery Larbaud, Discussions. Paris: A. G. Nizet, 1975.

Journal

Valery Larbaud. *Journal 1912–1935*. Préface et notes de Robert Mallet. Paris: Gallimard, 1955.

D.A.

Valery Larbaud. *Ce Vice impuni la lecture. Domaine anglais*, nouv. éd. augm. Paris: Gallimard, 1936.

D.F.

Valery Larbaud. *Ce Vice impuni, la lecture. Domaine français*. Paris: Gallimard, 1941.

Delvaille

Bernard Delvaille. *Essai sur Valery Larbaud*. Coll. Poétes d'aujourd'hui. Paris: Seghers, 1963.

CHAPTER 1

Notes for a Psychological Profile

I *"Divers et ondoyant"*

CERTAIN formative influences of Larbaud's childhood and early manhood persist throughout his work: his family, their social situation in Vichy, his life as the only son of a widowed mother, his nostalgia for childhood, his conversion to Catholicism. These influences create a cluster of key polarities among which constantly fluctuate, "divers et ondoyant," the personality of Larbaud and the themes of his work: mobility and immobility; affirmation and negation; fervor and derision; departure and return (often stated in more complex and all-embracing terms as "conversion and procession"); lyricism and irony; cosmopolitanism and provincialism ("a citizen of the world and of Valbois"); solitude and companionship; "work" and pleasure; attachment and detachment. In other words, a personality (like most human personalities once the surface is scratched) full of contradictions, of discordant elements, always changing while somehow always remaining the same.

II *The Redoubtable Matriarch*

The room in the Municipal Library of Vichy, housing Larbaud's books, manuscripts, memorabilia, is dominated by a life-size portrait of Mme Veuve Larbaud, monumental in black silk, lace, and leg-of-mutton sleeves. Just as the portrait dominates the room, so the matriarch dominated the life of her only child, until the moment of her death at the age of eighty-eight. Mme Larbaud, née Melle Isabelle Bureau des Etiveaux, was the daughter of an ardently Republican Huguenot lawyer from the town of Gannat, near Vichy. A friend of Gambetta and of Eugène Sue, he was exiled by Napoléon III because of his political opinions.

19

(The family passed several years in near poverty in Geneva, a period evoked in Larbaud's story "Rachel Frutiger.") On his return to France, after the downfall of Napoléon III, Maître des Etiveaux handled the legal affairs of Valery-Nicholas Larbaud, the owner of the Source Saint-Yorre in Vichy. This rich (for Vichy and for the period) bachelor of well over fifty, thinking it was high time to provide an heir for his fortune, asked in marriage the hand of Melle Jane, the younger daughter of his lawyer. She refused. But Isabelle was willing to take him on. After all, she was going on forty and the suitor had money. (Money. Money was the dominating passion of Larbaud's milieu.) Valery-Nicolas accepted the switch. After all, no "romance" was involved, the marriage was a purely "business" arrangement. He was far from an ardent suitor, seldom called on his mature fiancée. She was just as pleased. "If I saw him too often, I don't think I'd have the courage to marry him." Valery-Nicolas conveniently died eight years after the birth of his only son—the business of providing an heir had been carried out expeditiously—leaving behind him a rich, satisfied, and masterful widow. Speaking with one of her friends concerning the dear departed, she is alleged to have declared: "Eleven years of slavery, my dear. Well, I've certainly earned my money. And there's really nothing better than being a widow."[1]

Those who knew her very often disliked her but nevertheless considered her "a remarkable woman," vital, energetic, and shrewd, with a peasant vitality and shrewdness. She evidently disdained any trace of softness, tenderness, sentimentality. "Love" apparently was unimportant for her and she never gave much of it to anyone, whether to her husband, to her friends, or to her only son. This "Protestant" coldness would explain Larbaud's enduring quest for warmth, friendship, close human relations, love. But at the same time he always maintained a reserve in dealing with others and many of his friends remarked on his secretiveness, his unwillingness—dictated by timidity?—to enter into any close and enduring human relationship. Characteristically, like Felice Francia in "Amants, heureux amants," he wanted "love" and "liberty" at the same time, and when he saw that they were incompatible, was usually inclined to sacrifice "love."

After the death of her husband, Mme Larbaud invited her sister Jane to live with her, in her three impressive residences—the house on the avenue Victoria in Vichy, the villa in Saint-Yorre and the country property of Valbois near Saint-Pourçain-sur-Sioule. (Larbaud, as we can see from his letters, had a genuine affection for his aunt, who often "took his side" in his differences with his mother, which increased in frequency and intensity as he grew older.) But in his early years, even as a sickly, over-weight, only child, spoiled by his mother and aunt, cut off from contact with children of his own age, dividing his time between Vichy and the country estate of Valbois, he seemed to be happy enough. He writes in his *Journal* (February 24, 1935): "When I think about it my life up to the age of 12, when I left Sainte-Barbe was quite happy, in spite of bad health." He apparently was an obedient, submissive child, if we are to judge from his many letters to his mother, written in the neatest of handwriting and expressing the most filial of sentiments. In a typical letter (from Ste. Barbe) he speaks of his affection for "ma chère maman": "I think of you every day. . . . I need to be close to you . . . ," and continues: "I have inherited my father's ideas. I work harder when I think of him and remember that he was never lazy. I willingly forego many pleasures, since I remember how serious my father's life was, and what firm, solid ideas he upheld."

This acceptance of the "idées bien assises" of the father-figure naturally did not last; Larbaud had violently rejected them by the time he had reached his stormy adolescence. And, according to his own testimony, it was very stormy adolescence indeed, after the three happy, tranquil years spent in the Catholic college of Ste. Barbe near Paris. As he notes (*Journal*, p. 360) he became "less and less happy" and was "really wretched from 17 until I came of age." Reading, in 1912, a life of Leopardi, the poet's sufferings at Recanati at the hands of the *mamma cattiva* (*Journal*, p. 29, entry in English)

made me think about my own bad times. Really I wonder how I could suffer so much without losing anything of my optimistic view of life. . . . Mother, and generally my educators (but, of course, Mother especially) thought they had crushed my will; but they had only

postponed the realization of my wishes. I am quite sure now that
M. was quite unconscious of all that, thought me very happy; did not
imagine for one minute that I could suffer deeply when my will and
ends had been defeated by her (perhaps thought I repented or was
corrected and amended by the defeat)....

Larbaud had been an excellent student at Ste. Barbe. But he
hated the *lycées*—Henri IV, the lycée Banville in Moulins, Louis-
le-Grand—in which Mme Larbaud had subsequently placed him
against his will, and his academic record while studying in them
was a very spotty one. In a sense, he was avenging himself on
his mother, who felt that *her* son should necessarily be "un
brillant sujet," pass competitive exams with flying colors and
prepare himself for a "serious" career as a lawyer, politician, or
diplomat.

Larbaud began to hate school more and more—it was the
beginning of his enduring prejudice against academicians, especially professors of literature—and, determined not to "make
good" according to his mother's standards, devoted himself more
and more to the study and writing of poetry. Already Vichy
middle-class society was feeling sorry for Mme Veuve Larbaud
—her only son was turning out badly. Its prejudice against him
was still another reason for Larbaud to detest the narrow,
materialistic, provincial world of his family. In later life, he
avoided as much as possible any contact with his parents' milieu.
He understood that his family's friends were "always under the
influence of the judgments that my family passed on me when
I was in my twenties." But this harshness and lack of understanding encouraged the young man in his revolt and "finally gave
me the courage to throw off the family yoke completely."

The showdown with Mme Larbaud was not slow in coming.
On August 21, 1902, his twenty-first birthday, he writes a formal
letter to his mother, announcing that he has now reached his
majority. He proceeded to demand an account of her management of his inheritance and insisted that thenceforth he be given
full control over his own fortune. Mme Larbaud replied that he
was impractical and spendthrift and would quickly delapidate
his patrimony if she permitted him to get his hands on it. A
compromise was finally arranged by which he was granted an

annual allowance. This sum enabled Larbaud to live comfortably but not lavishly and, contrary to the legend that grew up around him, particularly after the publication of *Barnabooth*, he was very far from being a millionaire. When he did come into his capital, he was quite incapable of managing it, spent unwisely, and died very nearly a poor man. Old friends of the family, of course, said, "we told you so!" In a sense, he had remained his mother's "little boy" up until the end. He refers to that tumultuous summer of 1902 in an entry (in English) in his *Journal* (August 1912, pp. 29–31):

I wonder who of us suffered most; I from fourteen to twenty-one or she during the année infernale; I recall that I too suffered during that year. (I wish I could express the feeling of that young man, when, everything being ready, he said good-bye to his Mother at Charing Cross St. and thought he had seen her face for the last time and when precisely during that last hour she had been as sweet and good and frank with him as when he was a little boy) at that moment he thought: I cannot do otherwise; and had given anything to be able to do otherwise.

Master at last of a small income of his own, Larbaud went off to a sanatorium near Dresden to soothe his shattered nerves and, inspired by his newly won independence, began to write what eventually would be an early version of the *Journal de Barnabooth*, which he then thought of calling, "Journal of a Free Man."

But in spite of all the bitter fights, the umbilical cord was never cut. The son's dependence on mother persisted and the love-hate relationship with it. In a letter to Léon-Paul Fargue[2] written when Larbaud was going through one of his recurring bouts of depression ("the Mood," as he called them, in English), he confides to his friend: "I cling to my Mother, I feel the need to obey her, to be a little boy again." Larbaud's strong but often loathing dependence on mother may explain (as we shall see) a good deal about his attitudes toward women and his incapacity, until relatively late in life, to enter into a relationship more enduring than a casual liaison. And he entered into this relationship with an older woman, already a grandmother, who during the last twenty years of his life, after his paralytic attack, acted as a mother surrogate and cared for him as a child.

His mother never ceased to try to direct his life. She wanted him to obtain a doctorate, as a symbol of prestige. After all, if he couldn't be a lawyer or a politician, if he even refused to take over the profitable business of his father and sell Vichy water, at least an advanced degree would serve in some small measure to save the reputation of the family. If Larbaud dropped his project of doing a thesis on W. S. Landor, it was perhaps because he refused to bow to her will. She was also intent on marrying him off and had picked several suitable fiancées for him, including an heiress from Lyon. There, too, he balked. She disapproved of many of his "literary" friends, particularly of Léon-Paul Fargue, who, she suspected, was "corrupting the morals" of her son.[3] She was very much in evidence whenever they visited in Vichy. Jacques Rivière, in a letter to Alain Fournier,[4] speaks of lunching with Larbaud and "his extraordinary Mother" and observes that her son's attitude toward her was a curious mixture of submissive obedience and of hostility. Larbaud often suffered because of his mother's unpredictable behavior in the presence of his guests. He described a luncheon to which Francis Jammes was invited:[5] "M. as usual talked too much and gave misrepresentations of me (as usual still) and of L. P. Fargue, which is rather awkward, as Jammes, I think, did not see through what M. said and took it whole, in spite of all the grossness and evident exaggeration and misconstruction. . . ."

As the years went by, Mme Larbaud increasingly declined to receive his friends; it was "too tiring," she didn't want to invite anyone. Nor would she willingly lend him her car to go to see friends in the vicinity of Vichy. Her parsimoniousness persisted and, when Larbaud was short of money, it was of no use to look to his mother for financial assistance.[6] But he never broke off entirely; on the contrary he increasingly felt that it was his duty to spend part of the year near her and often went to great lengths to find some excuse, some justification, for any protracted absence. In 1926, when he wanted to spend six months in Portugal, he went through the elaborate comedy of obtaining a letter from the Cultural Services of the Foreign Office (where he had powerful friends, including Alexis St. Léger-Léger and Paul Morand) that he could show to his mother. It invited him officially to lecture in Lisbon on French literature. Mme Larbaud could have no objections to that; it might even please her to think that her "failure" of a son was obtaining official recognition. Larbaud gave one *conférence*. But, in order to make a better impression, in his usual letter to "ma chère maman," he reports that he gave four of them.[7]

Allen (1927), an homage to the Bourbonnais, is dedicated to her; for him, evidently, the native province is also a kind of mother-symbol, the maternal domain from which one departs but to which one inevitably returns. He feared, hated, loved her, and even after she was gone he is still aware of her presence in the house on the avenue Victoria and at Valbois. He never dared tell her of his long liaison with Mme Nebbia. It was only after her death that he felt free to bring his companion and her little granddaughter to live with him openly in Vichy.

III *Vichy and the Wide World Beyond*

His mother incarnated for him all that narrow, selfish "republican" middle-class society of the Vichy that he hated. In a letter to Marcel Ray,[8] he describes Vichy as "a hell of cold mud and of stinking water." His constant denunciations of provincial life reflect his attitude toward his mother. She was always trying to get him to "settle down" in Vichy, just as he was always bent on getting away from it—to Paris, to London, to Italy, to Spain. In his *Journal* (1931, p. 257), he asserts that "it is only outside of France that I can feel in a state of euphoria." Some of Larbaud's "cosmopolitanism" and his passion for foreign travel may be ascribed to his ultimately unsuccessful efforts to put as much distance as possible between his mother and himself. His dislike of Vichy and all it stood for is apparent throughout his work, and it is a cruel irony that he was condemned to spend the last twenty years of his life there, confined to a wheelchair and deprived of the power of coherent speech. In *Allen* (*Pl.*, p. 758), he writes that he had long hated the town, had associated it with "exile," "reclusion," "the grave." He adds (*Pl.*, p. 743): "They threw me out . . . they condemned me without a hearing; the way I lived, my literary activities, the opinions I

expressed were all suspect, odious." Elsewhere (*Pl.*, p. 744), he
speaks of "the ignorance, the vanity, the stupidity, the mean-
ness" of small towns.

But he never desired to cut himself off completely from provincial life and, as he advanced in years, he became increasingly
attached to his native Bourbonnais ("the sweetest part of
France") and spent more and more time in Valbois. He remarks
(in English) in a *Journal* entry of 1912 (pp. 27–28):

I like breakfasts in Mother's room between 7:30 and 8:00. (What
there is to be seen from the windows, etc.) It is curious how long it
has taken me to find something interesting or indeed worthy to be
loved about here, where I have been so long as a prisoner, and in
these places which I had come to hate so much.

IV   "*Cosas Chicas . . .*"

As a young man, in his frequent sojourns abroad, he rarely
lived in the capitals; London was an exception, but even in
England he often preferred villages in the countryside. In Italy
he chose to live for several months in Potenza; in Spain he spent
a winter in Valencia and several years in the rather dull, if
restful, small city of Alicante. Such choices may be linked to his
preference for the small scale, for minuscule countries like San
Marino or Lichtenstein, "toy-soldier" countries which have the
charm of diversity without pretensions of "national pride." Larbaud was constantly oscillating between the desire for a small,
protected space, a "Motherland," in which he would feel "safe"
and "enclosed," but which could also be confining, imprisoning
and the longing for an open "cosmopolitan" space, in which he
could feel free and unencumbered, but in which he would be
menaced with solitude and insecurity.[9] And he needed to move
freely from one state to another, from "open" to "enclosed" space,
from solitude to companionship. He seemed instinctively to fear
and reject anything static and immobile, even in the realm of
human relations. His sensibility and his art are in constant
flux, moving almost compulsively between opposite poles. His
own psychology and that of many of his most representative
characters reflect this apparent "instability," which is, in fact, a
recognition of the shifting nature of reality.

In his own relations with others, Larbaud observed the same strategy. He was fond of company, but only up to a certain point. He could remain for weeks in his out-of-the-way refuge on the rue du Cardinal Lemoine without seeing anyone. He disliked Paris literary and social life and remained aloof from it. He was always disappearing out of reach to some obscure provincial city where no one else ever went. Even with his closest friends he could be very secretive. His relations with the *N.R.F.* group, for example, were never "intimate."[10]

V *Money, Money*

From his mother he also inherited a preoccupation with money. Although he felt that money was a burden, although, like Barnabooth, he could sometimes feel the twinges of social conscience, he was well aware that the liberty he so cherished, "the integrity of the Sérénissime Republic," as he put it, depended on economic security. He was never a spendthrift playboy—if he lost his fortune after his mother's death it was rather for lack of experience in financial management—and was considered by his closest friends as rather tight and always reluctant to "pick up the check." (During the period when he shared a nightlife with Fargue, it was Fargue who usually paid.) He surprised his friends at the *N.R.F.* (who considered him a millionaire!) by insisting on being remunerated for his articles. He feared that he might be published, not on the basis of his literary talent, but simply as a rich dilettante who would be willing to pay to see his name in print. He steadfastly refused to play the role of "financial backer" of any of the small *avant-garde* reviews (like Jean Royère's *La Phalange,* of which he was a collaborator) and shared with Barnabooth the fear of being exploited because he was rich.

VI *"A Warm Treasure . . ."*

His dependence on his mother, both economic and emotional, influenced his attitude toward women in general. His early adventures, with "Isabelle" of "Mon plus secret conseil," with "Inga" the dancer of "Amants, heureux amants," with "Gladys," and with his other English housekeeper-mistresses would seem to

have satisfied not only his sensuality but also his desire to out-
rage his mother and to declare his independence from her. But,
as in that poem of Matthew Prior he loved to cite: "No matter
what beauties I saw in my way/ They were but my visits but
thou art my home . . . ," these numerous liaisons never developed
into permanent relationships, and the wandering prodigal always ended by going home. The young Larbaud, in spite of his
disdain for tourists, was certainly a "touriste du coeur." He
changed mistresses as he changed hotels. Of course, this attitude was a common one among upper-middle-class young men
of "the belle époque"—which was "belle" only for a privileged
bourgeois minority. Larbaud usually regarded women as objects
of pleasure, objects of which, however, like a child with a toy,
he usually soon grew tired. He could excuse himself, naturally,
as his contemporaries did, that he was not dealing with "women
of his own milieu. . . ." There are hints, in fact, throughout the
Journal that Larbaud preferred to make love to "women of the
lower classes," whom he could regard as his inferiors and toward
whom he had "no obligations." In 1911 he writes to L. P. Fargue[11]
from Chelsea: ". . . I really enjoy living (intimately) with a
woman who is without education and without culture. I'm crazy
about her. As for her daughter, I'll speak to you about that later,
it's really a charming adventure."

One senses in him that divorce between sexual love on one
hand and tenderness and respect on the other, which was so
evident in Gide, and which, to a certain degree, characterized
much of nineteenth-century European bourgeois society. In spite
of his physical appearance—he was always inclined to obesity—
he conceived of himself as something of a "lady-killer," and is
always on the look-out for an easy conquest. . . . ("a petite
dactylo, wonderfully Frenchy, all powder and legs . . ."). He
was not in search of "the great love of his life" (he was too
"classic," too discreetly disabused for that) but rather of "girls
who liked being kissed and who fill your arms with a warm
treasure of soft, white and well shaped limbs, breasts, etc."
(*Journal*, p. 149). "In fact," he muses in the *Journal* (July 1919,
p. 173), "I am too lucky with . . . that. One at home who literally
dotes on me; two in England who want to make it up with me
and begin anew, and then the thought of Ella! . . ."

The "one at home" is a young French servant girl whom Larbaud had engaged on his return from Spain in 1919 and who was performing as usual the dual functions of housemaid and mistress. He comments on how well she takes care of the apartment and of him and how pleasant it is to slip quietly into bed after a good dinner. No need to go out. His attitude toward her is a mixture of almost cynical egotism and of a certain condescending tenderness because of the devotion she has for him. He feels that in hiring her he is "giving her a holiday" (*Journal*, p. 173), but has no intention of letting her stay around very long. To prolong the liaison would "do her a great deal of harm. . . . Better leave her next month, after having made her as happy as possible." He had a special treat for Yvonne on their last night together, before he left for Valbois to rejoin mother. After their supper, "when it was quite dark," they left his apartment separately—no one should see him going out with his maid!—and he took her for a taxi-ride in the Bois de Boulogne. "It was a great thing for her who had never been in a taxi, poor thing! She said that she had never been so happy in her life" (*Journal*, p. 191). Her gratitude briefly touches him and he caresses the idea of "letting her continue in her present situation," only immediately to reject it: ". . . but this is not possible and, in fact, I am already tired of her." We never hear of Yvonne again.

Such an incident reveals how curiously insensitive Larbaud could be, in spite of his elaborate courtesy and the genuine kindness of which he was capable, to the feelings of women whom he considered his social inferiors. But he himself, as is clear from the tone of his journal entry, was apparently quite unaware that he may have treated Yvonne shabbily. He thought that he had done very well by her. And probably most of his contemporaries of his own class would have agreed with him. His relations with women also appear to have been motivated by a certain desire to conduct "psychological experiments" which might be used in his own work. Certainly the three "nouvelles" of *Amants, heureux amants* are derived directly from his liaisons with "Gladys," "Inga," and "Isabelle." Like Henry James, Larbaud's powers of narrative invention, as well as his range of observation, were limited and in his work he was forced to

utilize his own rather narrow experience as intensively as possible. He was also attracted, in a rather voyeuristic fashion (one
thinks of the opening scene of "Amants . . ."), by sexual devia-
tions, particularly Lesbianism. It surfaces in *Enfantines* ("Rose
Lourdin"), in the *Biographie d'A. O. Barnabooth* (in the personage of Anastasie, Duchess of Waydberg, who, dressed as a
man, accompanies Barnabooth on orgies in lower-class bordels),
and in the *Journal d'A. O. Barnabooth*, where the American
Amazon, Gertie Hansker, also dresses as a man during her more
questionable adventures. Larbaud's attitude toward sexual de-
viations is one of curiosity rather than of condemnation. He
was certainly aware of the unorthodox sexual preferences of
several of his friends, like Gide and Ghéon, in the *N.R.F.* group.
His insistence on the homosexual character of Shakespeare's sonnets, in the introduction that he wrote to a French translation
of them,[12] profoundly shocked and outraged the translator, but
Larbaud refused to modify his text. He also devoted an important
essay to the young homosexual English poet, Digby Dolben.

VII   *The Cult of Childhood*

Much has been written about Larbaud's cult of childhood
and of the childlike qualities that persisted in his own personality—his love, for example, for lead soldiers and little flags. No
Frenchman of his generation has written more perceptively of
childhood than Larbaud in *Enfantines*. He admired the child's
freshness, his instinctive knowledge of the world of nature and
of persons, a knowledge which most adults lose as they "grow
up." He retained throughout his life a nostalgia for the purity
and untarnished integrity of childhood. He often preferred, it
would seem, the company of children to that of his contemporaries. The *Journals*, during the years in Spain, abound in references to teen-age girls. And one of the great charms of English
life for him was the fresh, blonde beauty and unconscious grace
of those "kiddies" (as he coyly refers to them), whom he liked
to observe at play in public parks. In the 1930s Mme Nebbia
brought her little granddaughter, Laeta, to live with them; and
Larbaud's journal entries of this period reveal the joy he felt
in the company of his "adopted" daughter. He took her for

walks in Paris, entered her in his old school (Ste. Barbe), played with her, bought her toys. "Laeta and I walk hand in hand or she hangs on my arm. I feel more in love with her than the tenderest of suitors can be with the loveliest and most virtuous of ladies . . . as far as she is concerned, I am falling into a kind of 'child worship'" (*Journal*, p. 310). Larbaud is never condescending in his attitude toward children; he considers them equals of adults and in some respects superior to them. He regrets the inadequacy, the lack of comprehension of most literary treatments of them. Eugene Field, he points out (in an early review in *La Phalange*), cannot be a great poet of childhood because "he has forgotten his own," has forgotten that the child is a *person*. He finds that Alice Meynell's essays on children also fail in this respect (*Journal*, pp. 308–309).

But although he consistently defends children against adult misinterpretations and exploitation, Larbaud has no illusions about their "innocence." The child can also be cruel, deceitful, vengeful, like Julia, the tenant farmer's daughter in "le Couperet," who finds pleasure in tormenting the defenseless drudge, Justine, the little shepherdess. Claude Roy remarks[13] that Larbaud was well aware that childhood was neither "an animal life" (la vie d'une bête), as Bossuet presents it, nor "the Green Paradise" of Baudelaire, but simply "a marvelous and difficult period in the course of human life."

VIII   *The "Going over to Rome"*

Larbaud's vision of childhood has close ties with his religious sensibility. In "Gwenny-toute-seule," the narrator, informed that the little girl to whom he had been so attached—"my dream of a little Gwenny, who would always be close to me and to whom I would devote my life" (*Pl.*, p. 527)—is leaving the seaside resort where they had met to go back home, muses to himself that life seems inevitably to separate him from the children he has loved. More and more, he is weary of the stupidity and the uselessness of everything but innocence. "And that is why I turn towards You, gentle and invisible. . . . It was You that I was searching for among the children . . ." (*Pl.*, p. 531). For Larbaud, the Kingdom of Heaven is a kingdom of little children, whose values are completely opposed to the purely civic and pragmatic virtues of the agnostic Protestantism in which he had been brought up.

Reflecting on the life of Anne de Guigné (1911–1922), who died in the odor of sanctity, Larbaud remarks that this child-saint, "for whom the notions of country and property have no meaning," refutes the error of those blasphemous people, whether devout or unbelieving, for whom "Religion, Country, Property all go together" (*Journal*, p. 355).

Several factors contributed to Larbaud's very discreet, almost clandestine "going over to Rome," which took place formally on December 24, 1910, when he was baptized a Catholic in the Church of Notre-Dame-de-Grâce in Paris. The first was his early contacts with Catholicism at the Collège de Ste.-Barbe, where he was very happy, where he came to love the beauty of the Mass and the poetry of the liturgy. Larbaud's faith was aesthetic and emotional rather than intellectual and rational. In "Mon plus secret conseil," Lucas Letheil cites "Nunc et in hora mortis nostrae" as the phrase which made him understand for the first time what marvelous effects could be obtained with words (*Pl.*, 713). In *Allen* (*Pl.*, p. 727) he claims that "all good literature is a *Carmen Deo Nostro* and that everthing that is good in literature is finally "action de grâces, alleluia." It "rises," it is meant to rise, "like a song of praise." He was seriously interested in the Church as early as 1907, when he remarks in one of his letters to Marcel Ray (July 9, 1907) that "he had missed Mass this morning." Two of the contemporary poets he most admired, Francis Jammes and Paul Claudel, were both Catholics, both leading figures in an important "Catholic Revival" taking place in French literary circles at the beginning of the century. Linked with the rejection of Naturalism and of the cult of the nineteenth-century positivistic science, with what Larbaud (*Journal*, p. 89) calls the "platitude of free thought," it was drawing many young French intellectuals and writers into the Church. Claudel, perhaps the outstanding figure among them, gives an illuminating account of the reasons for his own conversion in *Contacts et Circonstances*.

But Larbaud's "going over to Rome" follows a different route from that of the majority of his contemporaries. They converted through an intellectual conviction of the need for absolute truth to combat the moral relativity about them, for order and discipline and the submission of the individual to divine authority. Larbaud, on the contrary, was drawn to Rome for emotional and sentimental reasons, highly subjective and occasionally of dubious orthodoxy. For him, paradoxically, Catholicism meant "freedom," freedom, at least, from the constraints of his mother's cold Protestant ethic. It meant "love," it meant poetry and color and the expansion of the personality.

A group of English Catholic writers, identified with the circle around the poet Alice Meynell and her husband, played an important role in Larbaud's conversion. He was introduced to the Meynells in 1907 by Daniel O'Connor, an Anglo-Irish publisher and minor writer, who suggested to him some of the traits of Maxime Claremoris in *Barnabooth*. Through the Meynells, Larbaud presumably became acquainted, or at least better acquainted, with an entire group of English Catholic poets, including Francis Thompson, the author of "The Hound of Heaven"; Digby Dolben; Coventry Patmore (translated by Claudel, with an introduction by Larbaud). Larbaud included essays on the three of them in *Domaine anglais*. He proclaims his admiration for Patmore (*D.A.*, p. 73), for him "a greater writer than Tennyson," who is "the poet of a certain period and a certain class," the poet of "a vague Deism and Darwinism," with an "incredible belief in Progress." In Patmore Larbaud found "joy, moral teaching, and lyric emotion," and also "a certain serene yet militant virtue, and that Peace which goes beyond—that is to say, which is more intelligent than—all understanding."

Larbaud, as usual, when dealing with authors he admires, finds parallels between Patmore and himself. When he speaks of Patmore's "going over to Rome," he might easily have been speaking of his own; the truth or falsehood of Catholicism, he insists, cannot be demonstrated mathematically, and it is very rare that a conversion is brought about by reason alone, but rather through the growth of a profound feeling, of a constantly recurring spiritual state, which little by little floods the entire soul (*D.A.*, p. 58). But the element in Patmore's poetry which appealed most directly to Larbaud was its insistence on love as the source of all life. Throughout his work—and especially in "The Angel in the House," and "The Unknown Eros"—Patmore represents human love, especially conjugal love (he was married three times), as the image and the forerunner of Divine Love. The love of creatures leads to the love of God. Larbaud eagerly accepted this consoling doctrine, which apparently made it possible for the "good Catholic" to enjoy the best of two worlds. Claudel, who worshiped a God of terror and majesty, sternly condemns (in a letter October 11, 1911)[14] a passage in the essay on Patmore in which Larbaud asserts that Patmore had been led into the Church by his "meditations on the sexual instinct."

Claudel would have none of this. "I regret your use of the term 'sexual instinct' (I know you employ it in the English sense). Sex is not all of love; love is a sentiment far more general and profound. Sex, of course, accompanies love and unfortunately sometimes stifles it." Although Larbaud admired Claudel, and Claudel tried on various occasions to come to know him better, the two never became close friends. Claudel, with his intransigence, his fierce dogmatism, and his intellectual and spiritual violence, had little in common with the fluidity, tact, discretion, and indulgence of Larbaud. Larbaud, in fact (like so many of his contemporaries, Gide among them), seemed terrified of Claudel and avoided any confrontation with him, much as he might have avoided a session with an Inquisitor. Certainly, the rigidly orthodox Claudel would have found Larbaud's easygoing, highly personal religiosity, from which the idea of sin, especially original sin and eternal damnation, seemed singularly absent, highly suspect, and probably heretical.[15]

If "love" for Larbaud is the first and fundamental Catholic virtue, humility is a close second. He regards it as a primary intellectual virtue as well, as one of the most necessary qualities of the good translator, even of the true artist. He approached God with the love, the humility, the intellectual innocence of a child; he approached Him with *pleasure* rather than with "fear and trembling" or mystical exaltation. He felt an instinctive sympathy for the popular religiosity of Italy, with its legions of saints, its taste for celebration and even for superstition, its vestiges of Mediterranean paganism. Larbaud's faith, if you like, was more Catholic than Christian, more Roman than Catholic. He has no objections to those Spanish "kiddies" of his, whose "chief occupations are flirting and the recitation of the Rosary"

(*Journal*, p. 71). In true Latin fashion, he finds that the Church is an agreeable setting for occasional amorous dalliance (*Journal*, p. 67): ". . . My best memories of her will be two or three visits to the Church of the Carmel, at the close of the day: I sat in a pew, and she knelt close to me." He practices popular forms of piety such as the wearing of scapulars—"I bought . . . a scapular, which is not the one I wanted, but which I intend to wear for a month" (*Journal*, p. 107). Later (*Journal*, p. 139) he speaks of buying a scapular which he promises "to wear until the day after my birthday" as well as a batch of holy medals "for the woman-hood at home." Putouarey, in *Barnabooth*, incarnates something of this aspect of Larbaud's religiosity: he "haunts the street at night, looking for girls and saying his rosary that he may not find them" (*Pl.*, p. 226). He prides himself that the walls of the bed-room of his adulterous young Neapolitan mistress are abundantly adorned with pious images. And finally, of course, although he is full of doubts about belief, his doubts incline Putouarey "in favor of the myth," which he finds more aesthetically satisfying than the "sterile" doctrines of agnosticism and free thought.

More and more, as he grew older, Larbaud's religiosity reached out beyond personal feelings to embrace larger conceptions. Increasingly, the Church assumed importance as a cultural insti-tution, as the successor of the Roman Empire, and as an expres-sion of his ideal of European unity. Rome also represented that universality and that continuity which he considered the funda-mental attributes of any authentic civilization.

His Catholic faith seems to have liberated him from much of the metaphysical anguish which had marked his youth and is so evident in *Barnabooth*. It enabled him to feel a part of an insti-tution, "Mother Church," which sheltered him and to whose security he could unquestionably confide himself. But spiritual security and religious certitude are not always a spur to artistic creativity. After his conversion, he was less and less tempted to descend into the darkness of "the Underground of the Abso-lute" (the term is Dominique Fernández's)[16] and to contemplate the existential abyss. He might have been (we clearly feel it in *Barnabooth*) one of those "flamboyant, tormented spirits who change the tranquil evolution of intellectual progress" (Fer-nández). But he drew back from the brink and chose happiness, the happiness of a quiet life with his devoted companion and her little granddaughter. Already in his *Journal* for 1917 (p. 95) he sums up his impressions of the year and notes with satisfaction that he is "learning how to live, and that without many shocks or much worry." And later he was apparently glad to cut himself off more and more from the literary world of Paris, to say farewell to any Faustian ambitions he may have nourished as a young man, and to enjoy an existence of spiritual and material security, in the company of his devoted friend, between the little flat on the rue Cardinal Lemoine and his "Free State" of Valbois, which he had lovingly restored (*Journal*, p. 328). Was this an abdication, as Fernández hints, when he notes that "the 'cultured' writer, of whom Larbaud is an outstanding example, can become great only when that rich culture of which he is so proud is called into doubt and becomes an object of dissatisfaction and of scandal?" Or is it the choice of a wise man, who in maturity prefers such quiet happiness (which, in Larbaud's case, never excluded a certain undercurrent of melancholy) to the "sound and fury" of Romantic exaltation?

We often regard Larbaud as an "aesthetic" Catholic, drawn to the Church principally because he considered it an integral part of the Mediterranean culture he so admired; as a Catholic without deep or fanatical convictions, indulgent, unconcerned about ultimate theological truth, something of a "fideist" à la Montaigne. But the ambiguities of Larbaud's personality also reveal themselves here. One has the impression that with the passage of the years, he became firmer, more intransigent in his adherence to Catholic doctrine. His "cosmopolitanism" evidently did not extend to religion—"The Occident and Rome, for me, are sufficient."[17] He firmly rejected the Romantic substitution of Art for Religion, the confusion of "Art"-"Dieu."

IX   *Political and Social Attitudes*

The "going over to Rome," as we have said, not only marked a decisive reaction against his mother's agnostic Protestantism, but also against her bourgeois values. Before his conversion, Larbaud had flirted with the left, less through natural inclination than as a declaration of revolt. In 1902,[18] he wrote to his mother that he was no longer publishing anything in *La Plume* (a small *avant-garde* review with which he was then collaborating) because it was "too reactionary" in claiming that art should be aristocratic, "a point of view," he protested rather unconvincingly, "which I do not share at all." But soon after, with characteristic mobility, he was flirting with the far-right *Action Française* and proclaiming himself "a reactionary." But whether from the point of view of the left or of the right, he continued to castigate the anticlerical republicanism of his family, and to denounce those "pseudo-democratic principles of Republican rottenness, of the manure heap of Gambetta-ism."[19] He was temperamentally sympathetic to those right-wing, traditionalist, Catholic, and sometimes Royalist elements that opposed Republicanism more and more vociferously during the early decades of the century and which briefly triumphed during the régime of Marshall Pétain.

"Le Couperet" (one of the best of the *Enfantines*), contains a devastating portrayal of this anticlerical, materialistic, "republican" milieu in which Larbaud grew up. The "notables" of the region are gathered in the country property of M. Raby, a prosperous manufacturer of agricultural tools, married to the daughter of a collaborator of M. Gambetta, to celebrate the birthday of Milou, the only child. At table, over the champagne, "the Senator" addresses Milou as "the little heir" and his mother replies, "Yes, a little heir who will really inherit something." His father adds, "Ah, yes, with the fortune I'll leave him, my son can really set his sights very high—a minister, an ambassador, the governor of one of our colonies." The senator turns toward Milou: "Young man, what do you want to be when you grow up—a General or President of the Republic?" And Milou, full of hatred for these people who were deciding his future, determined to shock them all as much as he could, replied (*Pl.*, p. 426): "I want to be a servant."

Larbaud, with his devotion to tradition, was naturally conservative and would apparently accept any political regime which did not threaten his own personal liberty. But he was, nevertheless, profoundly shocked by the First World War, which he intuitively realized would mean the end of the traditional European humanism that he loved. He tried to "do his duty," however, and volunteered for military service at the beginning of hostilities in 1914[20] but was rejected for reasons of health. For a time, in 1914 and 1915, he worked with the wounded in a Vichy hospital, but he grew more and more depressed and restless. Through friends at the Quai d'Orsay, he was able to obtain a diplomatic passport and a vague journalistic assignment and set off to neutral Spain in January 1916 to "sit out" the duration in Alicante. During these four years, he corresponded relatively little with his friends, and when he did, the subject of the war is rarely mentioned. Nor does he speak of it in his *Journals*, except on rare occasions, although it is clear that like his most perceptive contemporaries, Valéry among them, he was deeply concerned by what he recognized as a catastrophe of unprecedented dimensions. In his longish account of his impressions of Spain, he notes, in English (*Journal*, p. 123): "Now, in the year 1918, Spain is the largest of the few European countries which survive intact in the midst of the almost general eclipse of European civilization. She continues, without a break, European history, from which the greater nations have momentarily disappeared." Although he keeps working industriously all during the war years, he publishes nothing in the French or British magazines to which he normally contributed; most of them had suspended publication anyway at the outbreak of the war; "I don't like to contribute to any of the reviews that are published in other than neutral countries"; he notes, in English, "The mere idea of writing, as it were, under the watchful eye of the police, makes me sick" (*Journal*, p. 141). He cites with approval Baroja's condemnation of the war: "This is the best judgement I have read about that shameful period, 1914–1918" (*Journal*, p. 167).

Back in France in 1920, he could speak out, as he did in an article[21] in which he attacks the evils of war: "The very essence of the military life is passive obedience, by which the individual will is destroyed." His dislike of a narrow nationalism, his commitment to internationalism and European unity becomes increasingly evident during the 1920s, in essays such as "Paris de France"[22] and in *Allen* (1927). In "Paris de France," Larbaud insists that the true Parisian "knows the world in its diversity, or at least knows his continent," for Paris is not simply a "national capital," but a capital "far above all local, sentimental, or economic politics," the capital of a kind of International of the spirit" (*Pl.*, p. 783).

This current of generous internationalism circulates unobtrusively throughout that curious, crotchety, "multi-layered," and often tantalizing little book bearing the enigmatic title of *Allen*. It would seem to be a hymn in praise of the beauties of Larbaud's native province, the Bourbonnais, but in reality, like everything he wrote, it is considerably more complicated and ambiguous than it appears to be. A praise of provincialism? Yes. But also a tract (albeit one that political scientists would probably disdainfully dismiss as too "random," inconclusive, and "frivolous") about a united Europe, an ideal international community. In studying the history of the Grand Duchy of the Bourbonnais, Larbaud realized that, as a virtually independent state allied to France, it had played a considerable role in the history of Europe. This leads him once again to a favorite theme: the superiority of a political system organized in small units, like San Marino, or Lichtenstein, or the old Duchy of the Bourbonnais, but held together by "a single, undisputed power," the Empire, Roman or Holy Roman, "ut subditas illi faciat omnes barbaras nationes" (*Pl.*, 757). (We recall that Larbaud wrote an unfinished study on the "De Monarchia" of Dante.) Larbaud recognizes the quixotic quality of such a political ideal, an ideal accessible "only to a tiny minority." And he adds (in English): "So few," then cites *Henry V* (a play in which the Connétable de Bourbon appears): "We few, we happy few, we band of brothers."

But fantastic as this talk about the independence of tiny, individual states within the framework of an all-embracing, universalizing empire may seem to practical, "republican" politicians, Larbaud's poetic fancies have a certain appeal, and more than simply a poetic appeal. A growing number of people are increasingly persuaded that "small is beautiful," and not only beautiful, but humane and efficient as well. How can we achieve this ideal of unity in diversity, retain the virtues of large-scale organization, without submitting to the inevitable tyrannies of excessive centralization and dinosaurlike bigness? Larbaud has often been represented as an egotistic dilettante. But underneath his firm refusal of slogans and political involvement, there remains an unshakeable belief in the liberty and in the autonomy of the individual, which zealots all too willingly sacrifice to the demands of a party or a doctrine. A distrust of abstract ideas and of sweeping political or philosophical generalities was deeply anchored in him.

Already in *Barnabooth* he writes, "What poor things they are, ideas. You have to be very young not to realize right away that they have less reality than the mist rising of an evening, some thousands of years ago." He had an enduring hatred, too, of all the feverish rhetoric of "nationalism" and "patriotism." In Spain, after receiving a questionnaire from a French review concerning "national poets," he blasts (*Journal*, p. 161): "Everything 'national' is silly, archaic." In the midst of all the violent nationalistic activity of the right at the beginning of the 1930s, he could define "being French" very coolly indeed: "In reality, it's simply a question of material interest for most Frenchmen. They 'love France' for the sake of their pensions and their unemployment insurance and because of their fear of the aggressiveness of other national states" (*Journal*, p. 357). Certainly during these tense years his aloofness and detachment were often construed as a sign of "decadence," both by the right and by the left. Larbaud took no part in the fierce debates of that period, during which European intellectuals increasingly felt that they must make a choice, a choice, admittedly, that most of them did not really care to make, between fascism and communism. But there is no doubt that Larbaud's natural conservatism inclined him to prefer the authoritarianism of the right to that of the left.

Like many of his contemporaries, he approved of Mussolini's regime, which he praises enthusiastically on his trip to Italy in 1932; fewer beggars on the streets, better train service, cleaner public toilets (!) (*Journal*, pp. 266–69). And, "as an Italian," he can only "thank the government which made this possible." The amateur of uniforms, of lead soldiers, and of flags experienced a childlike delight in Fascist demonstrations. He was pleased, too, to receive honors from the Italian government (in 1934, he was named Commander of the Order of the Crown of Italy), to contribute to official publications, to lunch with Bottai, a "liberal" Fascist minister, who was also a patron of literature and the arts. Larbaud, more and more enchanted with

Italy ("notre vrai pays," *Journal*, p. 259) and the attention he received there, did not try to look behind the pompous facade. His instinctive attitude politically was one of non-involvement; meeting Edy du Perron (the Dutch translator of Malraux) outside the Sainte-Geneviéve library, shortly after the February riots of 1934, he declared "quite simply" that if there was serious trouble, "I'll simply get out of France and wait until it blows over" (*Journal*, p. 298). It appeared to him to be the only reasonable way to behave.

Such "socially irresponsible" detachment on the part of writers like Gide, Valéry, and Larbaud early provoked blasts from critics of the left; in May 1926, in the review *L'Esprit*, Georges Friedman published an article attacking those intellectuals whom he labeled "les Disponibles" (the "unattached," the "uncommitted") and accused them of "avoiding reality, of having no political or moral convictions, of being unconcerned about the catastrophes of their time."[23] (Barnabooth, we recall, wishes to "close his window on all the cries coming up from the street.") Friedmann's portrait of "le jeune disponible" certainly bears a resemblance to the young hedonists of *Amants, heureux amants* and to Larbaud himself.[24] These accusations of Friedmann simply state once again an often-repeated view concerning the complex, long-debated problem of the social responsibility of the artist. Larbaud consistently defended an opposing one. Barnabooth at the end of the *Journal* rejects, as unsuited to his character, the total political and social dedication of Stéphane. And this detachment and this seeming indifference become increasingly evident in Larbaud's own attitudes. His paralytic attack in 1935 enforced a total seclusion. He was not to be confronted with the choices that faced his countrymen in the years immediately before the fall of France and during the German occupation. We can only observe that many of his most distinguished friends (Claudel, Gide, Fargue, and Valéry among them) either refrained from all political militancy or "got out of France and waited until it blew over." There is no indication that Larbaud would have done otherwise, and we can easily imagine him sitting out the Occupation in Lisbon, perfecting his knowledge of Portuguese and feeding the hippopotamus in the zoo. He was of the family of Erasmus and heroism was not his forte.

X *The Primacy of Pleasure*

But, we may well ask, what ideal, what goal, in the absence
of religious ardor, dedication to a cause, great passion, could
give direction to this life? The pursuit of pleasure? The satisfaction of personal desire? Throughout Larbaud's work we
observe the elaboration of what we might call an "ethic of
pleasure." He writes (*Journal*, p. 290): "Maxim: 'Pleasure above
all'; is always fruitful—scandalous and fruitful." Barnabooth, at
the end of his long and tormented "quest of the Absolute," finally
settled for "a peaceful, comfortable, obscure and studious existence" (*Pl.*, p. 277). "I've got 30 years ahead of me. How best
to use them? And I replied without hesitation—to do what I
like, first of all . . . for I know I'll do well only that which I really
like to do." Larbaud did do what he liked to do and nothing
else. His privileged situation as a "rich amateur" liberated him
from any obligation to "write for a living." He translated and
wrote about those authors, and only those, with whom he felt
an affinity, whose company he enjoyed. (It may be that Larbaud
would have written more, and written differently, under the
pressure of economic necessity.) He wrote essentially to please
himself and a small minority of people like himself, whose culture
permitted them to appreciate his art. He never aspired to reach
a "mass audience"; his readers never numbered more than a few
thousand. The postwar "publishing industry" with its "promo-
tion," its obsession with "best-sellers," its intensely, almost exclusively financial orientation, would have been anathema to
him—and very probably would have declined to publish his
works.

His interest in Epicurus (evident from several manuscript
notes) does not surprise us. In his lecture on Butler he establishes
a parallel between Epicurus and the author of *Erewhon*, and
makes it clear that this Epicurean strain in Butler appeals to
him.[25] Larbaud's fictional characters often echo the same devotion
to pleasure that is a constant theme of the *Journals*. The heroes
of *Amants, heureux amants* are all disciples of the cult of "Godersela"—according to Larbaud an Italian expression that translates
as "enjoy yourself"—and devote their days and nights to the
pursuit of pleasure, of the flesh and of the spirit, with an elegant,

unruffled amoralism. As we have often observed, Larbaud always shied away, almost instinctively, from the abstract and the theoretical. He agreed with Butler that life is fundamentally sensual. He had an unlimited capacity for enjoyment, and his pages constantly testify to the pleasure he was capable of finding in the smallest details of the spectacle of daily life: the beauty of a girl in the street, the agreeable taste of his morning chocolate, the contours of a landscape, the shimmer of light on water, the music of silence.

With Larbaud, sensuality goes beyond the senses to become a sensuality of the spirit. In *St. Jérôme* we shall note the infinite pleasure that words, the sound and the color of words, words in all the enchanting complexity of phonetic and semantic change, give to him. In fact, his love of literature and learning, the dominant passion, really, of his life, is a *sensual* rather than a purely intellectual passion. He was never primarily interested in "ideas" ("Ah, pauvres idées . . .") and would certainly have disclaimed any pretensions to being a "thinker." What he writes of his friend Marcel Ray in the review *Vient de paraître* (June 1927) might easily apply to himself: "Essentially, he is somewhat lazy, a lover of refined leisure. And even his studies were really the undertaking of a fundamentally lazy man, but one spurred into activity by curiosity and the desire to know. More than anything else, he wanted to know, to understand, and to love."

XI *The Supreme Pleasure of Work*

But that supreme pleasure, the pleasure of coming to "know, to understand, and to love" is a pleasure which must be earned. The young Barnabooth, in the *Poèmes par un riche amateur* (*Pl.*, p. 71), cries: "Oh, to learn everything, to know everything, to speak all languages." But such a vast culture cannot be acquired passively. Larbaud, Epicurean as he might proclaim himself to be, would be the first to agree with Alain that "man is formed by effort" and that "arts and letters are not candied fruits." Learning, in other words, is not "fun." For this self-declared sybarite, this "riche dilettante," this devotee of pleasure was also a dogged worker, for whom work, finally, was the greatest pleasure of all. Even Felice (how deliberately significant the surname is!)

Francia can declare, after the party is over and the girls have gone, that he is rather happy to be alone and to be able to get down to work again (*Pl.*, p. 645).

Numerous entries in the *Journal* confirm this passion for work. On November 5, 1917, he writes, in English: "What with a change in surroundings, bad health, voluntary solitude and returning 'ganas de trabajar' [desire to work], I live really apart from the world." Later in the same month he writes (*Journal*, pp. 87–89): "After an illness, and after some sentimental experience out of which we emerge free at last . . . one day there comes back the wish to work . . . and at last comes the day when we take up Work [note the capital!] again. Then a great, sweet, innocent silence falls about us. We have found again our 'raison de vivre!' The world cannot, has no right to interfere with us; we do not care for what it does, or thinks, or says. We live in our work and are at peace with ourselves." In December (*Journal*, p. 95) he rejoices that he is "feeling better" (from earliest childhood he was plagued with ill health and a tendency to hypochondria) and that nothing prevents him from working. "I lead a very quiet life, with work always in my thoughts. I live by and in my work." It is work and work alone that conducts him to "This Peaceful District of the Most Serene." For him writing, and specifically what he calls "living," that is, "creative," writing is the most important thing in the world: "It is action, research, worry, delight, all that makes life worth living and book writing a part of life." In comparison, concern with politics (he had been worried about the closing of the frontier between France and Spain) seems a very frivolous business indeed—"To think that I have given a thought to politics!" (*Journal*, p. 95).

This almost religious devotion to work remains a ruling passion up to the very end of his active career. In 1931, in a letter to Princess Caetani (*FVL*), he tells her that his doctor has given him the permission to work "with moderation," adding that, for him, it is difficult to work with moderation. And shortly before his attack in 1935, when Europe was torn with political strife and menaced by the growing threat of another world war, he notes (*Journal*, p. 368) that "it is in times such as these that work seems like a mountain top touched by the light of dawn, the glorious center of our thoughts and of our lives." Although Léon-

Paul Fargue was perhaps Larbaud's closest friend, one whose poetic gifts he deeply admired, he often reproaches him for not working and from preventing others from working: "L. P. Fargue more charming than ever, but a dreadful waster of time" (*Journal*, p. 185). But his fragile health and his own temperament preserved him from being a "workaholic." Periods of intense concentration would be followed by even longer periods of creative loafing. When Martin Roger du Gard (very organized, he) queried Larbaud about his "working methods," he got this reply: "'Live to work.' Yes. Work equals pleasure, it's not 'organized.' A minimum of 'method.' No 'regular hours' except for meal times, for a few social duties which have been reduced to a minimum, and for the hours when libraries are open." And as far as creative work is concerned, one is always "working," even when one is not consciously aware of it.[26]

This devotion to work also testifies to his exalted conception of the writer's art, to his veritable cult of literature. And he loved it, certainly not for the money it would bring him, nor for the sake of literary celebrity during his lifetime. "There's only work and the desire to work as well as possible, and with the resolution not to be concerned in the slightest about what people think of it. . ." (*Journal*, p. 367). And musing on the vanity and pettiness of the Paris literary establishment (of which he never wished to be a part) he is "happy to bury myself in work in order to defend myself from it and to get away from it" (*Journal*, p. 364). Normally so tolerant of human feelings, he is intransigent when professional integrity is at stake. He disdains those writers who start off well and then "soften and run like certain cheeses" the moment they are tempted by money, success, or critical acclaim. "This is inexcusable when a writer doesn't need to earn a living; lamentable when he does" (*Journal*, p. 245). He respects poets like Saint-John Perse, or Claudel, or Valéry, who remain "difficult," who make no concessions; for him, Valéry (*D. F.*, p. 276) is "a great moralist of the intellectual life." He deserves the same title himself. He could claim, with Putouarey (*Pl.*, p. 297), that "I love my vocation and for its sake I have given up the easy life they [his family] mapped out for me."

But such a total devotion to the writer's art and the leisured pursuit of pleasure as well, both depend on individual liberty.

We have seen how the loving tyranny of his mother early incited Larbaud to rebellion and roused him to break away, to be his own man. The opening pages of *Barnabooth* exult in newfound freedom: "At last, I travel as a free man! I have liberated myself from social obligations, escaped from the class in which my birth imprisoned me . . . I shall no longer be confronted with the demon of property and of real estate" (*Pl.*, p. 88). Young Lucas Letheil, fleeing from his demanding and disagreeable mistress, forgets even his ideal, his "beloved Irene," in the "wild jubilation of freedom recovered" (*Pl.*, p. 682). The hero of *Luis Losada* refuses to marry since it would compromise his personal liberty. In his journals, as so often in his fiction, Larbaud constantly speaks of "the defense of the integrity of the Sérenissime Republic," that is to say, of his liberty. But external freedom in itself is of small account unless it is accompanied by spiritual freedom, by intellectual independence, by a detachment from "the world" and an indifference to the values which the "world" seeks to impose. However, such freedom implies its own obligations (*Journal*, p. 248):" . . . First of all, my duty toward the one I love; then my duty toward the memory of my family; my duty toward friends and toward my profession."

In spite of this pressing need of liberty and of solitude, Larbaud, as we know, was far from being an ascetic hermit. He loved life, and the presence of others, and the beauty of the external world. Here again we remark an aspect of that "oscillation" which reveals itself in so many different forms in his life and his work. In spite of an intense devotion to "Art," he always subordinated it to life; and the works of art he admired most were those in which "the blood circulated." Valéry's "Jeune Parque," for example, moved him very deeply because it gave him the impression of literally "sharing the physiological life of a strong, beautiful young woman" (*Journal*, p. 102).

XII *"What Are Books Compared to Friendship?"*

Back in Paris after the long wartime retreat in Alicante, he reflects: "Work: very little. Friendship, almost too much of that, but it is never too much: what is work—such work as I can do— what are books compared to friendship?" (*Journal*, p. 183).

Despite his timidity, his need for solitude, Larbaud possessed to a very high degree the gift of making and keeping friends. The thousands of letters in the archives in Vichy speak of his kindness and concern for others. From childhood onwards, he sought in friendship the warmth and understanding often denied him at home. His devotion to Charles-Louis Philippe is a case in point. And he did everything in his power, as their collected correspondence reveals, to try to obtain for Fargue the recognition he felt he deserved. He was unfailingly generous in helping young and unknown writers like Marcelle Auclair, Emmanuel Lochac, Audiberti among many others. Generous, too, in writing reviews and articles to launch them. In 1911, he published the first article to be devoted to Saint-John Perse, whose genius he had immediately recognized. Friendship was one of the determining motives behind his efforts to introduce outstanding foreign writers in France, writers like Ramón Gómez de la Serna, Joyce, Gianna Manzini. He sincerely admired the work of his friends and with a characteristic humility considered it as more important than his own. Many sought him out for the sake of the help they hoped to receive from one of the most influential arbiters of international literary taste of the time.

Only a few of those he helped remained in touch after illness had removed him from the scene. His friendship was not of the "hail fellow, well met" variety and even casual relations were often difficult for him. As Francis Jourdain has remarked,[27] he was "naturally complicated" and oversensitive, which may explain his break with Léon-Paul Fargue and the termination of his relations with Adrienne Monnier. A letter (of April 1928) written directly in Spanish to the widow of Ricardo Güiraldes, the Argentine writer whom he had known so well, testifies to his exalted conception of friendship. He tells her that one night, overcome with a sense of "absolute and eternal solitude," he felt that his existence was "absurd." Then he remembered some lines of Güiraldes: "Sólo así quiero merecer . . ." and a certain equanimity returned to him. He realized that he still had as companions in this solitude "my mother, my wife, and three or four friends who have departed, to whom I shall be eternally bound. Ricardo was one of these friends . . . My desire to serve them is enough to make my life worthwhile."[28]

XIII *The Majesty of Death*

Larbaud was always "a delicate child." His chronic ill health had a definite impact on the way he lived and the way he worked. He probably had a touch of hypochondria, too, encouraged by a mother who wanted to assure his dependence on her. But sickness fostered his love of solitude and of reading and his precocious acquaintance with mortality and universal transience (*Pl.*, p. 982). In the essay "200 Chambres, 200 Salles de Bain" (*Pl.*, p. 891ff.), he recalls, with a certain pleasure, the many days of illness spent in hotel rooms, especially as a very young child when he was being treated in Paris and his mother had engaged an apartment in the Hôtel du Louvre. He often remained there for days on end without ever leaving his room. There he thought about death, his own death. "Next year, he wouldn't be a burden to anyone and he would be better off. He'd leave all the mean business of living to those who had made him suffer, spied on him, systematically discouraged him. And his father, who was always complaining about him, would speak tenderly of him once he was gone..." (*Pl.*, pp. 905–906).

Larbaud reveals a certain Pascalian acceptance in the face of sickness. In the shadow of mortality, this "limpid" shadow, "you see yourself more clearly. One's spirit, cut off from the world, increases in strength and wisdom.... Perhaps in life, as at the bullfight," he concludes, "the best seats are those in the shade" (*Pl.*, p. 897). At twenty, he was already telling himself that he probably wouldn't survive his mother. But this awareness of death did not unduly depress him. Rather it spurred him on to make the best possible use of the time he had left. The early death of Charles-Louis Philippe, whom he so loved and admired, made a profound impression, intensified his spiritual life, may have hastened his conversion to Catholicism.

His religious faith, of course, gave him courage. But he was also fortified by the conviction that he might overcome mortality, survive, even ever so obscurely, through his art. More modestly, more discreetly than Malraux, he also deeply believed in art as "anti-destiny." This belief explains in part the importance he attaches to cultural continuity and to tradition. Literary tradition represents a long succession of human achievements that have overcome time; within it, even the most modest creators deserve a place. The smallest link is also a part of the great chain. He frequently insists on the idea that "la poésie est une oeuvre collective" (*D.F.*, p. 159). In hailing Antoine de Nervèze, a very obscure precursor of Georges Scudéry, "truly a 'minimus' among the minors," he wryly hopes that when he, "a little known writer too," has become "a completely forgotten one" some scholar may "write my name next to yours" (*D.A.*, p. 28).

Rome, in its historical as well as its religious dimensions, became for him the supreme symbol of such continuity. Each time he returned, the city became more deeply meaningful. Nowhere else did he feel so intensely "both the joy of living and the sense of mortality" (*Pl.*, p. 982). Rome seemed to offer him the dual consolation of eternal life for the spirit and, within the framework of a millenary tradition, survival for the work of art as well.

CHAPTER 2

The Poet

I   The Question of "Poetry" and "Prose"

LARBAUD'S old friend Marcel Ray always insisted that Larbaud was essentially a lyric poet and regretted that he wrote
so little poetry after the publication of *Poèmes par un riche amateur* in 1908.[1] A journal entry for April 14, 1934, recording a
conversation with Emmanuel Lochac, notes that Lochac is constantly reproaching him for having abandoned poetry.[2] Larbaud
pretends that "his best argument" for doing so (after having
pointed out humorously that writers can't earn money with
poetry and that he already owes his publishers some 6,000 francs
in advances) is that the prose he tries to write aspires to be "as
strictly constructed" as poetry.[3] What he has said of the Spanish
novelist, Gabriel Miró, could well be applied to his own work:
"His poems have the form of novels and are written in prose."[4]
Such a position is in accord with the main line of development
of modern poetry from Baudelaire onwards. As Ezra Pound con-
tended, poetry is not simply a question of external form, but
rather of "language charged with the highest possible degree of
meaning." Moreover, Larbaud was temperamentally opposed to
rigid genre distinctions, in fact, to "categories" of every sort. He
consistently prefers the flowing to the fixed.

II   *Juvenilia:* Les Portiques *and* Les Archontes

Most of his poetry was written when he was a very young man,
a good deal of it before 1908, when *Poèmes par un riche amateur*
appeared.[5] He made his debut as a poet at the age of fifteen
with a slim volume of thirty pages, entitled *Les Portiques* and,
with a schoolboy's parading of erudition, subtitled in Greek. It
was printed by a local printer of Cusset, near Vichy, at the ex-

pense of his mother, who evidently wished to demonstrate to disapproving friends that her son, despite his being difficult and having a spotty school record, did, nevertheless, have some talent. The collection consists of some fifteen very derivative, sub-Parnassian *pastiches*, clearly written under the influence of Leconte de Lisle, with echoes of Hugo, Hérédia, and occasionally even of August Barbier. The longest piece. "Les Northman" (*sic!*) attempts an imitation of Nordic heroic poetry: "Cependant qu'un guerrier, debout, la tête haute/ Défiait l'ouragan. ..." Twenty-five copies were printed on vellum. For Larbaud, these poems were probably a thing of the past by the time they had appeared. He had left Parnasse behind him and was now attracted by the Symbolists and especially by Verlaine.

Four years later, in 1900, the local printer was again pressed into service to publish another youthful effort entitled *Les Archontes*. Presented as a "comedy translated from the Greek of L. Hagiosy" (Larbaud was always very proud that he had received the grade of 18/20 on his Greek examination in the orals for the *baccalauréat*), it was, of course, an original work, expressing all Larbaud's youthful disdain for the "Republicanism," the materialism, and the bourgeois complacency of his family's milieu. There are even deliberately "shocking" passages, composed in Latin, designed doubtless to "épater la bourgeosie." One of the Archontes proclaims: "We have well served our Country and Humanity, as well as Progress, in which we all believe." The concluding chorus chants: "We all belong to the religion of the Crucified God. Of course, we don't believe in Him, but we simply can't stand all those imbeciles, those Jews, Moslems, Buddhists, who criticize the plans we have made to further the glory of Free Thought, Progress, and Humanity." One can imagine Mme Larbaud's reaction as she read this abominable text, especially since she realized that it was "her own good money" that had paid for it.

Larbaud subsequently disowned both of these *juvenilia*, which were never reprinted.

III Poémes par un riche amateur *(1908)*

But the poems in his next collection, in spite of their obvious and often deliberate reminiscences (especially of Whitman and of Henry J. M. Levet) reveal that he had found a voice of his own. Notes to the Pléiade edition indicate that they represent the result of an attempt to avoid "self-expression," to create a type of poet not to be wholly identified with himself.[6] In fabricating the mask of "Barnabooth, le riche amateur," Larbaud may have been following the example of Whitman, an inveterate wearer of many different masks, as were Yeats and Pound (one of whose volumes is entitled *Personae*) and especially of the bilingual Portuguese poet, Fernando Pessoa, who created some nineteen different identities or "voices" to express diverse and contradictory attitudes in his verse. Every artist, of course, is a maker of masks. But this process, which involves a questioning of the concept of the "sincerity" and the "authenticity" of the poet, may be particularly characteristic of a self-conscious period such as our own, one which is indeed sometimes in doubt about the very possibility of literary expression at all. Modern literature, a literature of shifting and unstable identities, has posed more and more insistently the problem of the relation of the writer to his writing, the problem of the "I," the problem, too, of a certain "depersonalization." Larbaud's early preoccupation with such questions bears witness to his awareness that a significant reaction was taking place against traditional Romantic literary norms. He insists that in these poems he has no intention of "expressing himself" but rather of creating a personage outside of himself. In a letter of September 1908[7] to Henri Buriot-Darsiles, a young professor in the lycée of Moulins, he writes that their only value is that they reveal the character of M. Barnabooth and that from the purely artistic point of view they have been "botched" ("bâclés"). The implication, of course, is that they have been deliberately "botched" in order better to reflect the character of Barnabooth. And he goes on to state that they are very much influenced by all the authors that Barnabooth presumably may have read, "his compatriot Whitman, among others." Yet we may be justifiably skeptical about such self-proclaimed intentions. The device of presenting Barnabooth as "the author" does not convincingly eliminate the possibility of "personal" expression, since clearly many of Larbaud's own characteristics have been incorporated in his portrait of "the rich amateur."

Poèmes par un riche amateur exists in two separate editions. One, entitled *Poèmes par un riche amateur ou Oeuvres françaises de M. Barnabooth, précédées d'une introduction biographique*, was tricked out in a pink and green cover, purportedly designed to resemble "the labels on American canned goods" (*Pl.*, p. 1208). As an homage to Barnabooth's American citizenship, it was published on the fourth of July. The regular trade edition, with a plain yellow cover, bore the title *Le Livre de M. Barnabooth, prose et vers, précédé d'une vie de Barnabooth par X. M. Tournier de Zambie.*

A certain flippancy, a certain tone of self-mockery runs through the volume. Both Claudel and Gide sometimes deplored this side of Larbaud,[8] although Gide in reading the poems expressed regret that he had not been "plus cynique" in *Les Nourritures terrestres.*[9] But it is precisely this tone, a combination of *persiflage* with "seriousness," of lyricism with cynicism which confers on the work of Larbaud its very personal charm. Clearly, he admired the spirit of "the rich amateur" who couldn't care less about acquiring literary fame or about competing successfully with those "professionals" whom he disdained. Larbaud, too, was writing "pour son déplaisir" and for his own amusement. But his amusement did not exclude all the seriousness of "homo ludens" nor a sincere but discretely concealed sensibility. Barnabooth-Larbaud is often writing very much in earnest and we should not be put off by the surface frivolity of some of the poems and especially of the texts of Tournier de Zambie. Underneath their flippancy, they provide clues about the nature of the very original enterprise upon which Larbaud had embarked.

He had begun to write the preliminary version of the "biography" of Barnabooth as early as the autumn of 1902, in a sanatorium near Dresden, where he was recovering from a bitter emotional conflict with his mother. It consisted of eleven brief sections, recounting, tongue in cheek, details concerning the birth, the nationality, the childhood, education, literary tastes, and so forth of this sympathetic personage, whose name, to French ears, sounded so very exotic. The "biography" also provides background information which enables the reader better to understand allusions in certain of the poems (a number of which were eliminated from the 1913 edition). For example, in

referring to Barnabooth's family holdings in Peru, it clarifies
the opening lines of "Aspiration" (*Pl.*, p. 1178): "My workers
are up to their necks in guano/ In order to make money for me."
It identifies the subject of "I. M. Anastasie Retzuch, Duchesse de
Waydberg" (*Pl.*, p. 1180) as the girl with whom Barnabooth
had fallen in love at the age of fifteen during a trip to Con-
stantinople and also "la vieille Lola," the old Chilean servant of
"Dialogue" (*Pl.*, p. 1182) and of "Voix des servantes" (*Pl.*, p. 52).
Many of Barnabooth's witticisms, such as "I am a genuine cos-
mopolitan patriot" (*Pl.*, p. 1165) could easily be attributed to
Larbaud. They share, moreover, common tastes in art and litera-
ture. They both defend the "amateur" against the professional:
"I'm an amateur and proud of it," asserts "the rich amateur"
(*Pl.*, p. 1167). On discovering Whitman, Barnabooth, like Lar-
baud, was so overwhelmed that he forgot to go to meals (*Pl.*, p.
1170). There are other common literary enthusiasms: for Viélé-
Griffin, Henri de Régnier, Francis Jammes, Henri Bataille,
Claudel, Maeterlinck, and (surprisingly enough!) for James
Whitcomb Riley.

IV Origins of Barnabooth

"Barnabooth" was not created on the spur of the moment. Larbaud had been assembling the elements of this mask for many
years. At the age of nine, he tells us, he had read a novel by
Louis Boussenard, *Le Secret de M. Synthèse*, the story about a
man "so rich that he could buy up the world" (*Pl.*, p. 370).
When, as a *lycéen* in Paris, he was studying Duruy's *Histoire
Romaine*, he (like Barnabooth) was fascinated by the young
emperors of the decadence, who were given the power to rule the
world "before they had acquired the power to rule themselves"
(*Pl.*, p. 1161). In 1896, the French press made much of the case
of Max Lebaudy, the heir of a great sugar-refining fortune, who,
because of the lack of proper medical attention ("mustn't coddle
the rich boy") had died at the age of twenty-three during his
military service (*Pl.*, p. 1150). His fate made Larbaud who,
in Vichy, was considered "a rich boy," all the more conscious
of the disadvantages of wealth, wealth which separates the
possessor from the world about him. This theme recurs through-

out the *Poèmes*, in lines such as those in "L'Eterna Voluttà" (*Pl.*, pp. 48–50): "Hélas, je suis trop riche...." as well as in many passages of the *Journal intime* as well (*Pl.*, p. 85): "I abased myself in order to persuade the poor to accept me as an equal" and is presented as "the moral" of the short story, "Le Pauvre chemisier."

These various elements crystallized during a trip to London in 1902 ("that infernal year") in the company of his mother and of a school friend from Moulins, Pierre Colombier. Columbier had recently come into an inheritance and was proceeding, to the envy of Larbaud whose mother never loosed the purse strings, to spend it as quickly as possible (*Aubry*, p. 73). During this trip, Larbaud invented the name of his "riche amateur" by combining the name of a village near London, Barnes, and Booth's, the name of a chain of drugstores. "Barnabooth," after further fleshing out, appears as the leading character of the short story, "Le Pauvre chemisier" begun about this time and published as part of the volume *Poèmes par un riche amateur* in 1908. He is clearly the product of the adolescent fantasizing of a young man from a narrow, provincial, upper middle-class background, timid, too fat, crushed by a domineering mother, who dreams, like an earlier Walter Mitty, of wealth, liberty, and power.

V *Poems in* A. O. Barnabooth: Ses Oeuvres complètes (*1913*)

The poems included in *A. O. Barnabooth: Ses Oeuvres complètes*, some fifty in number (fifteen from the 1908 edition of the poems were eliminated), are organized in two sections: "Borborygmes" ("Intestinal Rumblings") and "Ievropa" ("Europe"). On the most obvious level, they constitute a record of Larbaud's travels. But they also testify to a triple liberation. A spiritual liberation, encouraged by his ardent reading of Whitman which incited him to reject the prudery and the restraints of his milieu in Vichy, to accept the physical side of life, to recognize the importance of the body. They also record an esthetic liberation, a breaking away from a "refined" Symbolist tradition, which preferred an abstract "otherworldliness" to daily reality.

The "author," Barnabooth, as we have said, is represented as immensely wealthy and one of the recurrent themes of the poems is the problem of being rich and consequently of being cut off from others. The rich man is able "to buy everything except the essentials." But the attitude of Barnabooth-Larbaud toward the problem of the relationship between the rich and the poor, as in so much else, always remains ambiguous. It reflects one of Larbaud's basic convictions that man is never "all of a piece," never reaches definitive solutions, but always remains "divers et ondoyant." Rich, Barnabooth prides himself on being able to remain an "amateur." In the "Biographie" (*Pl.*, p. 1167), he protests: "You're insulting me when you consider me a professional man of letters. I am an amateur and proud of it." And later, in the essay "Ecrit dans une cabine du Sud-Express" (*Pl.*, p. 948), Larbaud echoes this sentiment: "Haven't we jealously preserved, in the face of all the temptations of a specialized career, the independent status of the amateur?" To be an amateur, naturally, implies the means to afford it. We read in the *Journal* (p. 351, January 29, 1935): "The spirit 'rich amateur' implies a certain breadth of vision in the face of circumstances and in regard to money; a certain lack of concern for the morrow; the habit of preferring pleasure to material gain, of choosing liberty with limited means rather than the social servitude imposed by affluence. It wasn't so much the actual 'fortune' of my family as the *idea* of the 'fortune' which sustained me when, in reality, my financial means were rather modest." Indeed, much of the European literature of the early twentieth century was a literature of "riches amateurs," like Proust, like Gide and the majority of his friends at the *N.R.F.*, like Thomas Mann, like the members of the Bloomsbury group.

Money bought leisure. And culture was the fruit of leisure. But this leisure, this culture was sometimes accompanied by a certain sense of guilt. Even Larbaud had occasional twinges of bad conscience, which never incited him, however, to social action or to political involvement. These poems testify to the efforts of "the author," a man imprisoned in self, to turn outwards and embrace the exterior world, even the world of contemporary technology, with something of the extrovert exuberance of Whitman. These efforts were rarely successful. For although Barnabooth might proclaim his longing to embrace the universe, to identify himself with the crowd, as in "Europe, III" (*Pl.*, p. 71): "Come, let us take off our evening clothes; I'll put on/ A threadbare suit and you a woolen dress/ And we'll mingle with the masses we do not know," he never is able to pull it off. A younger cousin of Mr. Prufrock, he always remains the spectator, rich and privileged, viewing the tumult of daily existence from a favored vantage-point: from the bridge of a yacht, as in "Nuit dans le port" (*Pl.*, p. 46), from the window of a luxury train, from the balcony of a room in an international *palace*.

"Prologue," the opening poem of the first section, "Borborymes," invokes "the rumblings of the intestines" and proclaims the intention to heed "the wisdom of the body," so long downgraded in classical French literature in favor of the analytical mind. Whitman, bard of "the body electric," taught Larbaud to listen to these "rumblings," indeed to listen to them reverently, as "the only human voice which does not lie" (*Pl.*, p. 43). This physiological tone offended some of his literary contemporaries, notably Claudel, especially when love-making was associated with this visceral "song of ourselves": "Loved one, we have often interrupted our love-making/ In order to listen to this song of ourselves. . . ." (*Pl.*, p. 43).

In the "Prologue" and throughout the collection, we are aware of a deliberate "prosaisme," of the conscious avoidance of the conventionally "poetic." "Centomani" (*Pl.*, p. 45) bluntly states: "They told me that the place was called Centomani/ I often went there during the winter of 1903." In the spoofing "Opinions of the Press," cited by X-M Tournier de Zambie in the "biography," one critic declares that such verse is "almost journalism" (*Pl.*, p. 1205). Another comment complains that it is only "a gross parody of Whitman" (*Pl.*, p. 1205). Some of the more obvious of these imitations (or parodies?) like "Chant de la variété visible" (*Pl.*, p. 1178) are eliminated from the 1913 edition. The "Prologue" ends, as it began, with an apostrophe to "borborygmes": "Maybe we have them in the brain as well/ Only we can't hear them through the thickness of the skull." The mind, Larbaud reminds us, cannot be separated from the body.

VI   *The Poems as a Travel Diary*

In part, as we have said, the poems constitute a kind of travel-diary. They record sojourns in Russia ("Images: Un Jour à Kharkow...."), in Southern Italy ("Centomani," "Et toi, Italie"), in North Africa ("Nuit dans le port," "Mers-el-Kebir"), in England ("Matin de novembre près d'Abingdon," "Mme Tussaud's," "Trafalgar Square la nuit," "Londres," etc.), in Scandinavia ("Carpe diem," "Stockholm"), in Germany ("Berlin," "Never-more"), in Holland ("Scheveningue," "Images: Un Matin à Rotterdam...."), in Spain ("Images: Entre Cordoue et Séville," "Europe, IV"), on the Dalmatian coast ("Europe, IV"). From these titles, it appears that Larbaud's "globetrotting" was less wide-ranging than that of a number of his literary contemporaries, Cendrars among them. He scarcely ever ventured outside of Europe. Although as a young man he was deeply interested in North American literature, he never visited the United States. Although he became one of the leading French connoisseurs of Latin American literature, he never traveled in Spanish America. He preferred countries of old humanistic culture; the Mediterranean had a particular attraction for him, an attraction that became stronger with advancing years. The New World did not really suit him. "Fi des pays coloniaux" Barnabooth exclaims in "Europe II" (*Pl.*, p. 70)—"they may have their natural wonders, but they have never produced a Theocritus."

Man for him remained always the measure of all things and the works of man delighted him more than the marvels of nature. In many, most of these "poems of places," the human visage, especially the feminine visage, is seldom lacking. Cities are associated with a woman's presence. Kharkow? A girl returning from the fountain, lowering her pail of pure water down to the cobblestones, "on the level of the lips of the child kneeling there to drink" (*Pl.*, p. 63). Rotterdam? The vision of two girls on their way to work, embracing amorously as they part (*Pl.*, p. 63). In Spain, at a little station between Cordova and Seville, he remembers a child who "dances for pennies./ In the thick dust, her feet were black" (*Pl.*, p. 64). Trafalgar Square recalls a beggar woman, "a woman dedicated to the city" (*Pl.*, p. 67). Here the great, modern city sheds the hard impersonality that others, like Verhaeren, found in it; in these poems of Larbaud, it is constantly humanized, constantly eroticized.

A travel diary? If you like. . . . But a new kind of travel diary, quite different from those of the Romantics. Something has been added: the exoticism of modern technology, of locomotives, of electricity, which Larbaud set about to assimilate poetically. He shared this ambition, of course, with a number of his contemporaries. With Marinetti, whose "Futurist Manifesto" declared that a racing car was more beautiful than the Venus of Milo. With Cendrars, who fell in love with "American" civilization, with its skyscrapers, electric signs, transcontinental railroads. With Apollinaire of "Zones." With Fernando Pessoa who, using the heteronym of "Alvaro de Campo," exalts the excitement of machines, in poems such as "Ode triunfal":[10]

> Ah, poder exprimer-me todo como um motor se exprime!
> Ser completo como uma máquina!
> Poder ir na vida triunfante como um automóvil último modelo.

Many writers of this generation shared Larbaud's taste for globetrotting and exoticism. The Far East attracted Claudel, Segalen, Saint-John Perse. Cendrars embarked on long treks across Asia on the Trans-Siberian and experienced mystical illumination during an "Easter in New York." Morand recorded his journeyings in *Ouvert la nuit*. Larbaud was a pioneer in this poetry of the exotic, and he consciously underlines the element of strangeness by the use of phrases in English, Spanish, Italian, as well as of foreign-sounding turns of phrase which are not "purely French" as in "Voix des servantes" (*Pl.*, p. 52), "Yaravi" (*Pl.*, p. 54).

VII *Literary Influences*

The major influence, obviously, is Walt Whitman, who made a profound impression on Larbaud when he discovered *Leaves of Grass* when he was barely eighteen. Whitmanian echoes resound, uncamouflaged, throughout the collection. "Prologue" (*Pl.*, p. 43) that "chanson de nous-mêmes," frankly acknowledges them. The luxury train of "Ode" (*Pl.*, p. 44) is a sophisticated offspring of

the locomotive of *Leaves*. Whitman and, to a lesser degree,
Francis Jammes, revealed to Larbaud the poetry of the commonplace, those "splendors of daily life and of hum-drum existence"
celebrated in "Alma Perdida" (*Pl.*, p. 54). Splendors such as the
sensual satisfaction of digesting well or the pleasure of sleeping
in a completely darkened room. Like Whitman, like Baudelaire,
he is a poet of the city. One of his dominant themes is the concept of Europe as one vast, glittering city, of which Berlin, Paris,
London, Stockholm all form a part. In "Europe III" (*Pl.*, p. 72),
he declares: "For me/ Europe is like one great city" (A fine page
in "Mon plus secret conseil" [*Pl.*, p. 690] also celebrates this
unity: "For him, Oxford Street began at the end of the avenue
de la Grand Armée, and Holborn was around the corner from
the Corso of Rome.") His Muse is a city-girl: "O my Muse,
daughter of capital cities, you recognize your rhythms/ In the
endless rumbling of endless streets" (*Pl.*, p. 71).

Whitman's delight in naming things, in stringing out long
litanies of places and objects impressed Larbaud who frequently
employs this device of enumeration, notably in the opening section of "Eterna Volutta," a listing of apparently unrelated sensations: smell of the perfume of faded flowers, music in mid-ocean,
the almond flavor of certain cosmetics, the sound of a cock-crow
in the center of a city. As Gide observed:[11] "Like Whitman,
Larbaud achieves a perfect lyricism by the simple juxtaposition
and presentation of objects." He shares Whitman's passion to
embrace the world in all its plentitude and variety, to explore
every form of experience. But in both of them, this appetite, this
ardor is accompanied by a sense of solitude and of metaphysical
anguish. In "Europe V" (*Pl.*, p. 74), he addresses his "vagabond
heart" which "needs the movement of trains and ships/ And a
joyless anguish kept ever alive." In "Le Don de soi-même" (*Pl.*,
p. 61), he cries: "Wherever I go, in the entire Universe/ I always
encounter/ Outside of myself and within as well/ The infinite
Void/ The unconquerable Nil." Love of life is intensified by a
constant awareness of death ("Europa IX"): "So all these trips
on ocean liners and on crack trains/ Will end one day in a hole
in the ground./ They'll put this vagabond heart in a box/ Nail
down the lid and that will be the end of it" (*Pl.*, p. 78).

But in spite of his admiration for *Leaves of Grass*, he found its grandiloquence, its epic quality alien to his own temperament, which was more attuned to sophisticated irony, elegant understatement, discreet self-mockery. As he put it in his preface to the poems of Levet, he wanted to be "a Whitman à la blague," "a Whitman with some humor in him." He wanted to write verse in which ardor and irony would be paradoxically intermingled, in order to achieve that ambiguity of tone which would increasingly characterize some of the most significant writing of our century. He discovered models in two of his near-contemporaries, minor poets almost forgotten today, although they made a deep impression on Larbaud and his friends: John-Antoine Nau and Henry J. M. Levet.[12]

Nau (Eugène Torquet) was born in San Francisco in 1860. On the death of his father, he returned to France with his mother and studied in lycées in Le Havre and Paris. Nau was a nonconformist who rejected the middle-class respectability of his family to live the life of an artist and a wanderer. He hated cities and always managed to live far from them—in Martinique, on the Côte d'Azur near Saint-Raphael, in Brittany. Like Larbaud, he made no effort to become a part of the literary world of the capital. It was a surprise to everyone, including himself, when he was awarded the Goncourt Prize in 1903 for his novel *Force ennemie*. Larbaud was especially impressed by his poetry and praised *Hiers bleus* (1904) for its skill in "capturing the modern sensibility of space." Reading Nau today, in spite of much which is declamatory, one occasionally encounters a poem like "Lily Dale" about an English barmaid who dispensed "corrosive gin and torrid whisky" which has the wit and the irony Larbaud admired.

The influence of Levet is even more visible. His importance in Larbaud's poetic development is made clear in the course of the "conversation" with Léon-Paul Fargue, presented as the preface to the edition of Levet's poems which the two friends prepared for Adrienne Monnier's collection of *Cahiers*.[13] Larbaud first ran across him in 1902, in the "little review" *l'Effort*, where several of Levet's *Cartes postales* had appeared. He liked them so much that he learned them by heart. Levet, born in Montbrison in 1874, died in Menton in 1906, after a brief career in the French consular service that took him from Manila, to Indochina,

to Majorca. He had spent his student days in Bohemian circles
in Paris, where he had written a good deal of somewhat improper
satirical verse. Delvaille[14] claims (excessively) that "a good deal
of modern French poetry is inspired by Levet" and proceeds to
list those who had imitated him: Luc Durtain, Paul Morand,
Philippe Soupault, Louis Brauquier, Louis Chadourne . . . as well
as André Salmon in "Calumet," Mac Orlan, Cendrars. Levet's
smart cynicism often recalls the early T. S. Eliot, who may have
known about him, and combines irony, contemporary references,
colloquial language to achieve his distinctive effects. Among the
Cartes postales, "British India" is typical:

> Sur son trône d'or, étincelant de rubis et d'émeraudes,
> S. A. le Maharajah de Kapurthala
> Regrette Liane de Pougy et Cléo de Mérode
> Dont les photographies dédicacées sont là. . . .

Why did these flip and clever verses so impress Larbaud
and his friends? Perhaps such wit was a revelation after the
"majesty" of the Parnassiens and the misty other-worldliness of
the Symbolists? To these influences might be added others: Rimbaud, Laforgue, and, among contemporaries, Henri de Régnier,
Francis Jammes, Claudel, Maeterlinck, Saint-John Perse, and,
rather surprisingly, Henri Bataille.

VIII   *Plagiarism?*

In the "avant-propos de l'éditeur" of the 1908 edition of the
poems, Tournier de Zambie notes that certain critics have accused Barnabooth of "flagrant borrowings" that verge on "plagiarism" (*Pl.*, p. 1176). "M. Barnabooth has often simply translated
lines of outstanding foreign poets and scattered them here and
there throughout his own work." He gives several examples, such
as "J'aime à baiser une femme de flammes," a direct translation
from the Cuban, Gabriel de la Concepción Valdés (Plácido):
"Quiero abrazar una mujer de llamas." Certain poems, he continues, are evidently copies from others: "for each line in them,
one could find an equivalent in other poets" (*Pl.*, p. 1177). Such
criticism left Barnabooth quite unmoved, for it is evident that

what his detractors asserted was "plagiarism" was, for him, a deliberate literary device, a procedure, moreover, employed consciously and systematically by greater poets before and after him. Larbaud was challenging Romantic notions of "originality" by implying that every poem is derived from other poems.

In the brief essay, "Le Fait du Prince,"[15] he recurs to this question, by presenting an "original" poem, ascribed to another "persona," Charles-Marie Bonsignor, and entitled "Pour le jazz-band de l'hôtel Excelsior," of which each line has been "borrowed from another poem." "Originality" here is nothing more than the rearrangement of existing elements: "Je tiens à vous faire remarquer qu'il n'y a pas un seul de ces 16 vers qui soit tout à fait de M. Bonsignor—ni de moi."[16] He proceeds to enumerate sources, line for line: the *Vita nuova*, the 26th Psalm, Propertius. Larbaud admits that in reading a text he is always asking himself the question, "Now where did that come from?" But he is fully aware that mere source hunting is of little real importance. He is persuaded that with these "formes communes" (which his friend, Ernst-Robert Curtius, would later designate as "topoi" in his magisterial *Europäische Literatur und lateinisches Mittelalter*), with "these expressions that are not really *clichés*, but which have been used so often that they no longer 'belong' to anyone," the poet miraculously succeeds in creating something "new" and personal. Half a century later and a good deal less lucidly, Struc-turalists like Julia Kristeva (*Semiotiké*, 146) are telling us much the same thing: "Every text takes shape as a mosaic of citations, every text is the absorption and transformation of other texts. The notion of intertextuality comes to take the place of the notion of intersubjectivity." Or, as Jonathan Culler sees it (in *Structuralist Poetics*, p. 261), the text is composed of a set of voices, identifiable and unidentifiable, rubbing against one another and producing both delight and uncertainty.

IX *Techniques*

Although most of the poems are composed in *vers libre* (but in free verse of a very deliberate construction and of great subtlety), many passages are written in conventional meters, with a preference for alexandrines. Apostrophe is frequently em-

ployed: "Borborygmes! O Borborygmes!," "train de luxe," "Voya-
geuse, O cosmopolite," "O paysage neutre," "Et toi, Italie." Such
direct address establishes a tone of immediate communication.
Parantheses are numerous. They are used to add details to a
statement, to make a comparison, and, most importantly, to
confide in the reader by means of a murmured aside. Larbaud
often introduced the "infinitif exclamatif" to achieve verbal
effects more suggestive than are possible with either the sub-
junctive or the imperative. Everywhere his handling of *vers
libre* testifies to his linguistic skill and to the sureness of his ear,
as he creates rhythms and phonetic patterns best suited to express Barnabooth's complex states of consciousness.[17]

X   Dévotions particulières *and* Poésies diverses

Barnabooth appears in only one poem of the six comprising
Dévotions particulières.[18] In "A M. V. L." he asks "his old
Valerio": Is there no way of leaping outside this particular
moment in time, outside of this end of a Middle Ages, "like the
goldfish at Valbois that on hot days used to try to leap out of
what that fellow at your Mother's place called 'the Arau-
quarium,'" Most of these little poems reflect Larbaud's rather
childlike piety and seem oversweet after the self-mockery of
"the rich amateur" and need not detain us as poetry. Several of
them are linguistic *tours de force* of the sort that Baroque poets
often composed as exercises in multilingual verbal virtuosity.
"Milan," for example, dedicated to Our Lady, a sentimental
piece in three languages—Italian, French, and English—concludes: "Je portais Votre image, avec les noms d'Ambroise et de
Milan dans un scapulaire/ Et mon ange gardien/ When he looks
into it/ He will find in it/ Just a Tiny Girl." "Valence-du-Cid,"
composed in Spanish, French, Latin, with one line in Valencian
dialect, portrays the Cid paying homage to the Virgin Mary. "La
Neige" in *Poésies diverses*, is written in a mixture of six different
languages: Portuguese, Spanish, Italian, English, German, and
Latin and was first circulated to Larbaud's friends as his New
Year's greetings for 1935.[19] It is followed by Larbaud's French
version of the text.

XI *Critical Reception*

The total printing of the 1908 edition of *Poémes par un riche amateur* numbered only some 200 copies. Nevertheless, it reached and impressed most of "the happy few" of the turn-of-the-century Paris literary establishment: Gide, Henri de Régnier, Henry Bataille, Mme de Noailles, Gustave Kahn, Octave Mirbeau. It earned for its young author the beginnings of a reputation. Charles-Louis Philippe wrote an enthusiastic letter (dated July 8, 1908) describing it as "one of the most original and astonishing books to have appeared in France for years . . . I had no idea that you were capable of writing a poem like 'Don de soi-même.' Or rather, I had no idea that anyone writing today was capable of it. . . ."[20] Gide not only wrote a flattering letter (regretting, however, the "insuffisance" of the biography by "Tournier de Zambie") but also did a review for the *N.R.F.*: "Barnabooth has traveled everywhere. I like his impulsiveness, his cynicism, his *gourmandise*. . . ."[21] Other contemporary reviews included those of Jean Clary in *Pan* and of Jean Royère in *La Phalange*.[22]

But, despite the success obtained by "the rich amateur," Larbaud was to write practically no more verse, but rather embarked on his long and arduous quest of a prose which would be "as strictly constructed as poetry."

CHAPTER 3

Fictions and Semifictions

LARBAUD was quite aware that he had small powers of narrative invention, little talent for "making up" and "telling a story" in the traditional sense. Moreover, he early revealed a certain impatience with conventional patterns of any sort. In his work, the frontier between fiction and nonfiction is never clearly defined. Most of what might be called his fiction (so dependent on autobiographical sources) was written in the early part of his career, the bulk of it before 1920.

I *Juvenilia:* Gaston d'Ercoule *and* Le Pauvre Chemisier

Larbaud began this unfinished *récit, Gaston d'Ercoule* (based on memories of the Lycée in Moulins) around 1906, when he was spending the winter in Montpellier writing and preparing his *licence.* In 1908, while in Paris, he showed the unfinished manuscript (now in the FVL) to Charles-Louis Philippe,[1] whom he had come to know and admire through their mutual friend, Marcel Ray. It was Ray who suggested that they ask Philippe what he thought of it.

Philippe advised against publication and Larbaud accepted his advice; consequently, *Gaston d'Ercoule* appeared only nearly half a century later, in 1952, in a limited edition prefaced by Robert Mallet.[2]

In it figure many of the recurrent themes of Larbaud's later writing: cosmopolitanism (*Pl.*, p. 7), a disdain for narrow nationalism (*Pl.*, p. 7) and for the middle-class complacency and obtuseness that he so despised in Vichy (in the *récit* "Riveclaire-les-Bains") and the towns around it ("Mortboeuf," "Somnole sur Lente"). Gaston, "ce sans-le-sou," with all his faults and his ridiculous affectations, was finally superior to those around him

66

(*Pl.*, p. 17) "bêtement contents d'eux-même," for he possessed that quality of "civility," which Larbaud so esteemed. Otherwise, Gaston was not an attractive young man, physically or morally. He was pale, plump, stooped, short-sighted and his hands—with their fingers like sausages—were "toujours visqueuses." He was a liar, a snob, and a kleptomaniac. But for the narrator, Gaston remains an admirable and even courageous figure. He refused to accept the narrowness around him and created, by lying, thievery, self deception, a glamorous, unreal world of his own (*Pl.*, p. 17). *Gaston d'Ercoule* already reveals Larbaud's skill in the composition of a portrait, in the analysis of character; it also reveals the limitations of his talents for fictional invention.

Le Pauvre Chemisier, a modern version of the *conte philoso-phique*, begun early in 1903, was finished in Naples in the spring of the same year. In it, "Barnabooth" makes his first appearance in Larbaud's work. After considerable revisions, it was published (in 1908) as a part of the volume *Poèmes par un riche amateur* and reprinted in the 1913 edition of *Barnabooth*, from which the "biography" and a dozen of the poems had been eliminated. The tone of *Le Pauvre Chemisier*—flippant, clever, and cynical—has much in common with that of the "biography" of Barnabooth. "Barnabooth" has not yet acquired the human dimensions which he will reveal in "le journal intime." It is also a satire directed against certain popular novels such as Octave Feuillet's *Jeune homme pauvre*.

The "Poor Shirtmaker" of the title has fallen on evil days. Obliged to give up his shop in the Palais Royal, he has moved to a less aristocratic location near the Grands Boulevards and has been forced to take his only daughter, Hildegarde, out of the convent to help him make shirts. He is, of course, a most unusual shirtmaker, who quotes Mallarmé and whose favorite authors are Martianus Capella (!) and Lautréamont. Hildegarde and "Le Jeune Homme Pauvre" fall in love at first sight.

One day, M. Barnabooth ("I prefer to speak of myself in the third person") strolls by, sees Hildegarde, and is smitten. His great wealth is already a burden for him: "In spite of his in-calculable fortune, he was badly dressed—such was his current affectation—and very timid." The next day he returns to gaze at Hildegarde and to order a dozen dozen shirts; the following

day, he comes back to order a dozen dozen underwear; and the
following, a dozen dozen silk nightcaps (although he never wore
them). He then invests 10,000 francs in the business and the
shirtmaker's financial problems are over. He invites the shirtmaker to dinner, avows his passion for Hildegarde, but confesses
that he cannot marry her since he is "already engaged to several
young women" and has a duchess as his mistress (*Pl.*, p. 33).
The shirtmaker is at first outraged, but economics prevail over
sentiments, and he consents to the idea of "selling his daughter."
Even "le jeune homme pauvre" urges Hildegarde to accept "the
vile proposition of the infamous M. Barnabooth" for the sake
of "their future happiness." He also demands that she sleep with
him before surrendering herself to "the sinister millionaire."

But when she dutifully goes to the rendezvous, Barnabooth,
after taking her on his lap, tells her to return, pure and unsullied,
to her father's house, warning her that she will never forget
that she "behaved like a prostitute" and that she will think of it
when she embraces her children, the children of "the other man."
But Hildegarde returned home, quite untroubled, in spite of
Barnabooth's dire predictions. Her wedding with "Le Jeune
homme pauvre" (on whose manly face one could discern "Love
of Country," "Devotion to Duty," and disdain of literature) was
magnificent. The bride proposed a toast: "To the health of that
idiot, Barnabousse . . ." and the appended "moral of the story"
reads: "Il y a des choses qu'il faut savoir saisir au vol." *Le
Chemisier*, clever, but of an obvious "boulevard" brand of witty
cynicism, would have been a very suitable contribution to one
of the small, satirical magazines like *Le Courrier français* for
which many of Larbaud's acquaintances wrote around the turn
of the century. John K. Simon has well characterized it in his
article "Larbaud, Barnabooth, et le journal intime."[3]

Cette phrase ("il y a des choses qu'il faut saisir au vol"), comme
beaucoup d'autres aspects du conte, semble annoncer des romans
de Raymond Queneau. On reconnaît la même parodie de la sagesse
classique (et plus particulièrement les contes du 18ème siècle) des
personages et situations types.

II Le Journal intime de A. O. Barnabooth

A. *In the Tradition of the* Bildungsroman

Le Journal intime ranks as Larbaud's most ambitious work, the one in which he risked the most, in which he took chances, chances he would no longer hazard in his later, smaller scale, more cautious writings. It has usually been approached on the surface level as a pioneer example of a "new cosmopolitanism" in French literature. It is very much more than that.

In spite of its originality (the creation of the *persona* of Barnabooth, the pre-Joycean use of a form of *monologue intérieur*, among other innovations), the *Journal intime* continues the European tradition of the *Bildungsroman*, the novel of initiation, of which *Wilhelm Meister* and Flaubert's *Education sentimentale* are two outstanding examples. It records Barnabooth's "education" through travel, through his experiences with women, and most particularly through his conversations, endless, probing, intelligent, sometimes overly self-conscious, conversations with his friends, with the Irish art critic Maxime Claremoris, with the French provincial nobleman, the Marquis de Putouarey, with Stéphane, the Russian prince. Each of these friends incarnates— though always in an ambiguous and complex way—a different attitude towards life; each proposes, directly or indirectly, a choice to the young millionaire, who has the possibility of living just as he chooses—the life of "art," the life of pleasure, the life of purposeful action and social involvement. Barnabooth can identify momentarily with each of them, even with the snobbish and insignificant Italian, Bettino, in his ridiculous attempts to pose as an Englishman. Barnabooth recognizes his own talent for "putting himself in another's skin," for seeing the world through another's eyes, for accepting provisionally another's "reality" (while recognizing that every "reality" is also unreal). He thinks this may be a "bonne qualité" (*Pl.*, p. 99). But, characteristically, in the same breath, he fears that this endowment, instead of being a positive thing, is only yet another proof of his "sempiternelle nullité." Barnabooth recounts the drama of a young man—very much the drama of Larbaud himself when

he was writing the *Journal intime*—in search of an identity, a
man cut off from normal everyday life by his vast wealth, a man
who is haunted by the fear that he has no real existence of his
own (*Pl.*, p. 93), a man tempted by the adventure of the
absolute.[4]

Barnabooth is a "big" book, a youthful book (although the
author was thirty-two, he had had a prolonged and protected
adolescence) which dares to confront the insoluble questions;
never again, as we shall see, does he attempt such an audacious
enterprise. He resigns himself, he takes in sail, he navigates
closer to the safety of the shore. In the end, Vichy and Mme
Larbaud and Cartuyvels have made their point—"ça viendra"
and "ça est venu."[5]

The *Journal intime* (which Gide had suggested be entitled
Journal d'un homme libre) appeared first, as *Journal d'un mil-
liardaire*, in the February through June numbers of the *N.R.F.*
It was issued as a volume by the *N.R.F.* under the title *A. O.
Barnabooth, Ses oeuvres complètes; c'est-à-dire un Conte, ses
Poésies et son journal intime* in July 1913 and has been frequently
reprinted. (The original manuscript, given by Larbaud to Léon
Hennique, was lost during a bombardment in Normandy during
the war).

B. Organization

The work is organized in four "cahiers"—"Florence"; "Florence,
San Marino, Venice"; "Trieste, Moscow, Serghiévo"; "St. Peters-
burg, Copenhagen, London"; and concludes with an "epilogue,"
a poem (written in London in 1913) with the final line "La
Mort, avec sa main d'os, écrira, Finis" (Death, with its bony
hand will write, Finis). The travels of Barnabooth closely follow
the pattern of Larbaud's own voyagings and the text is closely
linked—both in terms of the places described and the sentiments
evoked, sentiments of guilt, of loathing of self, of the sense of
aridity and nothingness—with *Poèmes par un riche amateur*.
The *Journal*, moreover, is based on Larbaud's own journals
written during the first decade or so of the century. These personal journals, however, were destroyed by Larbaud since he
considered *Barnabooth* as a literary creation, not as a personal

journal,[6] and insisted that a clear and categorical distinction should be made between the two, as he points out in the essay "une Journée" in *Jaune bleu blanc* (*Pl.*, p. 839).

The *Journal intime*, as we have said, consists primarily of A. O. Barnabooth's endless conversations with his friends. (The book in many ways is a typical product of the small, closely knit, highly self-conscious French intellectual and literary society of the early years of the century, a society in which everyone was always talking, analyzing, criticizing, and recording in diaries—which, naturally, like that of Gide, were designed for publication— everything that was being said.) It analyzes Barnabooth's inner states, often in the fashion of the great French classical moralists, with whom both Larbaud and Gide had so many affinities. It describes impressions, always subtly observed, of the places visited by Barnabooth-Larbaud. Very little "happens," although A. O. Barnabooth himself is always hoping it may (*Pl.*, p. 236).

The predominantly discursive text is enameled with a few dramatic incidents such as the rather sinister comedy of Florrie Bailey, the cheap English music hall artist whom A. O. Barnabooth meets in Florence and to whom he proposes marriage. She refuses him since she is in the pay of A. O. Barnabooth's administrator to spy on the young millionaire and couldn't imagine being married to him anyway. We may also mention his visit to a bordel in Nice, accompanied by the sadistic American heiress, Gertie Hansker, dressed as a man; his love affair with Anastasia; his adolescent adventure with Marika, the young Cypriote he met in Constantinople; as well as Putouarey's stories of Winifred, of his entanglement with "la famiglia Caccia"; and the incident of "the Man of Sorrows." These constitute the quasi-entirety of what might be called "stories" or anecdotes. They are all fragmentary, unresolved, antifictional—and deliberately so.

C.   The Evolution of the Character of A. O. Barnabooth

The Archie Barnabooth of the *Journal intime* is quite a different person from the smart, pseudosophisticated, shallowly cynical young man who appeared in the "Biographie" of Tournier de Zambie. He has matured, become compassionate, and more concerned with fundamental moral problems.[7] The early death of Charles-Louis Philippe,[8] whom Larbaud admired as an artist and venerated as a man, as well as Larbaud's conversion to Catholicism in 1911,[9] may account in some degree for this greater seriousness. And, of course, Larbaud had grown older, had acquired with the years a greater experience of life.

Let us consider first the shifting, contradictory character of A. O. Barnabooth himself, as it is revealed in the *Journal intime*; then let us look at the various stages of "the education of Barnabooth." First, through long discussions with three of his friends, each of whom proposes a different view of life: Maxime Claremoris, the Marquis de Putouarey, and the Russian Prince Stéphane; then through his relations with women, the little cockney music hall artist, Florrie Bailey; Gertie Hansker, the American millionairess; the Duchesse of Waydeberg; and finally his Peruvian wards, devoted, simple, pure, one of whom, Concha, he finally decides to marry; and finally through his travels and his observation of foreign countries and customs.

A. O. Barnabooth's constantly expressed desire is to acquire self-knowledge. In spite of all the obstacles of his birth and fortune, he is determined to reach an honest "definition of self."

The *Journal intime* begins on a train, a luxury train carrying Barnabooth from Germany to Florence. As he looks out the window at the little towns rushing by, he feels that same Whitmanian desire already expressed in *Poèmes* to identify with them, to be able to share the humdrum lives of their inhabitants (*Pl.*, p. 84). This desire to share the lives of others impels the young millionaire to leave his private salon car in order to share a third class compartment full of young Prussians on their way to Florence. Their reactions illustrate for him the differences between the Nordic and the Latin sensibility. Barnabooth, we learn at the beginning of the *Journal*, in a radical effort to liberate himself from at least a part of the burden imposed by his vast wealth, has just sold all his possessions: his châteaux, his yacht, his racing stables. His only baggage on this, "his first trip as a free man," is a small trunk filled with money. Whatever he needs, he buys on the spot and gives everything away on his departure (*Pl.*, p. 88). But ironically (and irony permeates the text), this altruistic gesture caused a panic on the stock markets throughout the world, since it was interpreted as an indication that the vast

Barnabooth enterprises were bankrupt. "Small investors" were "tortured" by the fear of losing everything they possessed.[10] But Barnabooth can feel no sympathy for the frugal "small investors" so sentimentally exalted in bourgeois mythology. He condemns them, rather, for their "moral filthiness."[11]

Liberty, then, is what Barnabooth wants more than anything else. But he fully realizes that it is money which buys leisure and economic independence. Yet money, as Barnabooth proclaimed in several poems of *Un Riche Amateur*,[12] is also the enemy of *genuine* liberty and leisure, since it imposes social and personal servitudes of its own.[13]

Barnabooth then is both the beneficiary and the victim of his vast fortune. The problems created by it constitute one of the primary preoccupations of the journal: he is aware that money can buy everything except true relations with others. But here, as elsewhere, his attitudes are characteristically shifting and ambiguous.

He sometimes feels that money is a force of evil and that vileness, naturally and in spite of his own will, emanates from his great fortune (*Pl.*, p. 92). Business and moneymaking are finally no better than criminal activities (*Pl.*, p. 131). But he has no more illusions about the poor, simply because they are poor, than he has about the rich. Poverty does not necessarily ennoble. Barnabooth ruefully admits that only among the rich and powerful has he found "esprits fins" and "âmes delicates" (*Pl.*, p. 85). The poor cannot afford such luxuries. And, as in the poems, A. O. Barnabooth sometimes lashes out irrationally against them—"I hate the poor—they've trampled on me enough, they've spat in my face . . ." (*Pl.*, p. 95)—while longing at the same time to be accepted by them, to be one of them.

For the poor, since they don't have any, it is only money that counts. Florrie Bailey, whom A. O. Barnabooth wished to marry in order to do a "good deed," willingly serves Cartuyvels to spy on her lover. Cartuyvels calmly tells Barnabooth that "naturally" she consented to do so since he offered her money (*Pl.*, p. 133).

The *Journal intime* continues the tradition of the French moralists in its overriding concern with very conscious self-analysis. Prince Stéphane (at A. O. Barnabooth's request) reads the *Journal intime* and comments on it. Note Larbaud's fondness for

setting up a kind of maze of mirrors in which the same image
is endlessly reflected back and forth. A. O. Barnabooth keeps a
journal, which he lends to a friend to make an analysis of the
original analysis which will then be analyzed in its turn by A.
O. Barnabooth—an analysis of an analysis of an analysis. This
kind of tricky lighting calls to mind other literary experiments
of the same nature—such as Gide's later *Journal des Faux Mon-
nayeurs*, which comments on the composition of his novel about
a novelist who is writing a novel about a novelist writing a novel.
Stéphane reproaches A. O. Barnabooth for allowing himself to
feel guilty about being a millionaire. Why torment himself with
the idea that wealth has given him an unfair advantage in life?
As a matter of fact, the opposite is true—talented people are
often handicapped, downgraded, and discriminated against if
they happen to have money (*Pl.*, p. 262). And he cites some lines
by that arch-bourgeois, Emile Augier, claiming that money pro-
tects its possessors from "Les details répugnants et bas de l'existence," only to mock at them. Wealth rather forces one to
confront "these low, repugnant details" (*Pl.*, p. 263).

But as the *Journal intime* breaks off—it does not really "end"
for nothing is definitely resolved—A. O. Barnabooth has apparently, for the moment at least, resigned himself to being rich. He
has discovered that the asceticism of Prince Stéphane is not
for him; he loves worldly things—beautiful objects and luxury
shops and the pleasure of buying things in them. Engaged to
Concha Yarza, prepared to marry and to return to his own country, he goes on a spectacular spending spree with his fiancée
(as Reggie and Queenie, on a more modest scale, do in *Beauté,
Mon beau souci*) (*Pl.*, p. 302). Concha, he is persuaded, does
not "love him for his money," but, from his own experience with
Florrie Bailey and from that of his friends, like Putouarey, he
is convinced that most women are mercenary. With Angiolina,
Putouarey's Neapolitan mistress, "the question of 'how much a
month' was uppermost in her mind. The words most frequently on
her sweet lips were 'denaro' 'roba' 'risparmio.'"

Yet money, as he is quite aware, gives him the leisure to
devote himself "to the one thing which can satisfy me, that is to
try to see things clearly . . ." (*Pl.*, p. 116) to pursue the task
of self-definition. But at the same time, characteristically, he is

conscious that such "self-definition" is simply the result of self-deception, of seeing oneself as one would like to be seen and not as one is. "When we think we are analyzing ourselves, we are often simply creating, out of the whole cloth, characters in a novel" (*Pl.*, p. 93). A. O. Barnabooth freely recognizes that he is unsure of himself, a nullity. His "image" has not yet taken definite form.[14] Ambivalence about identity persists throughout the work. The reader is not convinced (and certainly Larbaud does not expect him to be) by Barnabooth's declarations that he has finally "found himself," in deciding to marry and to return "home," to lead a life of quiet satisfaction. Barnabooth obviously will never be "satisfied," in spite of his protestations that he envies bourgeois complacency, that he would like to accept a "philosophy of a watering place" (another dig at Vichy!), "the metaphysics of the Riviera" and turn his back on "the Central Africa of his soul." Looking at the Sunday crowd in Florence (*Pl.*, p. 95) he observes that perhaps they have found "the only real wisdom in life, a resigned mediocrity" (*Pl.*, p. 95). But soon after he rejects this "sagesse" as being simply the result of "the cooling of ardor" (*Pl.*, p. 103). For, in spite of his resolve to "abdicate my interesting personality" (*Pl.*, p. 244) and to accept the role of "the Merchant Prince, the society sportsman and the Rich Amateur," he cannot resist the temptation of the Absolute —"cette faim d'absolu" (*Pl.*, p. 90).

D. Barnabooth's "Education": His Friends

He looks to his friends, three of them in particular, to give him guidance in this quest of the absolute. At the beginning of the *Journal* in Florence, A. O. Barnabooth is deep in talk with Maxime Claremoris, a young, brilliant art critic, editor of an *avant-garde* review "Le Pèlerin passioné." (The portrait of Claremoris was inspired in part by Daniel O'Connor, a young Catholic writer whom Larbaud had met in London in 1907 when he frequented the circle of Alice Meynell.) A. O. Barnabooth had a certain fondness for Claremoris since he was "the only poor man who ever gave me the pleasure of lending him money" (*Pl.*, p. 91).

Claremoris, typical of a generation of Pre-Raphaelite aesthetes, has dedicated himself to the "Cult of Beauty."[15] "Aesthete! Yes, that's the word for him. When it comes right down to it, he's very 1880; Oscar Wilde's his ideal; he loves Cathedrals and the Middle Ages, he's the Leicester Square version of Montmartre" (*Pl.,* p. 104). Claremoris hates all the vulgarity of modern life, hates machines, hates modern democratic society. He regrets the unification of Italy, despises Garibaldi and drinks to the restoration of the temporal power of the popes. Barnabooth— like his creator—is much more tolerant and often prefers the living spectacle of the street to the culture of museums. He prefers finally, life to art. "What do you find so beautiful in Your Beauty?" A. O. Barnabooth asks Claremoris one evening when he has taken him to the Savonarola, a cheap music hall (Claremoris disapproves of such "base pleasures") that he himself frequents assiduously and where Florrie Bailey performs.[16] A. O. Barnabooth has little confidence in Claremoris; he has cut himself off from life. "How can he understand," Barnabooth asks, "the passions which move and guide me?" (*Pl.,* p. 103).

He cannot share the aesthetic obsessions of Claremoris. In fact, he has returned to Florence with the firm intention of not seeing any more museums. He has had enough, too, of seeing pictures through the eyes of art critics. Moreover, in trying to know a foreign culture, he prefers the marketplace to the museum, finds the popular café or music hall more enlightening than libraries. How instructive it is "just to watch people going by in the street!" (*Pl.,* p. 155).

He has a keen eye for local color and local customs, such as the spectacle, for example, so characteristic in Italy, of the housewife lowering a little basket from the top story window to receive her mail from the postman (*Pl.,* p. 88). He likes to sit among the beggars on the benches in public parks; to listen to the talk of children as they play (*Pl.,* p. 107); feast his eyes on the spectacle of piles of oranges and melons heaped up in street markets (*Pl.,* p. 113). He finds aesthetic pleasure in the color of Strega or in the tang of Cremona mustard. Like his creator, he has "gone beyond" the official culture of museums.

Near the end of the *Journal,* another meeting with Claremoris is recorded, this time in Copenhagen. The "Aesthete," in a state of deep depression, admits that his "Cult of Beauty" no longer sustains him. "The small flame" (*Pl.*, p. 286) has burnt itself out; he no longer has anything to say. He has "touched bottom," he can no longer believe in the absolute of Art, in the "monument more lasting than bronze," to which he once thought he would ardently devote his life. He has sensed "the vanity of it all" (*Pl.*, p. 287). The works of art which the *avant-garde* considers so supremely great today will become in fifty years (if they survive at all) mere objects of historical curiosity, "simply philological monuments" (*Pl.*, p. 288); and he finally wonders why he ever yielded to the temptation of writing at all.

After *Barnabooth*, Larbaud himself skirts any discussion of the insidious question "why write." Writing had become Claremoris' *raison d'être*, and he had to keep on writing even—especially—if he no longer believes in it. Larbaud well may have shared the anguish of a Valéry and other of his contemporaries about the "impossibility" of literature. Underneath his apparently tranquilly convinced literary humanism, he certainly had wrestled with demons of doubt and destruction, whose ravages—from Dada and the Surrealists onward—have become ever more evident in contemporary literature and art. "Why did I write?" Claremoris asks (*Pl.*, p. 288).

So that some young critic, anxious to make a name for himself, should take apart my work according to methods often incapable of dealing with it? Should pry into my life without sympathy, perhaps even without intelligence? Or so that a commemorative plaque be placed on the wall of the house where I was born, in Cork, the only city I could never live in.

(One thinks of the posthumous honors paid to Larbaud by his native Vichy, whose officials were finally persuaded that he was a literary celebrity and not simply the widow Larbaud's spendthrift son!) No, the cult of Art, as Claremoris makes it only too clear, is not the solution. All he wants finally is to marry a rich woman, a *very* rich woman, and to try to "enjoy life"—even though he knows that finally the nada is always there ". . . il n'y a rien. . . ."

On the surface, at least, the Marquis de Putouarey shared none of the complexity, none of the aesthetic and philosophical

torment of Claremoris. He seemed to be the very incarnation of
l'homme moyen sensuel, whose sole concern in life was to "have
a good time," chase women, eat, drink, and be merry.

Barnabooth, in despair and hating himself at the conclusion
of his tragicomic affair with Florrie Bailey, fell into a deep
depression, wandering for days and nights through the streets
of Florence, scarcely eating, scarcely sleeping, "sucking, like a
sick bat, the breasts of the night." Then, early one morning, in
a low bordel, he met by chance the Marquis de Putouarey, to
whom he had sold, during the recent liquidation of all his
property, his car, "Vorace." Putouarey, seeing the state Barnabooth was in, drove him back to his hotel and remained with
him for the next few weeks, accompanying him on trips to San
Marino, Venice, and Trieste, during which the two of them
exchanged endless confidences. Barnabooth felt more at ease
with Putouarey, for all his apparent vulgarity, than he did with
the "aristocrat," Claremoris. No need to talk about "Culture," no
need to keep up any intellectual pretenses.

"Tant pis pour la grande, la grande littérature!" exclaims
Putouarey, as he starts telling Barnabooth about his latest affair
with a Neapolitan girl, Angiolina, already married and the
mother of two children. Her husband had gone to Argentina
in order to make money and to be able to send for his wife
and babies. Meanwhile, the Cacace family saw no reason why
Angiolina's charms should not be turned into a collective asset.
Her "mamma" accompanied her to the first meeting with
Putouarey, a meeting arranged by the neighborhood pimp, Don
Pasquale. The whole negotiation was carried on without a hint
of lasciviousness, "the question of how much a month dominated
the entire discussion." Once Putouarey paid, the family recognized his position as "vice-époux de l'Angiolina." Soon all
the Cacace tribe began to exploit him. He bought garments to
cover the immense expanse of Mamma, he gave money to "all
the Cacaces of the Kingdom of the Two Sicilies," even provided
money to send to Angiolina's husband in Argentina. At the end,
Putouarey realized that not only were the Cacaces lying to him,
but that they were all lying to each other. But he harbored no ill
feeling. His affair with Angiolina and his experiences with her
family had taught him more about Neapolitan life than "all the

novels of Mme. Serao" (*Pl.*, p. 200). What do you know of a country, he asks Barnabooth, unless you know the people, unless you have lived in direct contact with them, indeed in mouth to mouth contact? He draws shrewd conclusions from his erotic adventures in Italy. We northerners, he explained, think that Italians are a passionate, impulsive, and romantic people—nothing further from the truth. "In reality, they are practical, and calculating" (*Pl.*, p. 206).

Putouarey's earlier adventure with an English girl, Winifred, was quite a different experience, one tinged with strangeness and a bizarre poetry. He picked her up one night in the streets of Birmingham and took her to a cheap hotel. She had been drinking and told him a wild story of having arrived from New Zealand a few days before "to visit an uncle," who, she learned, had disappeared, after having gone bankrupt. Putouarey, moved and troubled by her strange behavior, does not touch her. She asks him to "wash her feet," and he even acquiesces to this request. He then leaves the hotel room, after giving her an appointment for the next morning and promising to help her. She never shows up. Putouarey goes back to the hotel to try to find her, but she had disappeared. That—and nothing more.

As the two of them roar along the Italian roads in "Vorace," as they pause in Rimini and linger in San Marino, their dialogue extends and deepens. Putouarey observes that his life—was "faite d'avance" by a kind of conditioning "less radical than castration, but somewhat more serious than the Chinese habit of binding the feet" (*Pl.*, p. 201). His parents both died when he was a very young child and he was brought up by his authoritarian grandmother (how the presence of Mme Veuve Larbaud haunts the creations of her son!) and by an old priest, the Abbé Vernet. Immediately after the completion of his military service, he was married off to a noble cousin. But he rejected the pattern of life imposed by his training and his class. One night, alone, he suddenly realized, as Barnabooth had realized, that he could be a "free man." Leaving his young bride in the provincial château, he embarked on his career as an "irregular," and as an eccentric. He writes letters to himself, passionately collects stamps, small principalities, and attractive young women, drives recklessly, aspires to a career devoted to research in chemistry.

Paradoxically, he is tormented by the problem of faith and religious belief, and the words of Renan, Haeckel, Nietzche are often on his lips.

Barnabooth comes to realize that this young man, who appears, at the first glance, to be "so well adjusted" had, in reality, an extremely complex personality. Larbaud, with his distaste for the traditional novel, fully realizing the conventionality of "convincing psychological motivation" and aware of the inherent contradictions of human beings, refuses to present them as "all of a piece." He endows them with the ambiguity which he recognized in himself, and Barnabooth, meditating on the character of Putouarey, expresses a sentiment which recurs like a *leitmotiv* throughout Larbaud's writing (*Pl.*, p. 229): "Que la nature humaine est belle qui peut contenir cette folie et cet équilibre...." (How beautiful human nature is that it can contain at once such madness and such measure).

Putouarey and Barnabooth meet each other again by chance on the eve of Barnabooth's departure to take up a new life with his young bride in his own country. Putouarey too has "settled down." He has wearied of his brief liaisons with "girls of the people," who "laugh too much and too loud when they eat, their mouths shining with grease." He is devoting himself seriously to his scientific studies and he has gone back to live with his wife (*Pl.*, p. 299). He will end as a member of the *Institut* or perhaps even as deputy from Putouarey. Things seem to have fallen all too predictably into place.

After a brief and inconclusive encounter in Trieste with "the American heiress," Gertie Hansker, Barnabooth leaves for Russia to visit his friend, Prince Stéphane, with whom he had shared many adolescent adventures, when the two of them were growing up together on the estate of the Prince's father near Kharkow (*Pl.*, p. 147). This part of the *Journal* utilizes many of Larbaud's own memories of his trip to Russia. His judgments about Russia quite possibly reflect his reading of Dostoyevsky, who, around the turn of the century, was being seriously "discovered" by the French literary world. We know that Larbaud, at seventeen, had devoured *"Notes from the Underground."*[17]

Stéphane, seven years older than Barnabooth, had changed radically since the days when the two of them had led a life of dissipation in the international world of Constantinople. He had become an important figure, especially after having subdued and "civilized" the turbulent province of Kharzan.

Stéphane, dubbed in the Western press, "the killer of Kharzan," incarnates "the imperial vocation," is animated by a high, intransigent, disciplined passion to serve the State, serve mankind. His ideal is order, an order imposed by force if necessary. He exhorts Barnabooth to serve this ideal, "Your country needs a Porfirio Díaz," he tells his friend, "go back home and serve" (*Pl.*, p. 271).

As we shall see in several other contexts, Larbaud (by temperament a political conservative) had a sympathy for "order" and for "benevolent" Fascist regimes, as evidenced in the *Journal* where several admiring references to Mussolini can be found.[18]

Barnabooth and Stéphane talk, tirelessly. What is "behind" all the joy and sorrow of this world, behind history, behind everything we observe about us? They agree that their early education had been of little use. They had been warned against "idleness," which in reality had given them the desire to work and to reflect. Their wealth, cited as an advantage, had revealed itself to be completely the opposite. Stéphane exhorts Barnabooth to stop feeling guilty about being rich, since in reality money crushes the individual (*Pl.*, p. 262). He exalts poverty, austerity, in a mystical half-Spartan, half-Franciscan fashion (*Pl.*, p. 264). And continuing his thought, Stéphane proclaims, on a truly Slavic, Dostoyevskyan tone (*Pl.*, p. 264) that "disdain, suffering, tribulations" are the "treasure" he has always desired. He is aware that Barnabooth had come to him looking for guidance, looking for "the Formula." But he insists that there is no "formula" and that the individual experience is "incommunicable." If you wish, there are "formulas" for conducting a life, but they are "la marchandise la plus inutile et la plus frivole qu'on trouve au marché." Most people "buy" a formula and follow it their whole life through, "the way savages wear a ring in their nose" (*Pl.*, p. 269). The only counsel Stéphane feels he can legitimately give is to have nothing to do with the "Ignavi," "passive, inert, people of inferior morality."

In the midst of all this psychologizing, this prolixity, this pursuit of the shifting image reflected in a series of mirrors, the few

pages devoted to the account of a visit to the monastery of
"Serghiévo" (a reminiscence of Troitsa that Larbaud visited on
his early trip to Russia) stand out in strong, concrete relief. It is
one of those little incidents, like the story of Winifred, or the
chilling account of Gertie Hansker's sadistic torture of a broken
down old prostitute in Nice, that appear, incongruously and
memorably, in the midst of all these intellectual conversations,
like menacing thugs who unexpectedly burst into a drawing
room. These incidents reveal the "shadow" side of Larbaud's personality, a fascination with perversion and cruelty, which rarely
appears in his later writing. The superficial observer might easily
criticize Larbaud as a "grand bourgeois dilettante," whose "culture" had removed him from "life," and especially the dark and
sinister aspects of life. But those who look more closely cannot
fail to see that he was well aware of them and that they had a
sometimes morbid fascination for him.

There, in the huge, vulgar, commercialized pilgrimage-center,
something of a Slavic Lourdes, the Prince and Barnabooth are
invited to lunch in the refectory with the Community. As they
wait for the arrival of the abbot, a curious spectacle catches their
attention. They are struck by the sexual ambiguity of the young
monks, underlined in Larbaud's delicate but specific description
(Pl., p. 266): "les trois Grâces déguisées en moinillons"; others
resembled "Diane et ses compagnons." Among all this androg-
ynous beauty, appeared a shockingly ugly, old, crippled apparently half-witted lay-brother, who, maliciously pushed down the
stairs by the young monks, fell at the feet of the abbot. When
the meal was finished, "une dizaine de belles nymphes cour-
roucées" continued to torture their victim, "and the prettiest
among them tore off his ear" (Pl., p. 269). Leaving the refectory,
with its heavy atmosphere of primitive religious practices, incarnated in the porcine figure of the Abbot himself, of sexual
perversity, of torture—and of the pleasure and the peace the
victim apparently found in his torment, Barnabooth "suddenly
understood it all." "And Stéphane, reading his thoughts, observed:
'So you love him too, the Man of Sorrows.' . . ."

Barnabooth is deeply moved by his conversations with Stéphane, by far the most impressive and impassioned of his three
mentor-friends. But with his inability to involve himself totally,

with his characteristic rejection of the Absolute (by which he is nevertheless attracted), he realizes that Stéphane's noble, "imperial vocation" is not for him. To try to embrace it would betray his own nature, as he has come to know and to accept it. He had made a mistake, trying to "identify" with everyone (*Pl.*, p. 277), listening to everyone's counsel. He will go his own way and lead the kind of life he feels is the life for him, "une existence paisible, aisée, retirée, et studieuse" (*Pl.*, p. 277). Rejecting the influence of Stéphane (he would be "unable to breathe on those heights") in a moving and quietly eloquent passage, he defines the ideal life in terms in which Larbaud might very well have defined his own.

I love the world, love it in my way: I love luxury stores, streets full of the movement of daily life, old palaces, the gentle facades of ancient towers, new churches all decked out on feast days, all the concrete reality of history, all the past that I savour, all the future that I sense—I sit there a little away from the crowd, I don't want to be mixed up with it, in order to be able to understand and appreciate better all that goes on about me. I don't want to lose sight of anything; I want to be aware of the continuity of things, watch the fruits of time as they ripen. (*Pl.*, p. 278)

But at the end of the journal, on the point of marrying the simple and devoted Concha and returning to live "in his own country," he finds that he is still closer to Stéphane than he thought (*Pl.*, p. 302). He wishes to "lose nothing"—and nothing has been lost, for from each of his friends, each one so different from the others, he has retained certain elements which have become a part of his own gradually maturing self.

E. Education by Women

Barnabooth, physically unimpressive, shy, plagued by moral scruples, is in no sense a "womanizer" like Putouarey or Felice Francia; nevertheless, he was strongly drawn to women, who played an essential role in his education. At seventeen, he had a love affair in Constantinople with Anastasie Retzuch (who figures in *Poèmes par un riche amateur*). She subsequently married, thanks to the money which Barnabooth had settled on her, the debauched and ruined Duke de Waydeberg. Barnabooth was youthfully vain about the union of his ex-mistress with a great noble. He paid the Duke's gambling debts and accompanied the newlyweds on their wedding journeyings.[19]

Then began a "vie à trois," marked by the most extravagant and excessive debauch (*Pl.*, p. 1162). The Duchess, dressed as a man, would accompany her two partners to the lowest dives of the capitals of Europe, in search of curious sensations. She died a few years afterwards in Naples. Barnabooth's sentimental education continues with an inconclusive liaison with Gertie Hansker, the *richissime* American, who had left her middle-aged millionaire husband at home in order to lead a life of dissipation in Europe. Something of the usual caricature of those "long-stemmed American beauties," imperious, vigorous, "unfeminine," who descended on Europe at the turn of the century to acquire titled husbands, Gertie Hansker, at twenty-seven, "had never yet worn a corset." She was "so beautiful, so independent, and so terrible that she could have got along without being rich" (*Pl.*, p. 230).

Larbaud's portrait of Gertie is not an attractive one. At Trieste, she appears in his hotel room to borrow some of his clothes (*Pl.*, p. 234) for an evening on the town, a request which does not surprise him after his previous experiences with her. One evening, returning very late from Monte Carlo, with Gertie, dressed as a man, and with a group of other friends, it was decided to visit the "red-light" district of Nice. They burst into the rooms of two old broken-down whores. Gertie demanded that one of them take off her nightgown. The woman refused. She had just undergone a serious operation. The scars were too ugly, she did not wish to "horrify" such "fine gentlemen." Gertie, furious, proceeded to obtain scissors and to hack violently away at the nightgown, wounding the terrified victim in the process, and then, apparently excited by the sight of blood, buried the scissors in her victim's thigh. Her friends pulled her away. As she was hustled out the door, she flung her lighted cigarette on the bed. After having witnessed this hair-raising spectacle, it is curious that Barnabooth (always literary even in his most intimate emotions!) should recite to her "Come live with me and be my love" (he also quotes Whitman, Petrarch, Statius, and Roger de Colleyre to her!), propose marriage, and evoke the child that would be born of their union. But then how innocent she looked as she sang "Rock of Ages" there at his side during services in the English chapel! Possibly the coexistence of the "innocent" surface and the hidden perversity constituted, for Barnabooth, Gertie's most irresistible attraction. But no marriage took place. The old "dégoût de toutes choses" oppressed the ever-vacillating Archie. He knows that nothing is really farther from Gertie's mind than founding a family and that very quickly they would be reduced to "having separate yachts." So Archie, renouncing "these sterile loves" ("ces amours inféconds") (*Pl.*, p. 238), leaves Trieste without saying goodbye. (Such precipitant flights before the female characterize Larbaudian antiheroes, like Lucas Letheil, as well.)

Indeed Barnabooth appears less passionately drawn to women than to philosophical speculation. Even at the height of his very brief passion for Gertie "he suddenly was overwhelmed by all the sadness of the world" felt the need to "flee and hide away somewhere in order to savor my despair" (*Pl.*, p. 235). He realized that he was no longer thinking about Gertrude Hansker, but about "certaines doctrines philosophiques" (*Pl.*, p. 235).

But Barnabooth really preferred girls of "the lower classes" to these American millionairesses and debauched duchesses (*Pl.*, p. 147), girls who would permit him to play—quite sincerely— the role of the generous benefactor, girls who would not make, as persons, excessive demands on him. In Florence he assiduously frequented a cheap music hall, the Savonarola, where he met one of the dancers, a Cockney named Florrie Bailey, whose stage name was "Désir de Coeur." Bent on degrading himself (*Pl.*, p. 131), on making a gesture which would alienate him from his own world of wealth and privilege and proclaim his solidarity with "the lower classes," he proposes marriage to her. Florrie receives the offer calmly, to the disappointment of Barnabooth, who had expected "an explosion of joy, a delirium of gratitude" (*Pl.*, p. 123) and informed him that she would "think it over." Meanwhile, Barnabooth's administrator, Cartuyvels, arrives in Florence and informs him that one of the spies employed to "protect" him is precisely Florrie Bailey, who is paid to report on his actions. Naturally, she refuses to marry him, especially as she informs him in their last, rather comic interview, that she is "a gaiety girl" and that she'd rather become a nun than to be his bride.

At the end, Barnabooth, rather relieved that he will not be saddled with Florrie, decides that she rather disgusts him with "her vulgar sensuality and her viscous kisses" (*Pl.*, p. 139). Neither his *affaire* with Florrie, nor his youthful adventures with girls like Marika, "une Smyrniote au visage doré" (*Pl.*, p. 148) really procured him great pleasure. Sexual passion, "l'amour fou" is evidently not Archie's *forte*. He finds a solution—at least a temporary one—to his sentimental problems in his marriage with Concha Yarza, one of the Peruvian sisters he had long generously and altruistically supported, for whom his feelings are essentially fraternal. "I finally came to know a new kind of friendship that was not based on common tastes at all, a kind of passion of which desire is only one of the elements" (*Pl.*, p. 295).

F. Education by Travel

Barnabooth's deepest passions perhaps were for places and for poetry rather than for women. Travel formed him, gave him both the joy of feeling at home everywhere and the pain of really belonging nowhere. Archie was one of the first of those "hommes de nulle part," those displaced persons who have become stock figures in modern literature (*Pl.*, p. 97). He evokes landscapes lovingly, especially those of Italy, which is the setting of most of the *Journal intime*, as he travels from Florence, to San Marino and Rimini to Venice and Trieste. Coming from Northern Europe, he is struck by "the gentle, indulgent, yes, intelligent light of Tuscany" (*Pl.*, p. 86). Barnabooth shared Putouarey's affection for San Marino, described in an overlong section which verges on the travel guide but which is redeemed by telling observations of small details. Barnabooth, like his creator, has an affection for *cosas chicas*, for pocket-size countries like Lichtenstein and Luxembourg, Andorra and San Marino. He has a certain nostalgia for the fragmented Italy of city states and miniature principalities, for Florence at the time of the Grand Dukes, when it was "the salon of Europe" (*Pl.*, p. 89). But to cosmopolitan cities like Florence, Barnabooth prefers the provincial towns like Bari or

Taranto, where "on est entre Italiens"; and naturally, as a cosmopolitan, he was attracted by the international flavor of Trieste,
with its mixture of Latin, Germanic, and Slav elements.

III   Enfantines

Enfantines constitutes an homage of Larbaud to childhood.
The texts comprising this collection—eight in all—first appeared
in little magazines (beginning with "Dolly" in *La Phalange* in
1909) before publication as a volume in 1918. Several of them
are clearly autobiographical ("Le Couperet," "L'Heure avec la
Figure," "La Grande Epoque," "Devoirs de Vacances"); one
("Rachel Frutiger") is based on school experiences of his mother
and his aunt when the family was living in exile in Switzerland;
others recall sojourns in England ("Dolly") and in Montpellier
("Portrait d'Eliane"). The *Pléiade* edition includes two other
"Enfantines," "Gwenny-toute-seule" and "La Paix et le Salut,"
as well as an unfinished, hitherto unpublished text, "L'Elève
Camille Moutier." One "Enfantine," "Pour une Muse de douze
ans," appeared in the *N.R.F.* of April 1, 1938, and is included in
Aux Couleurs de Rome.

The techniques employed in them are varied, ranging from
early, almost unconscious experiments with the interior monologue to more conventional third person narrative ("La Grande
Epoque"), although each one has elements of originality that set
them apart from most "short stories" of the period, notably a
quasi-identification of the author with the children about whom
he is writing. Works about children in the nineteenth century
(and the child really entered literature only with Romanticism)
usually viewed the subject from outside. In France more than in
England (and this was one of the reasons why Larbaud was
attracted to the Anglo-Saxon world), they were often patronizing,
sounded like accounts written by a dominant ruling class concerning the curious habits of an underdeveloped minority. Larbaud in *Enfantines* entered as an equal into the universe of the
child, a universe from which the adult is usually excluded because of his own insensitivity. For Larbaud never ceased to be
a child himself. In a moving and revelatory passage of "Gwenny-
toute-seule" (*Pl.*, p. 531–32), the narrator bursts out: "I've tried

long enough to play the comedy of the 'grown ups.' I've tried to get interested in their ideas, in their preoccupations. I just couldn't do it. . . . Perhaps I'm wrong. But now just let me be a child again."

Such an intimate identification of the narrator with the children who people *Enfantines* produces a tone of ambiguity, of uncertainty, of shifting roles. Often the "moi" of these stories is a double, but indivisible one—the fusion of the child participating in the action and of the adult remembering it, seeking to recreate it. On the first reading, "L'Heure avec la Figure" may be puzzling. It is only at the very end that we become aware that the narrator himself was the child who had imagined the friendly "face" discerned in the markings in the marble of the fireplace, one of those "made-up" characters—like "Rose" and "Dembat" in "Le Couperet"—that people the imaginary world of the child. The child-narrator confides in "the Figure" as he waits for the music teacher, hoping against hope that he will not appear. The Figure does not speak, but the two understand each other very well. And as he waits, the child takes the Figure on an imaginary voyage in the enchanted forest that he has invented. When they have returned, it is almost six o'clock—surely too late for the music lesson. It is only then that the narrator reveals himself: "The Figure in the marble will be still waiting there when we'll be grown-up and the children who come after us will discover him in their turn . . ." (*Pl.*, p. 434).

As E. R. Curtius has noted,[20] "the Figure" symbolizes the whole pantheistic world created by the child, in which the humblest objects take on a poetic beauty and a magical significance. It is the world of Milou's adventures with "Rose" and "Dembat" in the unexplored jungle of his imagination; of Arthur and Marcel and Françoise in "La Grande Epoque." A world in which the sense of wonder is always alive, a world in which boredom cannot exist. It may seem increasingly remote today, in a society from which the child's sense of the marvelous seems to be disappearing; where the "mass media" replace the individual imagination; where the most extraordinary events are greeted by a yawn; where boredom—even among the very young—seems to be the only universal sentiment; where everyone wants to be youthful, but where even the children have ceased to be childlike. Are *Enfantines* an anachronism, the product of an earlier age when the child was still an "oppressed minority," living in a closed and mysterious reserve of his own? Or do *Enfantines* express something universal in man, the need for poetry, and for wonder, that even technological pressures cannot entirely stamp out?

The need, too, for love, which is not merely another name for the satisfaction of sexual desire. Love, often in its most intense and passionate aspects, forms one of the major themes of *Enfantines*. In "Le Couperet," Milou, only eight, falls in love with Justine, the orphan who works as a drudge on his parents' country property. Justine, he notices, had badly cut her finger in the course of her heavy work. And Milou consciously manages, as testimony of his devotion, to inflict a similar wound on himself. (This self-mutilation is also linked, as we shall see, with a dawning sense of social injustice). As the blood spurted from his finger, he thought: "Justine will hear about it. And perhaps she will think 'The master's son cut himself just the way I did—and on the same finger of the same hand' " (*Pl.*, p. 427). Of course, his parents could understand nothing of this violent and gratuitous passion. At the end of summer, as the family is leaving to go back to town, Julia, the cruel and calculating daughter of the tenant farmer, comes up to say good-bye. And, noting Milou's reluctance to kiss her, his father reproached him: "I can see that you've never been in love!" (*Pl.*, p. 430).

Love and suffering are inevitably linked. In "Rose Lourdin," the narrator, a successful actress, recounts to someone—perhaps herself? the identity of the "vous" is never made clear—her youthful passion for an older student in the same pension, who was also named Rose, Rose Kessler. Rose Kessler never knew that she was the object of adoration of the younger girl, for whom it would have been a "pleasure to have knelt down abjectly before the beloved" (*Pl.*, p. 404). For a strain of masochism runs through Rose Lourdin's hopeless attachment. "O, I should have like to have made her angry so that she would have beaten me." After vacation, Rose Kessler did not return to school; nor did one of the young teachers with whom she was allegedly having "unwholesome relations." All this is recounted delicately. Nothing is crudely spelled out. Nevertheless, it is clear that Larbaud's

vision of childhood is closer to that of Freud than to that of
Eugene Field or of Alice Meynell.[21] Purity, innocence, sweetness
—these terms recur constantly in the pages of *Enfantines* to
describe the qualities of childhood. But Larbaud also discreetly
makes us aware of the darker, more disturbing elements that
inevitably accompany them.

"Rachel Frutiger" recalls stories Larbaud's mother told about
her impoverished and precarious existence in Switzerland. The
directress of the aristocratic pension in which she and her sister
were enrolled kept demanding that their father must pay their
tuition, otherwise they could not continue in school. They knew
that their father could not pay and were afraid of wounding
him if they asked for money, so they told him nothing about
being expelled. They left the house in the morning and wandered
in the streets all day, always afraid that they might meet someone who knew them and who would wonder why they were not
at school. As in other Larbaud texts, the title would seem to
have only a casual connection with the story. Rachel Frutiger,
a rich banker's daughter who publicly shows her sympathy for
her two impoverished French classmates before they are expelled, appears only in a brief scene, in which she exemplifies
the courageous and gratuitous generosity of which children are
capable.

"Devoirs de vacances" utilizes precise autobiographical details
of Larbaud's own summer vacations, partly at home, working
on his summer assignments, partly with his family in the watering place of La Bourboule. He recalls the deep pleasure he
always experienced in studying and writing. The child dreams
of all he is going to accomplish during the summer. "Nothing
will distract us from our studies." Here again, the narrator often
shifts *personae*. Sometimes it is the child who is speaking as
"we," sometimes, the man he has become. This device permits
ironic comments on official, exam-oriented French education,
as well as eloquent declarations about the pleasures of the
spirit of which even the most precocious child would scarcely
be capable. "We were suspicious of what they were teaching
us; the predigested intellectual nourishment they gave us made
us sick to our stomachs. And besides, we weren't angels, able to

understand everything abstractly, without the aid of our senses"
(*Pl.,* p. 493). And what a pleasure it was during vacation to
discover poetry for one's self, not the poetry of the textbooks,
but contemporary poets like Verlaine! Reading Verlaine, the
child loses all appetite for doing his vacation assignment on La
Fontaine and starts writing poetry of his own. But when he
reread his poetry, he thought that it wasn't very good. Maybe
his parents were right then and he would never succeed in anything. Back home, he confides once again in the familiar "Figure"
concealed in the veins of the marble mantelpiece, with whom he
has shared so many secrets in the past (*Pl.,* p. 486). He tells
"the Figure" how good it is to be alone with him again and
wonders why it is impossible to put up with the company of his
parents. "We're always reading about problem children; why
not problem parents too?" (*Pl.,* p. 487). Autumn comes too soon
and with it, going back to school. He didn't even bother to take
his vacation assignments back with him. "Only teacher's pets
hand them in."

Several of the *Enfantines* are set in England, the land of
"Alice," a country dear to Larbaud for its fresh-faced, blonde
little girls, whom he loved to watch as they played in parks. In
these stories, the narrator is no longer a small boy, but rather a
lonely, unattached gentleman of a certain age, in search of the
love and affection of little girls. The tone is delicate, sometimes
almost sentimental; but, nevertheless, a subterranean current of
sensuality runs through them. The earliest of these "English"
Enfantines, "Dolly" (1909), recounts the death of a rich American child, who is living with her nurse in an English resort
hotel, while her mother, a famous actress, is on tour. The narrator, her tutor in French, sometimes brings his little friend,
Elsie, to the hotel to keep her company. He had made the
acquaintance of Elsie one day when she was playing in the park
and had escorted her home to her parents, poor working people,
who saw no harm in confiding their daughter to such a nice
gentleman. After that, he and Elsie saw each other every day,
and he is delighted when he persuades her to tell him that she
loves him. Dolly dies soon afterward. And Elsie falls in love
with one of the girls in her class in school and makes up excuses

in order not to continue to see her old admirer. Sitting alone
in the park, he watches a sparrow, which promptly flies away.
"L'oiseau s'envole."

The little birds were always flying away, leaving "le pauvre
vieux garçon" alone. In "Gwenny toute seule," Gwenny looking for
her ball, strays into the garden of a house on the English coast
rented by the narrator for the summer. And the same old sentimental story begins again. The narrator always hopes that some
day his dream will come true, the dream of having a little
Gwenny all his own who would live with him and to whom he
would devote his entire existence (*Pl.*, p. 527).

For, as he confesses, the conversation of people of his own age
saddened him and he could only enjoy the company of "timid
little boys and gentle little girls..." (*Pl.*, p. 527). But as soon as
he found a little companion, it seemed that her mother would
always come looking for her, and off she would go, without even
looking back, leaving him alone once more. Gwenny continued
to come to see him regularly until one day she arrived to tell
him that her vacation was over and she was returning home.
"So she left me, as the others left me. Mabel, from Hammer-
smith, Lily from Fulham, Ruby from Chelsea whom I shall never
forget. The kisses of Ruby were the best I've ever had..." (*Pl.*,
p. 528). He realizes that all this is inevitable and that his only
consolation is "his gentle, invisible friend" who, we understand,
is the child Jesus, "gentler and purer than all the pure and gentle
little girls I have loved." Obviously, Larbaud saw nothing "suspect" in his obsessive interest in little girls, revealed so openly
and candidly in the *Enfantines* and in his journals. His love for
them, he assured himself, led him to the love of God, *was* the
love of God.

"Portrait d'Eliane à 14 ans," which fittingly appears last in
the collection, analyses the emotions of a girl passing from
childhood to womanhood. As she sits with her mother in the
public garden of Montpellier, we share her fantasies, fantasies
nourished by the clandestine contemplation of naked male
figures in the *Petit Larousse*. Her desire is awakened by the
sight of the young men strolling by, especially of one of them,
whose companions address him as "Lucien." She manages to
approach them. As she passes, Lucien happens to brush her

arm. He murmurs, "Pardon, Mademoiselle . . ." and continues on his way. And Eliane, closing her eyes, murmurs: "I love and I am loved" (*Pl.*, p. 518).

Technically, the very brief text, "La Paix et le salut" (originally written in 1914 as an epilogue for *Enfantines*) is one of the most intriguing in the collection. It is essentially an extended poem in prose and reveals how Larbaud was moving, in the course of his development as a writer, farther and farther away from any vestige of "story" or linear narrative. Composed of impressionistic evocations of Dublin, of Marienlyst in Sweden, of London, it suggests more than it "tells." It lends itself to a variety of interpretations, depending on the angle of vision of the reader, who, in a sense, must create for himself the "meaning" of the text. The author apparently has no precise "message" to convey. The prose suggests a late Monet, where clear delineation has been sacrificed to shifting effects of light and color, to sensual stimulation. The style artfully evokes luminous pulsations, trembling undulations (". . . des ondulations de clarté tremblante" [*Pl.*, p. 533]). It begins enigmatically, with a phrase of delicately erotic implications: "To the youngest rosebud, so tender and so hard, and so firmly closed . . ." (*Pl.*, p. 533).

"So tender and so hard": this phrase reveals, perhaps, an essential feature of the overall structure of *Enfantines* which might be described in terms of polarity between "tenderness" and "hardness." The tenderness of Milou towards Justine, for example, is paralleled by the cruel harshness of Julia. The "tenderness" of all those English "kiddies" is matched by their thoughtless abandonment of the "pauvre, vieux garçon," their lonely, rather pathetic adult admirer. And this alternation between tenderness and hardness is also established within a larger context in the opposition of the world of childhood (a world of "gentleness," of "douceur," a key word in *Enfantines*) and the harsh, insensitive world of adults. "La Paix et le salut" hymns the "need to love" through remembered images of childhood; "Marie all alone," sitting pensive in a crimson twilight; the little girl in a red beret; the naked child on a Swedish beach. And from these images arises an all-embracing vision of a new century of the child, a century that Larbaud hoped would be one of "peace and salvation."

The First World War broke out soon after these words were written.

The casual reader might be inclined to dismiss *Enfantines* as fragile sketches of little substance. Those who expect to find the "well-made" short story in the manner of Maupassant will be disappointed. There is no "plot," no "surprise ending," in fact really no "ending" at all. Many of them read like fragments from a journal. But the rare, really attentive reader, so beloved of Larbaud, the reader who reads "little but well," will soon find in them much more than meets the eye Nowhere is Larbaud's gift of making "something of nothing," or rather of capturing profound but fleeting sentiments rarely expressed in conventional narrative, more richly apparent. To achive his purpose he experimented with new techniques, but experimented with them so unobtrusively that their truly innovative character is often not immediately apparent. He employs in certain *Enfantines* a *proto-monologue intérieur* long before he heard of Joyce or Dujardin. He breaks down the traditional patterns of French prose into irregular cadences of poetry as in "La Paix et le salut." And as we have said, in *Enfantines* Larbaud explored a new area of expression: the life of the child as seen from within. He opened up a whole new domain, later to be exploited by Alain Fournier, Cocteau, Jacques Chenevière, and others after them. And "poetic" and subjective as they may appear, *Enfantines* also reveal Larbaud's concern for social justice. He observed, with contained indignation, the exploitation of the poor by the rich, of the workers by the *bourgeoisie*, as we see in the sympathy of Milou for Justine, in the shocked surprise he feels when his friend, Arthur, the son of the manager of his father's estate, addresses him as "Monsieur," because he is the boss's boy. But he seems to recognize the inevitability of such injustice in a rigidly divided society, in which the narrator-poet is quite aware that he, like the child, is excluded from what adults have decreed is the "real" world, unless he is willing to renounce his "childlike" ideals of innocence and purity in order to conform to it.

IV   Fermina Márquez

From the world of the child in *Enfantines,* Larbaud, in *Fermina Márquez,* moves on to explore another *terra incognita*—that of adolescence. And just as *Enfantines* was the first of many subsequent books on childhood, so *Fermina Márquez* launched the vogue for the novel of adolescence, as exemplified in works of Raymond Radiguet, Jacques de Lacretelle, Roger Martin du Gard, and many others of lesser talent. Like *Enfantines,* this subtle and poetic *récit* is constructed largely of personal memories, memories of the happy years he spent in the Catholic Collège Sainte-Barbe, from 1891 to 1894. As usual, the gestation of the book was slow and it developed through several preparatory stages. While still at Sainte-Barbe—in the book, St Augustin—he was thinking of writing a poem, *El Duendecito,* about his impressions of the school and of his fellow students, many of them Latin Americans. It was there that his interest in Spanish, awakened during his first trips to Spain with his mother, became more serious ("Spanish was the language most of the students used" [*Pl.,* p. 309]), and had a definite influence, as we shall see, on his future literary development. During the summer of 1905, in Vichy, he began a story, *Conchita,* to which, as he continued to work on it in Valencia in 1905–1906, he gave another title, *L'Histoire de la Encarnación et ses admirateurs.* By 1908, he had completed a nearly definitive version, which he entitled *Incarnación Barea* and, on the advice of C. L. Philippe, submitted it to *La Grande Revue.* It was refused, but Gide immediately proposed to use it in the recently founded *N.R.F.* which badly needed some good "creative" writing to balance its many critical articles. Larbaud accepted, having changed meanwhile the title to *Fermina Márquez,* the name he finally decided upon for his heroine. (In Madrid, in 1906, he had fallen in love, platonically, with an older woman, Señora Bosque de Flores, whose Christian name was Fermina.) Preceded by a quotation from Tibullus (IV, 2), the text appeared in four successive numbers of the *N.R.F.* in 1910, had considerable success, and definitely furthered the advancement of Larbaud's literary career.

Its structure clearly indicated his distaste for the conventional

realistic novel. In one passage, he comments pointedly that the
young Fermina, as she read popular novels, could not realize
how "insignificant and artificial" they were (*PL.*, p. 321). There
is no "plot"; Larbaud offers us rather a series of episodes poetic,
impressionistic, and presented with an artful absence of "logical
progression," which describe the impact of a beautiful Colombian
girl of 16 on the students of the cosmopolitan College of St.
Augustin, where her little brother, Paquito, is a *pensionnaire*.
He is very lonely, since it is the first time in his life that he
has lived away from his family. So his aunt, Mama Doloré,
accompanied by his two sisters, come out from Paris every afternoon to keep him company. (Mme Doloré and the children were
spending several years in Europe to "acquire the culture of the
Old World," as wealthy Latin Americans of the last century were
accustomed to do.)

From the opening paragraphs, Larbaud creates a shimmering,
shifting verbal atmosphere which has affinities with the visual
atmosphere of post-impressionist painting, with Bonnard and
Vuillard (of whom Larbaud wrote appreciatively in several of
the "Letters from Paris" which he contributed to the *London
New Weekly* in 1913–1914). The boys first perceive Fermina not
directly, realistically, "face to face," but rather as a reflection on
the glass door of the *parloir* of the school. (Larbaud has a pre-
dilection for such effects, for "images in a mirror," which were
more suggestive for him than "concrete," directly observed
reality.)

The cosmopolitan student body was dominated by the Latin
Americans, "who were convinced that they were the legitimate
descendants of the Conquistadores" and who proclaimed themselves "a hundred times a day,' 'we Americans.'" Their natural
leader was Santos Iturría, a Mexican, who had already acquired
the poise, the confidence, and the physical strength of manhood.
His exploits in Montmartre, on nights when he and a big Haitian,
Demoisel, scaled the wall and "went on the town," inspired the
universal admiration of his more timid classmates. Soon a group
of the boys, Santos in the lead, all smitten with the beauty of
Fermina, were regularly accompanying Mama Doloré and her
nieces on walks in the park during their daily visits. The park is
admirably presented in Larbaud's firm yet somehow fleeting

prose[22] with the everchanging play of sunlight on the great old trees, their ivy-covered, moss-encrusted trunks stippled with shadows. Walking adoringly, timidly beside Fermina, the boys become aware of the mystery of the "jeune fille," who is becoming a woman. And the narrator (one of them, obviously, since he speaks as "we"), as he evokes this experience long after it is over, thinks of the ambiguity of sexual differences:—"When life gives me a little time and peace to think things over, I discover feminine aspirations and feelings in myself; and I'm sure that women, if they take the trouble to know themselves, find that, in addition to their generous feminine heart, they also have something of the ordered and lucid 'masculine intellect'" (*PL.*, p. 322).

The dashing Santos, understandably, succeeds in winning the affection of Fermina. His physical attractions soon make her forget the severe Spanish piety that had obsessed her girlhood and set her to reading sentimental novels and dreaming of romance. The sacred retreats before the profane and human love takes precedence over the divine. Santos wears a band woven of her hair about his wrist.

But Larbaud is not essentially interested in telling a story of the innocent raptures of young love. The stellar role in the *récit* is reserved for an unlikely candidate—Joanny Liénot. Liénot, always the first in the class, vain, ambitious, calculating, obsessed with power and fame even to the point of being somewhat unbalanced, is of the same family as Lucien, in Sartre's short story, "L'Enfance d'un chef." He coldly decides that he must "win" Fermina, as he would win the first prize in Latin composition. "Why shouldn't I be the one?" (*PL.*, p. 128). He plans his strategy carefully. Posing as the champion and the defender of little Paquito, he quickly gains the confidence of the Márquez family. Meanwhile, the school authorities, aware of irregularities, forbid the boys to accompany the young visitors on their afternoon strolls. The only exception is Liénot, whom Mama Doloré has specifically requested as a companion, because of his kindness to Paquito and because she wishes him to "help Fermina perfect her French." Liénot is triumphant. He will be alone with her and will have a free hand to make her conquest. He engages her in a passionate dialogue. Dialogue? Rather a harangue.

For Fermina has little chance to say anything, as her fervent suitor seeks to impress her with his genius, his eloquence.

At first, these hours alone with Fermina were unalloyed bliss for Liénot. The desire to "conquer" was replaced little by little by the pleasure of comradeship. He was astonished at her ardent mysticism, nourished by her reading in the lives of ascetic Spanish saints, her humility, her self-abasement before God. Comparing her with the girls he knew, daughters of his parents' bourgeois friends in Lyon, he found her sublime and knew that he was in love with her. And encouraged by her confidences, he was emboldened to reveal himself to her as he never had revealed himself before in his life. To reveal all the torments of his pride and ambition and his dream to recreate European unity through the restoration of the Roman Empire. (As we have seen, the ideal of European unity is a theme which recurs throughout Larbaud's writing, in *Allen*, in *Saint Jérôme*, and many passages in the *Journals*.) Joanny, like Larbaud, had a passion for Roman history. For Joanny, as for Larbaud, "The Roman church is what remains of the Empire." He exclaims: "French? What do I care for a name derived from that of a barbaric tribe? French! I'm not French. My catechism teaches that I am a Roman Catholic. But in my translation, it should rather read: Roman and master of the world" (Pl., p. 354). For him the Pope is not simply the Holy Father, but the heir of the Caesars as well.

When they separated that afternoon, Fermina did not give him her hand. That evening he angrily reproached himself; he had displeased her—women are always afraid of ideas. At their next meeting, when Fermina asked why he studied so hard, why he won so many honors, he avowed his love: he wanted to be *worthy* of someone—and she was that person. She did not reply. She spoke only to ask him what class Santos was in. And they separated in silence and earlier than usual. After the spring holidays, he sought her out for the showdown and proclaimed, "I am a genius. And I lied to you when I said that I worked in order to be worthy of you. Or of anyone else. I work to achieve fame for myself. My ambition is so great that only immortal fame can satisfy me. And I'm astonished that you didn't understand sooner that you were dealing with a man of genius." And that genius, he added, is a genius which despises the critical spirit and the exact sciences, esteems only human passions for they alone count in the stupidity of the modern world. (Somehow, after reading the early letters of Larbaud to Marcel Ray, one can rather imagine him in the role of Joanny, vehemently denouncing the bourgeois and republican milieu in which he lived, intent on persuading himself, in spite of the low opinion that his family and his friends had of him, that he was a genius after all.) Joanny takes leave of Fermina announcing that he will no longer be free to see her, since he will be having watercolor lessons every afternoon. Thereafter, Santos and Fermina resume their walks and long talks under the arbor.

These vehement central chapters (XI–XVIII) are the least convincing of the *récit*. Joanny becomes more and more incredible in his ranting, his eccentric brilliance, his virtuosity in handling unusual ideas. The mask of Liénot slips and reveals the face of the author himself.

At the end of the school year, Mama Doloré insists on seeing Liénot to thank him for being so kind to Paquito and to offer him, as a token of their gratitude, a magnificent gold watch. He is beside himself with rage and humiliation: "They've given me a tip, a tip . . . they look down on me. And I'm so much better than they are!" (*PL.*, pp. 384–85). He took the watch and threw it as far as he could into an abandoned storeroom.

Years later, the narrator revisits his old school, now closed and no longer in operation. The buildings are falling into disrepair. The fine park is uncared for. The old concierge was still there, happy to greet him and to give him news of his contemporaries. Joanny Liénot had died during his military service; Mr. Martí, Jr., is visiting Paris; Santos Iturría married a German girl and his father became Minister of Defense in Mexico. And as he strolls through the deserted classrooms, the narrator wonders what has happened to Fermina. "I hope she's happy. . . ."

That's all. *Fermina*, unlike so many of the "novels of adolescence" that came after it, is no passionate defense of youth against adulthood. There is no perceptible "message" except perhaps that in our lives, human passions and feelings are more important than reason and abstract intelligence. Youth passes, everything passes and there is no bitterness about it, only a certain Larbaudian melancholy. Finally, if we can say that

Fermina is "about" anything, it is about being young and growing older. Once, talking with Fermina, Liénot compared St.
Augustin to an ocean liner, sailing on over the vast sea of
time: "... C'est sur la mer du temps qu'il s'avance" (*Pl.*, p.
342). It is a liner pursuing its course very far indeed from the
shores of the contemporary world, where adolescents are swiftly
adults, where sex is no longer a mystery, where the torments
of Joanny, the religious ardor of Fermina, the gallantry of
Santos all might seem anachronistic, remote, and even somewhat
ridiculous.

Fermina Márquez, although a youthful work, is already a
supremely "finished" one, possessing the essence of Larbaud's
art and sensibility. Technically, it testifies to his dislike of straight,
realistic narration. To cite his own words: "Narration and action
have been relegated to the background and have been replaced
by the description of states of conscience" (*Le Bulletin des
lettres* II: 19 [June 25, 1933]: 174–75). And such "description
of states of consciousness" leads us here, as in *Enfantines*, to
experiments, perhaps unconsciously, and still unsystematically,
with the use of the *monologue intérieur* which he will employ
so brilliantly in *Amants, Heureux Amants*. The style is of an
accomplished grace and suppleness, uniting, with characteristic
skill, tenderness and irony. But occasionally, here as elsewhere,
sensibility sometimes softens into sentimentality and produces
passages worthy of an archly refined, very "literary" maiden lady.
As in *Enfantines*, several passages testify that he had abolished
—indeed, if he had ever admitted them!—any absolute distinction
between poetry and prose. Larbaud was walking the tightrope
here, trying to do untried and difficult and often risky things in
writing French prose, although he refuses to "make a point of
it" and rather coyly conceals his intention to innovate, to invent
a fresh tone, to "make it new." He has at least one trait in
common with Whitman, the literary passion of his youth; he
can be, as Walt admitted of himself, "as furtive as an old hen."

Discerning critics—there were a few of them—recognized that
he was trying to break new ground in a new way. Victor Litschs-
fousse in *La Phalange* (February 20, 1911) notes that the work
"is of a very rare artistic quality" but that "the ensemble is not
absolutely 'organic'" and hopes that in the future Larbaud will

acquire "the talent of a real novelist." The critic of the *Grande Revue* salutes the work as a modern classic, esteems that the author can do anything he sets out to do and writes with a rare purity of style. André du Fresnois, in *Gil Blas,* is particularly judicious in observing that *Fermina Márquez* represents a reaction against the whole naturalistic tradition in concentrating on fugitive impressions rather than on intellectual analysis. In addition, the literary friends Larbaud most admired—Gide, Jammes, Claudel—all wrote warm congratulatory letters.

V   Amants, heureux amants ...

A. *Introduction*

In 1923, under this title, Gallimard published a collection of three of Larbaud's *récits*: "Beauté, mon beau souci," "Amants, heureux amants," and "Mon plus secret conseil." These texts incorporate the principal ingredients which he so artfully combined in his narratives: autobiography, the personal essay, psychological analysis, plus a slender, usually very slender, thread of plot to hold things together in a well-formed package. Well formed, certainly, but not of any conventional shape nor of any strictly definable content. Robert Mallet has suggested (*PL.,* p. 1255) that the volume might fittingly be called *Le Touriste du coeur* (The Sentimental Tourist) since all three texts present, scarcely disguised, several of Larbaud's own youthful adventures of the heart.

The first recalls his liaisons with two Englishwomen, "W" and "Gladys" (*Journal,* July 6, 1919); the second, an affair with a dancer of Swedish origin, whom he had met when she was playing an engagement at the Casino in Vichy during the summer of 1904 and with whom he traveled in 1905 to Stockholm and to a country inn at Finja, a sojourn described in *Barnabooth* and alluded to in *Poèmes par un riche amateur* ("Carpe diem" and "Stockholm"). The third, "Mon plus secret conseil," evokes his long affair with "Isabelle," with whom he traveled in Italy in 1903–1904 and with whom he shared a villa near Potenza.

It is in this volume that Larbaud makes his first deliberate and systematic use of the "stream of consciousness" technique, in which he had become deeply interested after his discovery of *Ulysses* and his close friendship with its author. "Amants, heureux amants . . ." indeed, is dedicated to Joyce: "To James Joyce, my friend and the only begetter of the form I have adopted in this piece of writing." Joyce, however, pointed out that he himself had "discovered" the "monologue intérieur" in reading the novel *Les Lauriers sont coupés* (1887) by an almost forgotten (though still living) French writer, Edouard Dujardin. Larbaud subsequently dedicated "Mon plus secret conseil" to him, devoted one of the essays of *Domaine Français* to his novel, and engaged in a considerable correspondence with him.[23] The question of Larbaud and the "monologue intérieur" has been variously studied, most recently by Professor Frida Weissman.[24]

Larbaud did not conceive of the "stream of consciousness" technique as absolutely innovative, but rather as an outgrowth of older forms, such as the intimate journal and the traditional novel of psychological analysis. In one of the mini-essays of *Saint Jérôme*, "Par Omission," he traces it back to the "monologue bavardé" of Montaigne, to *La Princesse de Clèves* and continuing through Stendhal, Dostoyevsky, Schnitzler, Paul Bourget. In his own use of it, visible already in the monologues of *Barnabooth* and of *Fermina Márquez*, he discreetly refrains from plunging too deep into the murk of the subconscious, from exploiting "free association" to the full. His Latin instincts (allied with his distaste for Freudian theory) impelled him to remain on the conscious surface of the mind. Of course, he was fully aware that the *monologue intérieur* was an instrument which could well serve his own strategy in freeing fiction from the constraints of a conventional plot, in fostering that process of the "inwardization" of narrative, in which he himself was engaged and which he identified with the future of prose writing. He was convinced that the conventional novel, after its great popularity as the dominant nineteenth-century genre, would not survive into the twentieth. In his *Journal* (12.3.35), he expressed doubts that a single "genuine novel" complete with its plot and its "characters," written or published after 1910, either in England or in France, would be considered as a literary monument. His predictions have been largely confirmed by the widespread rejection of Realism which has characterized "serious" prose writing from the end of the First World War onward.

The dedication of "Amants, heureux amants" to Joyce as "the only begetter" of the technique is a graceful expression of Larbaud's admiration for the author of *Ulysses,* but it is quite evident that he was aware that variations on the stream of consciousness technique had been employed by a considerable number of distinguished predecessors . . . including himself. For his self-conscious utilization of the *monologue intérieur* in "Amants . . ." may be seen as a development of earlier, more tentative experiments with this device in his own work.

The titles for all three *récits* are taken from French seventeenth-century poets. "Beauté mon beau souci . . ." comes from Malherbe's "Dessin de quitter une Dame qui ne contentait que de promesses"; "Amants, heureux amants . . ." from La Fontaine's "Les Deux pigeons"; and "Mon plus secret conseil" from "Les Amours" by Tristan l'Hermite. Larbaud, with his vast literary culture, was constantly quoting, sometimes, indeed, without realizing it. He defends the use of citations in a text in *Saint Jérôme,* "Des Citations," in which he claims that they constitute "un appel ou un rappel," a means of establishing tacitly a closer relationship with the reader, who discovers that he is in "no strange land." In using them, he reaffirms that his work is a part of an unbroken literary tradition, "just as Joyce uses the Hamlet theme in *Ulysses* to invite comparison between himself and Shakespeare."

B. *"Beauté, mon beau souci"*

The idea for "Beauté, mon beau souci" was suggested to Larbaud during a visit to Hastings in 1914 and the actual composition begun in the spring of 1916 during a visit to Barcelona. As usual, the text underwent numerous revisions and modifications (during the winter of 1917–1918 at Alicante—it is dedicated to "la ciudad de Alicante"—and in 1919–1920 at Alicante and Valbois).[26] It first appeared in the *N.R.F.* (numbers of July 1 and August 1, 1920). The title, as we have noted, is taken from Malherbe, for

Larbaud a "Baroque poet" whom he had long admired, as certain passages from *Barnabooth* reveal: "Malherbe, the father of modern poetry . . ." (*Pl.*, p. 114).

Marc Fournier, a young, sensual Franco-Italian businessman, with interests in London, has installed a "refined," middle-class English widow of thirty-eight, Mrs. Edith Crosland, in his Chelsea apartment as housekeeper-mistress. Mrs. Crosland's fourteen-year-old daughter, Queenie, who for obvious reasons lives with her aunt, visits her mother only occasionally. The first time Marc sees her, he feels "the savage and melodious charm of her youth," and loses no time in kissing her. Queenie, a Lolita *avant la lettre*, shows no alarm or surprise and rather enjoys the new sensation of feeling a moustache pressed to her lips. The mother discovers these goings-on, but with perfect British aplomb makes no fuss about it, for she is all too aware that at her age she cannot hope for the durable and exclusive possession of a young lover. In fact, in trying to persuade Marc to stay on in London rather than returning for business reasons to the Continent, she proposes that Queenie come to live with them, making a rather unconventional *ménage à trois*. "How much she wants to keep me," Marc reflects. "She would sacrifice her own daughter!" (*PL.*, p. 568).

A few days before his scheduled departure, Queenie appears in Marc's room, clad only in one of her mother's nightgowns, which she has left unbuttoned. In a typically ambiguous scene, she pretends that her "mother has sent her" (which is a lie) and begins to make advances to him. As soon as Marc, excited by this "tendre et mince nudité" (*PL.*, p. 570), begins to respond, she withdraws and threatens to scream if he continues. Queenie, of course, with the instinctive cunning of children, is quite aware that her mother is Marc's mistress. Is she jealous of her? Is she intent on winning this exotic foreign lover and keeping him for herself? Characteristically, Larbaud never "explains" her motives, and we are left to figure things out for ourselves. (Larbaud, willingly enigmatic, demands much more "reader participation" than the majority of his contemporaries.) She permits him one kiss before she leaves, warning him that he must stop when she says so, otherwise she'll scream for the police. Afterwards, Marc, shaken by this curious scene, goes to join

Edith in her bedroom. She is reading a French novel Marc has lent her. "But that passage where he describes the legs of the little girl sitting on the school wall! I think it's almost indecent," she modestly observes.

Marc's departure from London concludes the first and more original part of the *récit*. The portrait of Edith (based on "Gladys," the British mistress often mentioned in the *Journals*) reveals Larbaud's conception of the character of the English-woman, for him composed of a disconcerting mixture of public prudery and private sensuality. Marc described (*Pl.*, p. 549) Edith's life as "divided between a kind of vague, chaste dreaming—and the bedroom." The basic situation is as shocking as anything in Nabokov, but Larbaud handles the whole business with such grace and discretion, without ever raising an eyebrow, that the reader, until he begins to reflect, simply accepts everything as "quite normal." Marc Fournier appears here as a typical representative of what he himself described as the *"godersela"* school (*Pl.*, p. 610) of unperturbed self-indulgence, of the same family as Felice Francia in "Amants, heureux amants..." and Lucas Letheil in "Mon plus secret conseil," wealthy, egotistic, uncommitted, amoral, sensual without passion, and nominally Roman Catholic. Fournier, like these other young womanizers, would certainly be described today as a "male chauvinist." Woman, for them, is an object, often an object to be admired and cherished, but an object nevertheless, and exists only to serve man, to make him comfortable, to satisfy his sensual desires. Mrs. Crosland "never refused Marc anything." She was "the sweet, amicable woman," who was always there, ready to share his bed when he came home (*Pl.*, p. 547). She was a great convenience too. "Thanks to her, the house was always well kept...."

The second part of the *récit* begins when Marc returns to London after an absence of several years. He arranges to meet Queenie, with whom he had remained in sporadic correspondence, even after her mother's death in America, where Mrs. Crosland, with her daughter, had gone to "keep house" for a cousin. When he sees her, he is struck by her air of poverty, her shabby clothes, her melancholy. Queenie, as she confesses, weeping, after her return to England "had fallen to her shame" and had an illegitimate child by a man who subsequently deserted her. Fortunately, the child died. Marc attempts to help her financially, but she spurns him, lest he get the idea that he can "buy" her, but she finally accepts a small loan and the gift of a typewriter, so that she can earn extra money.

Money indeed becomes a central preoccupation. When Queenie comes in for a small inheritance from the American cousin, her aunt, Mrs. Longhurst, who had "kicked her out" when she had "fallen" invites her to come back and live with her again. Soon afterwards, a very wealthy suitor, Reginald Harding, miraculously appears, wins the support of the aunt when she learns he is a millionaire, and proposes marriage to Queenie. He assures her that it will be a very advantageous operation for her: "1,000 pounds for her trousseau, 2,000 for her jewels, 80 pounds a month for household expenses, 20 pounds a month of pocket money, and charge accounts up to 500 pounds a year." Queenie at first rejects him. She now "hates" all men, deceivers that they are, and accuses him of trying to "buy" her. Money, money. But she finally decides to accept him (it's certainly a better deal than Marc's offer to make her his "private secretary," and we know what *that* means), especially after he has given her a little talk on the difference between being married when you're rich and being married when you're poor. Larbaud admirably succeeds here, without making the slightest commentary, in conveying the sense of the asphyxiating materialism of the *grande bourgeoisie*, the class to which he so consciously belonged, even when in revolt against it, and the central role of money in their lives. So Harding acquires a bride and Queenie rapturously begins to sign checks. She even sends Marc (just to show him!) a very expensive crocodile valise, accompanied by her card as "a farewell gift."

The young couple is ready to settle down to a life "of perfect happiness." In the conventional phrase, they have "everything to live for" and absolutely nothing to do. For Harding's ideal of "happiness" (and in this he resembles Marc and Larbaud's other young men of the "*godersela*" persuasion) is, as he tells Queenie, "l'absence de toute ambition et l'oisiveté complète" (*Pl.*, p. 608) —he didn't want to do anything, except, as he gallantly adds as an afterthought, "to be the lover of my wife." Obviously there

is little all-consuming passion here. We are light-years away from
the *amour fou,* the cosmic passion which obsessed Breton and
the Surrealists.

The life of pleasure which Harding promises Queenie constitutes in itself a menace to genuine happiness. Even as Harding
is telling Queenie how happy he is going to make her and
Queenie is telling him how happy she is, they are both aware
that they're faking it. The story ends with their first spat, after
which Queenie gives in "just as her mother would have done"
(*Pl.,* p. 613), for Reggie has the money just as Marc had.
"Beauté, mon beau souci," once the surface grace has been
stripped away, is a sad and disillusioned tale that illustrates
some of the melancholy of Larbaud's complex approach to love
and sexuality. Certain Freudian overtones (although Larbaud
disliked Freud's theories) keep recurring, such as Queenie's desire "to carry the cane" of Marc and Reggie. The ambiguities
with which Larbaud confronts us are never resolved. Are we to
see in Marc a condemnation of those callous upper middle-class
Don Juans for whom women (particularly women "of the lower
orders") are simply disposable objects of pleasure? Was Marc
being outrageously cynical or simply honest when he admitted
that when he heard of Edith's death he was "sad for a quarter
of an hour"? Or is Marc less unfeeling than he would like to
appear? Does the mask of callous Don Juanism conceal a nostalgia for genuine emotion? But perhaps Larbaud is simply telling
us once again that people are complicated and contradictory,
neither as good nor as bad as we think or as they would like to
appear.

One aspect of "Beauté. . . ," however, poses no problems. The
descriptions it contains of London are among the most graceful
prose-poems Larbaud ever wrote, particularly the opening paragraphs describing Chelsea, where "tout est solitaire et discret;
les couleurs mêmes se taisent. . . ." (*Pl.,* p. 540), More than Mrs.
Crosland, more than Queenie, London itself is the heroine of
the *récit,* the object of "mon beau souci. . . ."

C. *"Amants, heureux amants . . ."*

"Amants. . . ," written in 1920 (first published in the November

1, 1921, number of the *N.R.F.*), also draws heavily on personal reminiscences. It is based on Larbaud's *liaison* (in 1904–1906) with the bisexual Inga. It also recalls his stay in Montpellier, the setting of the story, where he had spent the winters of 1906–1907 and of 1907–1908, studying Greek, preparing his *license*, and working on various literary projects, including *Fermina Márquez* and *Barnabooth*.

Of course, there is little or no "plot" in this first conscious experiment of Larbaud's with the "stream of consciousness" technique. Inga, an off-and-on mistress of "Felice Francia," an independently wealthy, introverted, cultivated, and somewhat perverse young man, arrives for a brief visit. She is accompanied by her lover of the moment, a dancer like herself, Romana Cerri. They are en route to an engagement in Nice. The night of their arrival, the three of them have a party in their connecting hotel rooms; the champagne flows like water, the girls get drunk, and Felice (always in search of novelty) possesses Cerri in the presence of Inga and with her complicity. (In the past, as Felice notes, the two of them have often [*Pl.*, p. 646] "shared the booty.")

The *récit* opens the morning after, as Felice watches the two girls still sleeping and ruminates on the pleasures of the night before. We follow the "inner monologue" of Felice throughout the day, as he takes his guests to lunch, walks with them in the public gardens, escorts them to the train, and then resumes his life of studious solitude, having resisted the temptation of following the girls to Nice or of returning to still another mistress who lives in Spain. Two themes preoccupy him in his musings: the various kinds of love and the inevitable human solitude which love, always doomed to end in boredom or disappointment, can never conquer. Felice knows that finally he wants solitude more than anything else and that he must be willing to pay the price for it.

The various kinds of love—in no other text has Larbaud approached more explicitly, yet with his usual discretion, the question of Lesbianism, which obviously fascinates him. Inga, of course, sleeps with men. Felice remembers the happy days he spent with her in Sweden in a little country inn at Finja and asks himself, "Does she have as pleasant a memory of it as I do?" But he quickly concludes that it doesn't mean anything much to her, for he knows that her real passions have always been for women. "At school," she confesses, "I had Greta Kromer, at the Conservatory, Rosele Mayer; then there was Carmela Savini and I thought I'd die when Maria Ferreira left me" (*Pl.*, p. 620). But Felice himself has never suffered the torments of the grand, the obsessional passion. He never wants to get too involved with "the others," he never wants to endanger his own liberty.

Inga, however, is prepared to "give all for love," subordinates her professional career to the pursuit of "lovely, gentle" creatures. But she demands total submission in return. "Tout donner, mais exiger tout." Inga, strong, complex, lovable, and terrifying, dominates the story. She is "more of a man," if you like, than Felice. In her relations with men, however, relations which have little meaning for her, she wears the mask of "the adoring slave," "aimable, obéissante—et perfide" (*Pl.*, p. 626). She prefers very young men, "rather effeminate ones," who, ironically, are often very jealous of her. "Jealousy," remarks Felice, like the observant *moraliste* he is, "jealousy, an illness of very young men just starting out on their career of conquest. A kind of measles of the emotions" (*Pl.*, p. 625). Inga's young men never realize that their real rival is the other young lady with whom they so often strolled, chatted, and dined in Inga's company. Inga never lets them know. She prefers to keep them around as a distraction and as a camouflage (*Pl.*, p. 626). Felice, in his observation of these *femmes damnées*, finds that they are basically very "innocent." Their pleasantries are as harmless as anything one would hear in a convent. They behave in public with impeccable propriety. Even as Felice speculates about his relations with Inga and Romana, he continues to fantasize about "the one I'm always dreaming of," a mistress with whom he has quarreled. She is a Spaniard, married, of the upper middle class, and given to an ostentatious and dramatic piety, which seems to inflame her sensuality. ". . . On her way to a *rendez-vous*, if she happens to pass in front of a church, she goes in, piously kisses the feet of the Saviour, and then ten minutes later . . . !" (*Pl.*, p. 634).

A third variation on the erotic theme is presented in the person of a girl Felice observes as he lunches with Inga and Romana.

Always accompanied by her mother, she is the very type of proper young woman that Larbaud finds so unattractive. The product of a prudish, materialistic milieu, she is incapable of the passion of an Inga or of the eroticism of "the one I'm thinking of," and is concerned only with making a wealthy marriage. He thinks how interesting it would be to set Inga in pursuit of her (*Pl.,* p. 632). "Amants..." has a Proustian flavor in its subtle psychological probings, its speculations about the mystery of love and about the impossibility of ever really "knowing" the beloved object. "No," Felice concludes, "it's really useless to try to see those whom we love or even those who interest us, as an indifferent third party would see them." He is also constantly aware of the complex interplay between "individuality" and universal human traits (*Pl.,* p. 642). Aware, too, of the comparable interplay between the "male" and "female" present in every individual and of the impossibility here, as elsewhere, of making sharp distinctions, of establishing well-defined frontiers. "Sex? Something added, a disguise. And there is an infinite modulation in the passage from one sex to another. Take Inga for example. In a man's suit she appears to be doubly disguised." Such observations recall the classical moralists, with whom Larbaud felt such a close affinity.[26] Felice is constantly delivering himself of "maxims" of a disenchanted worldliness such as: "We really can't be absolutely 'natural'—and there's really no great advantage in trying to be."

The girls gone, Felice prepares to resume his usual solitary life of study, reading, and writing. Walking back from the station through the public gardens, a statue of the three Graces starts him thinking about the transcendence of art. "The pleasures and the sorrows of artists," he muses, "are finally the only things in the world that count," for theirs are the only sorrows and pleasures which do not pass away "like a dream." Art means more to Felice than love, it would seem, as he fondly recalls his reading of Alfieri, of Lucian of Samosata, of Homer. But artistic creation, and the genuine assimilation of the work of art demand conscious effort. In spite of his apparent frivolity, Felice (like Larbaud) knew the value of work: "My projects: this city and the peace I find here; the parks, books, work ... live to work..." (*Pl.,* p. 645). But to work freely and creatively requires the liberty that comes from economic independence and emotional detachment. And such liberty means solitude. At the end, that's what it is all about. Felice knows that after all the diversions, erotic and otherwise, he will remain alone, he will go back to the solitude he both desires and fears. Even if Inga and Romana had stayed on, he soon would be bored with them and would have longed to be alone (*Pl.*, p. 627). He wants to learn to be alone in life, "as one day I shall be in death," to build a wall between himself and the world, a wall that the world will never be able to scale. From time to time he may go outside to satisfy his curiosity, only to return into his own private domain. At the end of the *récit*, Felice wonders when he may possibly see Inga again, for it is to Inga that he is most closely attached. Will it be in a hotel, on a train, aboard a ship? They will greet each other formally. She, of course, will be with a new lover, "la cara, la diletta, l'unica." And Felice? "All alone, probably."

D. *"Mon plus secret conseil"*

"Mon plus secret conseil," begun during a holiday on the Italian Riviera in the early summer of 1922, was completed in Paris early the next year. After having read the text at one of Adrienne Monnier's "evenings" on the rue de l'Odéon, Larbaud submitted it to the *N.R.F.*, where it appeared in the numbers of September and October 1923. Even more, perhaps, than the first two *récits*, "Mon plus secret conseil" draws on precise personal memories. It is not only an almost literal account, as we have said, of Larbaud's trip to Italy in 1903 with "Isabelle"; it also recalls Larbaud's years at the Collège Ste.-Barbe at Fontenay-aux-Roses; a visit to Nice with his mother in 1895; studies at the Lycée Henri Quatre; dealings with his legal guardian, Dr. Cornil, Senator of the Allier. Technically it represents Larbaud's most ambitious and consistent use of the stream of consciousness technique; he introduces, moreover, an innovation in its application by employing all three persons in close association to achieve shifts in perspective and changes in "lighting." Lucas may first address himself as "vous," then shift to "moi" as he speaks of himself directly, finally changing to "il" to refer to himself in the third person. As Patrick McCarthy has pointed out, this device was well adapted to express the various "voices" that struggle within each character.[27] The citation from Tristan l'Hermite's poem effectively indicates what Larbaud was setting out to do, in summoning up all the poet's conflicting thoughts about his mistress ("Pensers, chers confidents d'un amour si fidèle...") and begging them to "keep him company...."

The text is composed of twenty-one brief sections, some bearing the names of towns between Naples and Taranto, along the route of Lucas Letheil's "flight from love." It introduces us into "the stream of consciousness" of this very young man of twenty-two (the age of Larbaud himself when he embarked on his first "serious" affair) who has run off to Italy with an older married woman, Isabelle. He soon discovers that she is far from being the most delicious of companions with whom to embark on that "experiment in conjugal life" to which he felt he should give a try, after a series of brief and inconclusive encounters with occasional mistresses. Isabelle, he discovers, has a psychopathic fondness for unmotivated scenes, for outbursts of rage in public places, for dramatic suicide attempts. Soon Lucas is "fed up" and longs to get away. He doesn't have the courage simply to hand her a ticket and put her on the train for Paris. So, very early one morning, after a noisy quarrel the night before (he's been sleeping on the sofa in the salon, reading Thomas de Quincey!), he flees Naples (without even a clean handkerchief). He vaguely hopes that if he stays away awhile, Isabelle will somehow simply disappear and leave him a free hand with "Irene," the rich and beautiful daughter of a Greek banker with whom he now imagines himself in love. Isabelle, he has decided, is not only disagreeable—she is also too *bourgeoise,* not at all suited to be the mistress of "a poet like Lucas Letheil." On top of everything else, she is a liar and a kleptomaniac; in restaurants, she can't resist stealing the silverware which she hides under her garters.

Lucas, of course, is a callow, spoiled youth ("orphelin et héritier") with none of the mature and disenchanted sophistication of Marc Fournier or Felice Francia. Even he can recognize that he has "a child's need to be taken seriously" (*Pl.* p. 661). The serious and respectable friends of his serious and respectable family, of course, have no use for him, especially after he makes it clear to them that he doesn't want to go into business or to pursue any profession but simply to live for his own pleasure. They are convinced that he has been led astray by "all those artists and anarchists he runs around with." When he makes fun of their conventional patriotic sentiments and declares that he intends to live abroad, their rage knows no bounds—"an expatriate! You'll certainly end badly . . ." (*Pl.*, p. 660). Of course, he longs to fling off the restraints of this milieu he hates and to assert his liberty. The flight with Isabelle was designed to "show them" how free he was. But he soon discovered that the "expérience conjugale" was a servitude and a bore, and he longed to be "free, free of all this mediocrity" and "alone, in my own place, with my books" (*Pl.*, p. 655).

But, as the train puts the miles between him and Isabelle, he is honest enough to admit that "he is running away like a rabbit . . ." (*Pl.*, p. 665). Much of what goes on in Lucas' mind as we are borne along on his "stream of consciousness" is simply adolescent fantasizing. Near Taranto, he has a headache and (inclined to be a hypochondriac like his creator) decides that "this evening on arrival, he'll probably have a fever and come down with a serious illness." He coughs and concludes that "his behavior is that of a sick man. His premature death will explain, will pardon a great many things. His trip to Taranto is a journey to the grave." And he recalls that as a child (*Pl.*, p. 665) he could always get what he wanted when he declared himself ill. It might still work. He imagines "la belle Irène" hurrying to his deathbed and holding his hand in hers as he expires. He would bequeath his entire fortune to her. "Tutto il suo bene . . ." "Tutto il suo bene. . . ." Lucien frequently uses Italian phrases as he fantasizes—it's a part of his role-playing. He has a fondness for that. In the course of his twenty-two years, he has played a number of roles. Under the influence of some working-class fellows, he was briefly a Socialist, very much to the left, and marched in proletarian demonstrations in Belleville. Then he went through an aesthetic, Symbolist phase, read Moréas and Kahn, took des Esseintes as his model. There followed a period as a sports fan, when he sought out the company of bicycle racers and was flattered to meet champs like Amerighi and Daragon. Occasionally, too, he imagined himself as a man of deep but unconventional religious feeling (*Pl.*, p. 711) with a touching and poetic devotion to the Blessed Virgin. He repeats the Ave Maria in Italian ("it's better than in French") praying that Our Lady may take *both* Irene and Isabelle under her protection, so that the first "will let herself be loved, and the second will not suffer too much." (And he adds with an ingenuous egotism—"nor me either,—when we break up.")

Lucas emerges as probably the least sympathetic and least convincing of the young *dandys* who figure in the collection. He is callow and immature, but astonishing riches of the spirit and of the intellect incongruously float to the surface in the course of his *monologue intérieur*. Many passages—like the one of the beauty of Naples in the morning light (*Pl.*, p. 662) or the Proustian reflections on time (*Pl.*, pp. 664–65)—strike us as quite "out of character."

At the close, Lucas's musings, as he falls asleep in the train, are printed in the form of free verse.[28] This is still another, rather obvious hint that for Larbaud the frontier between prose and poetry is nonexistent. Dozing off, Lucas murmurs: "I'm going to join Irene. . . ." But, advancing a bit further into the tunnel of the unconscious, he caresses the notion of forgetting her as well as Isabelle, of "liberating himself" from both of them . . . he'll see about that when he gets back to Paris. Perhaps he'll spend the month of May in Sicily—or perhaps Corfu. . . ?

E.   *"La Dignité de l'amour": Larbaud's Comments on Amants . . .*

In volume V of the manuscripts of Larbaud (now in the FVL) Vincent Milligan discovered Larbaud's brief commentary on *Amants, heureaux amants*, "La Dignité de l'amour," a text written between 1931-1935.[29] In it, he contends that true love abolishes the hostility between man and woman to which society has accustomed us. A mutual esteem creates "the dignity of love." This esteem is not essentially sexual in nature, but rather belongs to a common domain over which sex does not reign, "the domain of the essentially human, common to both man and woman."

F.   *Luis Losada*

Larbaud' unfinished novel, *Luis Losada*, begun in 1919, records his impressions of the years he spent in Alicante. He worked on it sporadically for over five years before giving up the project. It was published only in 1971, together with *Le Coeur de l'Angle-terre*, edited with an introduction by Frida Weisman.[30] The five chapters which he completed are essentially devoted to descriptions of life in Alicante and to a portrait of "Luis Losada", a Spanish cousin of the young men who figure in *Amants, heureux amants . . .*

CHAPTER 4

The Essayist:
"Essai, Traité, Divagation, Esquisse. . . ?"

I *"Call Them What You Like . . ."*

LARBAUD was quite willing to admit (as we shall see in his note describing the collection *Jaune Bleu Blanc*) that his "essays" could be called almost anything the reader liked: "essays, treatises, divagations, sketches, fantasies, epistles, remarks, conversations, promenades...." They reflect his old and deeply-rooted distaste for "genre distinctions," for trying to put things (as he felt that French academicians were all too prone to do) into neat pigeonholes, to halt the flow, to falsify by categorizing. He increasingly wanted (and in this he announced future literary trends) to break down these distinctions and "put it all in," even though the Cartesian might feel that logically it all didn't belong together. But when he got through with them, these apparently random remarks, these apparently incongruous juxtapositions did really go together, orchestrated as they were by his own very individual talent. In spite of their often offhand tone, their "slightness," even the briefest and the least pretentious of them, woven together with a subtle art and a deceptive modesty, are "serious" without being solemn, take up once again with a smiling gravity some of his obsessive themes: the sensuous delight of this world, the importance of love and work and pleasure, the persistence of continuity even in the midst of apparent change, the inevitability of death. Technically, they testify to his rare verbal virtuosity, his intense (but almost clandestine) effort to cast aside artificial formal distinctions, to write the text and the the antitext, to approach "l'oeuvre totale," the total work of which his Symbolist predecessors, like Mallarmé, were always dreaming.

116

But in his first contact with them, the reader is scarcely aware of their innovative qualities, is conscious only of the delight that they give. They constitute one of the best of introductions to the literary achievement of Larbaud, an achievement which anticipated some of the tendencies which have surfaced in our own time.

II   Allen: *A Citizen of the Bourbonnais...and of the World*

Commentators have been very skittish about discussing this appealing, puzzling text, whose very title "Allen"—as even the author admits—is so "enigmatic." Perhaps they didn't quite know what to make of it and were afraid that Larbaud might be putting something over on them. It was not only the critics who were confused. Gallimard, his publisher, insisted, as Larbaud reveals in the copious "notes" (almost as long as the text itself!), that the "bande publicitaire" on the book should at least give a hint to the prospective reader as to what it was all about. Rather unwillingly, since he detested publicity and "popularization," Larbaud composed the following very brief description:

"An automobile trip from Paris to the center of France."
"A dialogue on provincial life in France."
"A eulogy of the Bourbonnais."

The text proper consists of only thirty-six pages in the *Pléiade* edition; it is followed by fourteen closely printed pages of notes, the self-conscious enterprise (somewhat comparable to Gide's *Journal des Faux-Monnayeurs*) of a writer writing about the writing of his book. "Allen" first appeared in the *N.R.F.* in the numbers of February 1 and March 1, 1927. It was published in book form with the addition of a prologue and the notes, by Gallimard in 1929. Larbaud dedicated it to his mother, the loved and feared matriarch, then in her eighties, as a work "devoted to our native province."

The text is entirely written as a conversation, between five friends: the "Bibliophile," the "Amateur," the "publisher" (modeled perhaps on Gaston Gallimard or A. A. M. Stols), the "poet" (modeled certainly on Léon-Paul Fargue), and the author himself. There is no indication of who is talking and Larbaud has captured with rare virtuosity the shifting tones and the uneven rhythms of actual speech—uncompleted sentences, sudden, illogical changes from one subject to another, modifications in pace. In his notes he claims that his models were Lucian (one of his favorite classical authors, as one can easily understand), Fontenelle (of the "Dialogue"), and Walter Savage Landor (of *Imaginary Conversations*). But in the works of these predecessors, there is usually—as in Lucian—a certain dramatic, narrative element or—as in Fontenelle—a definite subject, logically developed. In "Allen" there is no dramatic or narrative element, but instead an apparently random exchange of a number of ideas. We perceive in it a certain discreet kinship with passages of philosophical fooling in Rabelais, or with *A Sentimental Journey* of Laurence Sterne (the source of Larbaud's frequently cited phrase, "the Bourbonnais, the sweetest part of France"), or with perversely playful *tours de force* like *Pale Fire*. Many of the comments of Virginia Woolf on *A Sentimental Journey*[1] could be applied to *Allen*: "The utmost fluidity exists with the utmost permanence. It is as if the tide raced over the beach hither and thither and left every ripple and eddy cut on the sand in marble."

Of the three principal subjects which have been "woven together," Larbaud assigns first place to "provincial life." He had long been preoccupied with the relations between Paris and the provinces and came more and more to regret the hegemony of the capital, which had stamped out the vigorous regional life existing up until the implacable centralization imposed by Louis XIII and his successors. Larbaud, as we have seen, had long dreamed of a universal Empire, within which small states would keep their autonomy, their savor, their individuality; his ideal was an ideal of unity in diversity, and diversity in unity. He hated the national state and its thirst for power, its ruthless suppression of regional liberties and differences. He frequently evokes in *Allen* the period when provincial capitals flourished, capitals like Dijon in the late Middle Ages, which then was more powerful than Paris, a city with its bishop and its university, filled with scholars and foreign visitors (*Pl.*, p. 735). After the seventeenth century, these once great and flourishing centers became "des trous de province," provincial backwaters. Larbaud detested the narrowness and the pettiness to which provincial life had been reduced.

In his youth, he hated Vichy with a violence, as he often notes in his *Journals*, hated its refusal to "take seriously anything except its own petty daily concerns." But later he was more and more drawn to his native "land," his own "pays" in reaction against the tentacular, impersonal capital. And for him, provincial life was specifically most closely identified with the Duchy of Bourbonnais, that "sweetest part of France." Indeed the title *Allen* comes straight from an incident of its history. The Duke, Louis II, on his return to Moulins from captivity in England in 1366, founded the Order of the *Ecu d'or* to honor the knights who had remained faithful to him during his long absence. And he announced to them that the motto of the Order would be "Allen," evidently his garbled version of the English "all one"—all together.

In the prologue, Larbaud lovingly evokes, in a series of brief prose poems, the principal towns of the Bourbonnais—Souvigny, Chantelle, Bourbon-Archambaut, Hérisson—deserted villages now which were once important centers, when the Duchy was still a semisovereign state, before its confiscation by the French crown. "I realized that the Bourbonnais was more than a 'region,' a 'province,' a 'département'—it was a European state, smaller than Switzerland or Belgium, but bigger than Luxembourg; a state which, allied to the kings of France, had played a role in European affairs right up to the time of Charles III's secession from the kingdom" (*Pl.*, p. 754). Charles III is one of Larbaud's heroes. He adopted the winged stag, the insignia of Charles III, as his own and stamped it on his books and manuscripts (*Pl.*, p. 751). This "last Duke of the Bourbonnais," who joined forces with the Emperor Charles V against François I, was killed during the sack of Rome in 1527. "Republican" historians like Michelet brand him a traitor; but for Larbaud, the *Connétable* chose the better part, preferring European unity as represented by the Empire to the disunity fostered by the rise of national states.

For "in spite of all appearances to the contrary, in spite of all the political speeches, it is quite possible," claims Larbaud, "that the system of national states, which seemed the only logical and reasonable one in the nineteenth century, has now outlived its usefulness" (*Pl.*, p. 757). This conviction—which, in one form or another, he so often stated and restated—constitutes the ideological center of *Allen*. But Larbaud had no intention of writing a political tract, as he makes clear in note XIV (*Pl.*, p. 768), entitled "the thesis discussed." Discussed, yes, but not upheld ("débattue, non soutenue"). For he always disliked polemics, feeling they inevitably eliminated the complexities and the contradictions of "truth." *Allen* also provides a pretext to discuss at some length another of his recurrent themes—a theory of social hierarchy, "the three orders," composed of the "third estate," the great majority, for whom material well-being is the principal preoccupation; the "nobles"; and at the summit of the hierarchy, the "clerks"—ecclesiastics, thinkers, artists. The function of "the nobles" is to construct, organize, prevent social disorder, and generally to conform "to the most sacred aspiration of the 'clergy.'" The proportion of each "order" in the general population is a determining factor in the difference existing between "Province"—where the Third Estate constitutes the overwhelming majority—and "capital," where nobles and clerks form an important and creative minority.

But *Allen* is more interesting, perhaps, as literary experiment than as a restatement of Larbaud's ideas on European unity and the revival of the Empire. In spite of its surface randomness, the notes make it clear that the various themes and the various tones were artfully orchestrated. For example, in note IX (*Pl.*, p. 766), he points out that the chapters of "movement" (2–6) had been placed between two chapters of "immobility." This arrangement illustrates once again Larbaud's penchant for "gliding" for "oscillation"—from repose to motion and then back to immobility again. A similar "oscillation" is established between the diversity of small principalities and the unity of Empire; between Paris and province—an oscillation between the small scale and the large, a continuous movement back and forth between opposing states. He was also trying an experiment in recording conversation in such a way that, as we have said, it would approximate the randomness, the abruptness, the *non sequiturs*, the modifications of tone of actual speech. To do this, he rejected the usual literary conventions of dialogue, the repetition of the "he saids," the identification of speakers, the maintenance of a certain "logical" sequence in the discourse. There are abrupt modifications of tone: a poetic description of Moulins, "with its ghost of a great palace, surrounded by gardens with colonnades, fountains, and orange trees" is interrupted with "do you want a light?" Weighty observations concerning "the temporal abyss of geology" are suddenly halted by "Look over there—the first shepherdess." The copious notes form an integral part of the work itself, for, as we have seen, Larbaud was engaged in writing, not simply a text, but an account of the writing of that text, an exploration of the "creative process."[2] With a sinuous indirection, he makes us aware of the writer's duel with the work he intends to create (*Pl.*, p. 558).

The reactions of Paris critics disappointed Larbaud. Most of them saw in *Allen* only a satire directed against provincial life. The most understanding appraisals came, as might be expected, from readers who were also natives of the Bourbonnais. Larbaud singled out with particular approval the comments of H. Buriot-Darsiles in a Moulins paper, which underline the importance of Larbaud's plea for regional autonomy, for the revival of provincial life, "la renaissance de l'initiative, la fin de la saison d'ennui." These views have acquired a measure of contemporary relevance as programs of "régionalisation" and decentralization are being increasingly introduced by the French government as a means of countering the numerous separatist movements—Corsican, Breton, Alsatian—that have steadily been increasing in strength since the War. In "Montpellier" (one of the texts in *Septimanie*), he predicts (*Pl.*, pp. 881–82) that in the United States of Europe of the future, when the power-hungry nation-states have disappeared, "Occitanie" (that area in the southwest of France where the *langue d'oc* was spoken) will regain its independent identity and its autonomy. The contemporary agitation for "a free *Occitanie*" bears witness that Larbaud's poetic intuitions may become political realities.

In *Allen*, the cosmopolitan is wed to the regionalist, "a citizen of the world and of the Bourbonnais," ever more firmly rooted in his "Free State" of Valbois, which he lovingly restored after his mother's death and where he and his companion spent more and more of their time. The "open" space of Europe and the "closed" space of Valbois—as well as the liberty of moving freely between the two—were equally necessary to him. True cosmopolitanism, he implies, never excludes an intense attachment to one's small native place nor does the sense of the past, of tradition—so evident in *Allen*—exclude the sense of the modern. Larbaud early discovered and reveled in all the poetry of modern life, from the popular songs of Dranem and other music hall stars, to motorcycle racing, to luxury trains rushing through the night, to the exploits of Putouarey's racing car "Vorace," taking breakneck curves on Italian mountain roads. *Allen*, a hymn to the far-distant past of the Bourbonnais, also celebrates the pleasures of driving through it. He describes, in lyrical terms, the machine in which the five friends travel from the *parvis* of Notre Dame to Moulins—"long, slender, tranquilly powerful . . . more handsome than we had imagined—a sleek blue and silver object" (*Pl.*, p. 727). He dwells on the sensation of watching the landscape gliding by as he sits immobile, of enjoying the changing patterns that the leaves of trees lining the highway make on the surface of the road, of feeling simultaneously in movement and in repose as they speed along at eighty kilometers an hour. Long before the composition of *Allen*, he had written (in 1911) a "Journal de Quasie" (which he never published). It recounts in four parts the pleasures of an automobile trip (the car is named "Quasie") through central France. As was his habit, Larbaud used material from "Quasie" (the manuscript is in the FVL) in the composition of *Allen*.[3]

III   Jaune Bleu Blanc: *Essay? Treatise? Divagation? Sketch?*

The title? The author explains it in a "preface" of three lines: "The manuscripts which form the present work were tied up together with a yellow, light blue, and white ribbon." We recall that these were the colors of Larbaud's personal pennon which was hoisted over the Thébaïde when poet-friends were in residence. The eighteen texts offer an excellent introduction to the various manners and tones of Larbaud's work, sum up, so to speak, his varied interests as a writer and scholar. They include notes on travels in Portugal, Spain, Italy, England, essays on Paris and what it means to be "a true Parisian," a dramatic monologue, philological *divertissements*. They form an artfully arranged tray of literary *hors d'oeuvres*, all exquisitely fashioned, of unique savor, and presented with the confident modesty of an artist sure of his craft. An artist content to create on a small scale— but determined to create impeccably within self-imposed limits. All of the texts had seen previous publication in reviews—a number of them in the Princess Caetani's luxurious *Commerce*, of which Larbaud was the most active member of the editorial board—and in small limited editions.[4] He had described the volume in a letter to his friend, Jean-Aubry, which is reproduced in the *Pléiade* edition (p. 1270):

This book is a collection, or rather, held together by the tricolor ribbon of its completely arbitrary title, an odd lot of relatively short texts. Most of them could be designated by terms such as "essay," "treatise," "divagation," "sketch." Some could be labelled "remarks," "epistle," "conversation." Chapter X, "On Women's Names," is perhaps a "fantasy" (clearly inspired by Montaigne's chapter, "Des Noms"). XII is a "disque"—a phonograph record; XIII, "a presentation"; XVIII is something of a poem. . . . It would be possible to group some of them together as "A Portuguese Notebook"; others as an "Italian Notebook"; others as a "Paris or French Notebook." However, there is a certain order in the arrangement of these little works: —the first ("Paris de France") takes us out of Paris; at the end of the eleventh ("200 chambres, 200 salles de bain") we're passing through it, in a hotel; the 17th, takes us back to Paris again ("Rues et visages de Paris") and the 18th ("rue Soufflot") leaves us there.

In spite of his love of travel, in spite of his devotion to his native Bourbonnais, Larbaud recognized in Paris the spiritual and intellectual capital of his world. In "La Rue Soufflot," the poem which closes the collection, he confesses that in spite of all his traveling "we've never really left here and all our life will have been a little trip zig-zagging back and forth in Paris and all around it" (". . . et toute notre vie aura été/ un petit voyage en rond et en zigzag dans Paris"). The draft of "Paris de France," the opening essay, was written in Alicante in 1920. It celebrates Larbaud's rediscovery of the city after his long absence in Spain. He first knew Paris as a child and since that time he has always maintained "his principal establishment there." But does that mean that he can truly consider himself "a real Parisian"? Scarcely. For the "Parigots" he is a "provincial"—since for them the provinces and foreign countries are almost the same thing. But the "real Parisians" themselves are often narrowly provincial, with their disdain (rooted in ignorance) for everything outside their city, their contempt for "foreigners" and for the unfamiliar. But these are not the Parisians Larbaud admires. He and his friends had a completely different idea—their "real Parisian" embraced intellectual horizons which extended far beyond the city itself; knew the world in its diversity; was a Londoner in London, a Roman in Rome. For them Paris, liberated from the narrowness of all local politics, should be "a kind of intellectual International" (*Pl.*, p. 783). After all his wanderings, Paris, for Larbaud, is "the city of our youth and of our memories" that as a young man he had explored with his closest friend, Léon-Paul Fargue, the noctambule "piéton de Paris." Paris is "the fundamental theme of our life" (*Pl.*, p. 787). And "just as when a man grows older, he ends by marrying the least demanding of his mistresses, so finally we scarcely leave Paris any more" (*Pl.*, p. 788). And this return engenders a kind of "grave melancholy"— the sadness of having come back to the place you started from, and coming back very much aware of the brevity of life, of diminishing energy and curiosity. But you have come back with an "enlarged vision" of what it means to be a Parisian—a European, not simply a Parisian of "Paris de France." Come back, in middle age, to confront the city of your youthful ambitions and to ask yourself—"and what have you done with the time that was given to you?" Such discreet melancholy runs like a dark thread through the glowing fabric of the text.

But Larbaud's Paris was not only the international Paris of artists and intellectuals. From Fargue, probably, he had acquired the taste for the Paris of the people, of small cafés, of music halls, of open-air markets, and he celebrates this other Paris in "Rues et visages de Paris." He first came in contact with it through a school friend he met at Louis-le-Grand, who lived near the Place d'Italie, and who was a real "Parigot." Larbaud devotes sections 8 and 9 of "Rues et visages . . ." to a portrait of this "picturesque savage, Julot" who figures in "Mon plus secret conseil" as Pierre Goubert (*Pl.*, p. 706).

But he has many other memories "of the loyal, delicate, tender heart" of popular Paris, particularly of women of the people, more adaptable, more sensitive than the men, more capable of absorbing the culture of the city. Memories of his old cleaning woman, who advised him as he was leaving for a formal dinner that he ought "to take a Camembert along in his pocket—you produce it when the dessert comes and you'll make a hit" (*Pl.*,

p. 970). Memories, too, of the girls who did housework for him and doubled as mistresses in his bachelor flat on the rue Cardinal Lemoine. And he adds his comments on another Paris institution, "les maisons d'illusions" which he had evidently investigated under the guidance of Fargue during their youthful nights on the town. Here we again catch glimpses of a more secret side of his personality, as he recalls his "lovely foreign friend" (was she a model for Gertie Hansker in *Barnabooth*?) whom, dressed as a man, he used to accompany to "establishments of this sort."

Other essays recall impressions of travel in his favorite countries. England, especially Warwickshire, the home county of W. S. Landor, in "Le Moulin d'Inigo Jones"; Italy, in "Lettre d'Italie," which treats particularly of a visit to Recanati, the native town of Leopardi, the Italian poet Larbaud knew best and with whom he identified most closely.[5] Italy again in "Une Journée," a fugitive little piece, notations of a day spent on the Lake of Como, with its random memories of a puppet show, of the sound of wooden clogs on the stone pavement, of a chance conversation with "a woman from Cantù." Again in "Le vain travail de voir divers pays" (the title is from Maurice Scève) which is "about" —among much else—a trip to Elba which did not take place. But underlying the apparent hit-and-miss diversity of "Le vain travail"—remarks on the *fatras* as a *genre* and the observation that there is something of the *fatras* in the text he is writing, impressions of the Lake of Orta and recollections of Samuel Butler's sojourn there, descriptions of the Baroque villas in the vicinity of the lake—persists the barely articulated sentiment of "the vanity of seeing different countries," of the "dégoût du mouvement" which alternates, in Larbaud's spirit, with the need to travel. To overcome this "vanity," he simply settles down at Portofino for the rest of his holiday, in a setting and among people familiar to him—after change, stability. Or to use his terms, "conversion" after "procession" (*Pl.*, p. 870). The essay ends with an homage to Italy, a country that "he never leaves without regret," since "by the decree of Caracalla," he is "a Roman citizen too. . . ."

"Douze villes ou paysages" consist of a group of brief poems in prose (what else to call them?) each only a paragraph in length. Some, written as early as 1903, evoke places (in a fashion not without a certain connection with Gertrude Stein's more audacious experiments in subordinating objective descriptions to subjective impressions) which he had known in England (Shrewsbury, Chester, Wells, Tintern Abbey), in Scotland (Edinburgh), in Spain (Biar, Muchamiel), in Montenegro, and in the Bourbonnais (St. Bonnet-le-Désert). They are composed of passages selected and "arranged" from his journals and from the then unpublished *Au Coeur de l'Angleterre.* "Septimanie" (the Roman term for *La Gaule narbonnaise*) is a comparable sheaf of brief impressions of eight cities—Nîmes, Narbonne, Cette, and especially Montpellier, where, as a young man, Larbaud made several long visits and which would serve as the setting of "Amants, heureux amants." In "200 Chambres, 200 salles de bain," he recalls the many days and (often sleepless) nights that as a traveler and as a convalescent, he spent in hotels ... in the hotel in Bussaco, in Portugal, "a former royal palace," the hotel in Montpellier where he knew a fake countess who swindled the management, the hotel in Paris he remembered from his chronically ill childhood. In hotel rooms he has an "unlimited sense of isolation" (*Pl.*, p. 891), of being in a halfway house between a "normal, active life" and the hospital. In a hotel, he can enjoy both maximum care and security and maximum liberty—as well as that accompaniment of liberty, the certitude of not disturbing anyone.

And there in the silence and solitude of a hotel room, the "Invisible Ones" came to console him, especially the one dearest to him, "Mother of Universal Love," the Virgin Mary, whom Larbaud represents as a young Italian peasant woman, nursing her baby. And he cites once again a passage from *La Vie de Mélanie, Bergère de la Salette, écrite par elle-même*[6] which seemed to have a very special significance for him: "My child, close your heart against all the agitation of this world; don't listen to what the world says; don't do what the world does; don't believe what the world believes." And, after this moment of mysticism, of frequentation of "The Invisibles," he brusquely comes down to earth again to recall, incongruously, that in this same hotel, Nathaniel Hawthorne (one of his favorite American authors) had complained bitterly because he found no soap in the bathroom, and asserted (in print) that Europeans evidently didn't use it. Incongruously? The entire text is peppered with "incongruities." And given the self-consciousness of Larbaud's art, we must assume that they are calculated incongruities. In attempting to catch in words the fleeting, variegated, contradictory stuff of life, then you put everything in. A fake countess who swindles hotel managers coexists with the Blessed Virgin, and saintliness with Mr. Hawthorne's dismay in finding no soap in the bathrooms of the Hotel du Louvre. Human existence is incongruous, he seems to be hinting quite openly, as Sterne did before him, and the "little" things are perhaps as important as those the world considers as "big" ones, particularly if you are trying "to make, from truth and dreams, a little French prose" (*Pl.*, p. 894: "nous essayons de faire, avec de la verité et nos rêves, un peu de prose française"). "Congruity," "coherence," "unity of theme and structure"—what are they but theories? And we know the distrust that Larbaud had for theories and theoreticians—"the mania of constructing theories is a way of killing time as morose and vain as playing solitaire" (*Pl.*, p. 853).

And how determined he is not to be "theoretical," never to bore us with wordiness, never to kill our appetite "by heaping up the plate"![7] But occasionally one longs for more solid fare. One cannot make a dinner of *hors d'oeuvres*. And Larbaud, over-concerned with the *bienséances*, too discreet, too entertaining, too well bred, often sends us with relief to the unwashed, the uncombed, the savage elemental writers like Melville, or Dostoyevsky, or Whitman, a youthful enthusiasm which Larbaud later sacrificed to his need for elegance and *mesure*.

IV   Aux Couleurs de Rome: *The Purple and the Gold*

Aux Couleurs de Rome is made up of fifteen texts, some very brief, often witty comments on "ideas" ("sur le Rebut," "La Lenteur," "Actualité"); others, "semifictions," in which invention is fused with personal reminiscence ("Deux Artistes lyriques," "Une Nonnain," "Tan Callando," "Pour une Muse de Douze ans," "Le Vaisseau de Thésée"); others, "portraits," like "Flora" and "Denise"; others, shimmering prose-poems, whose meaning is multiple and less important than the suggestiveness of their verbal music ("Aux Couleurs de Rome," "Le Miroir du Café

Marchesi" two superb and quintessentially Larbaudian exercises).
Like the texts of *Jaune Bleu Blanc,* all of them had appeared
in periodicals or in limited editions, previous to their publication
by Gallimard in 1938.

Jaune Bleu Blanc revolves (as Larbaud indicated in his letter
to Jean-Aubry) about the axis of Paris, the point of departure
and the point of return. *Aux Couleurs de Rome* is a celebration
of Italy and especially of Rome ("O Roma nobilis") which, in
the course of the years, had become Larbaud's favorite city,
the center of his personal universe as well as the center of that
unifying Latin civilization of which he had been the ardent lifelong advocate. Just as Augustan Rome had brought peace and
order to the ancient world and the Roman church to the medieval
world, so he looked to Rome as the means of conferring order,
meaning, and unity to all the enchanting, yet disruptive, diversity
of his own experience. The colors of Rome—gold and purple—
expressed the two sides of his own temperament: a delight in
all the golden, burnished surfaces of the world about us and the
sense of melancholy, of mourning, and mortality which we asso-
ciate with purple. Lingering there in the courtyard of the Collegio
romano, for him the most "Roman" of Roman settings, he is
intensely aware both of the "voluptuousness" of this earthly
existence ("volupté" is one of his favorite words) and of the
inevitability of death. Greedily feasting his eyes on the light and
color of Rome, he knows that "we must leave all this too."

This collection, the gravest of Larbaud's works, affirms once
again the Protean quality of his art. The "essay" is constantly
turning into "fiction," fiction into personal reminiscence, prose
into poetry. Nothing is fixed, everything is flowing, gliding, im-
perceptibly shifting from one form, from one mood into another.
One genre is rarely sustained throughout the entirety of a text,
but the transitions are so skillfully manipulated that only the
very attentive reader is wholly aware of what is happening. "Une
Nonnain," for example, begins as though it were going to be
"a philological diversion": "This word, 'nonnain,' is no longer
currently in use," he explains, and continues with a citation from
Vaugelas. But in the next section, the philological dissertation
becomes personal reminiscence: "Years ago we knew a young
nun. . . ." And he proceeds to recount an incident of his young

manhood (lightly disguised and cleverly amplified) when he was ill at Valbois and his mother engaged a nun from a nearby convent of nursing sisters to come to care for him. (Shortly afterwards, jealous of the young woman, she dismissed her.) Sister Pamphile, as Larbaud presents her, "very feminine under her black habit," is indeed attractive—fresh-faced, animated, a lover of good food and drink, intimately informed about all the gossip of the neighborhood. Listening to her, the narrator regrets that he has no desire to be "a Naturalistic novelist," for she could have furnished him with "all the documentation he could possibly need."

A sometimes unsuspected aspect of Larbaud's personality is revealed in "Deux Artistes lyriques," based on his memories of a couple of Italian music hall performers, "la coppia Baretta," whom he had applauded in Naples and in Potenza and had met by chance in the station of Metaponte. With his gift for "enjoying things," he even took pleasure in their evident lack of talent. Always on the lookout for continuity, he recognized in the very banality of their "turn" many of the timeless "topoi" of popular art, the old "tricks of the trade" handed down through countless generations of clowns and mimes. For Larbaud was a great "fan" of the music hall, like Barnabooth who assiduously frequented the Savanarola in Florence, where Florrie Bailey danced in the chorus. He had a veritable cult for "Dranem," one of the stars of the Paris *caf' conc'* around the turn of the century and the idol of the young Maurice Chevalier.[8]

The most ambitious of these texts, "Le Vaisseau de Thésée," consists of the long *monologue intérieur* (in the form of diary entries) of Charles-Marie Bonsignor, a hotel tycoon of forty-seven (who appears elsewhere in Larbaud's work, notably in "Le Fait de Prince" [*St. J.*, pp. 185–89]). Bonsignor, a more mature cousin of Archie Barnabooth, shares his self-doubts, his "moods," his internationalism. Despite his financial success, he is acutely aware of his lacks and aspires to greater learning, to greater understanding of human destiny, preoccupied, as he increasingly is, with the approach of death. "Every man and every woman is on the way to the tomb, traversing a small, allotted moment of time, surrounded by eternity." He meditates on the changes which have taken place in him, changes which take place in everyone in the course of a life. Always changing,

yet remaining the same, stable yet endlessly in movement, the
human process seems to him to resemble the total transformation of "the vessel of Theseus," piously preserved by the Ath-
enians as a precious historical object. With the passage of time,
one part after another had to be replaced, until finally not a
piece of the original was left—but, nevertheless, it was still "the
vessel of Theseus." Bonsignor, a *persona* of the mature Larbaud,
sees in the vessel "a noble symbol of our condition": "Notre
forme change, mais l'idée de nous-mêmes en nous-mêmes, inde-
structible, demeure." It is the old question of "the permanence
and the metamorphoses of man," discussed, more passionately,
more rhetorically, by Malraux, in the central chapters of *Les
Noyers de l'Altenburg*. And what can save us from the never-
ending flux, from the crushing burden of time and death? Only
our work, our "métier." Bonsignor, like Larbaud, after having
lived in many different countries, reaches the conclusion that
his work is his only real homeland. "Mais mon pays plus proche
de moi ... c'est mon métier" (*Pl.*, p. 1101).

"Tan Callando" takes us back to the England of "Beauté, mon
beau souci" and of certain of the *Enfantines*. André, a no-longer
very young Frenchman, wanders through the sad, ugly streets
of the popular quarters of Birmingham, distressed by all the
misery about him, especially the misery of the children. His
long-time British mistress, Ruth, has left him to marry a rich
young Englishman, Leslie. (We recognize here a reutilization
of certain elements from "Beauté. ...") André now has regained
his once-so-cherished liberty, but is not at all sure that he really
wants it. And passing a cemetery, he observed that soon "Ruth
and Leslie and André will be only names on tombstones like
these." Larbaud then brings in the inevitable literary allusion,
the famous poem of Jorge Manrique, "Coplas por la muerte de
su padre": "Recuerde el alma dormida/ avive el seso y despierte/
contemplando/ cómo se pasa la vida/ cómo se viene la muerte/
tan callando"/ Death, death coming on so silently. "Tan callando ..." also reflects, in André's religious preoccupations, in
his desire to overcome self-indulgence and to embark on a
Franciscan existence of humility and of modest work, Larbaud's
own increasingly mystical piety.

One of the most memorable of these pieces, a prose-poem
made up of recollections of women he has briefly loved (es-

pecially "Trini d'Oranie"), as he imagines their images dimly reflected in the tarnished "Miroir du Café Marchesi" in Parma, repeats again and again, like an incantation, "un prénom, et parfois moins encore." "Only a name—and sometimes not even that." Our lives? As shifting, as ephemeral as these imagined figures in a tarnished mirror. The mirror, image dear to all the Symbolists, the mirror which can conjure up fleeting memories, almost forgotten emotions. Larbaud, as we have seen, loved the mirror world where he could explore "les avenues souterraines ...les celliers où sont entassées merveilles d'un jour, d'un instant" (*Pl.*, p. 999), guided only by the recollection of "un prénom et parfois mois encore."

After these longer, graver meditations, the brief, occasional pieces testify to Larbaud's wit and discreet humor. He not only loved the past, but he was also keenly aware of the world about him, in all its charm and absurdity. In his early verse, antedating Cendrars, he discovers the poetry of the luxury train. In *Barnabooth* and *Allen*, he celebrates the automobile. But in "La Lenteur," he regrets the ravages it has already caused. Its "Golden Age" is over and prophetically he announces that the servant is now the master, and is depriving us of the little leisure we have left. "Speed" has now become a commonplace and to be able to travel slowly becomes a privilege, a form of snobbism, "une marchandise rare et précieuse." "Actualité" warns us, again prophetically, against the tyranny of "modishness" imposed by the mass media and recommends, in a variation on Ezra Pound's dictum that to be very new you must be very old, that the truly civilized man should try "to imagine everything about him as 'out of date' since time reduces everything to archeology." Learn to look at best-sellers as philological documents of the future. Learn finally to consider as "out of fashion" even the phrase "imagine everything as 'out of fashion.'" Such an attitude, at first a source of anguish for the spirit, can finally provide an ultimate consolation.

V   Le Coeur de l'Angleterre: *"Qualche cosa per altri libri..."*

The travel notes which comprise *Le Coeur de l'Angleterre* were largely composed during a trip to Warwickshire in 1909. They

finally appeared only in 1971, in an edition prepared by Frida
Weissman, from the manuscript in the FVL.[9] The text, in the
years between, had been generously utilized by Larbaud as a
quarry from which to mine material for incorporation in other
works. Among the numerous examples, we may cite "Le Moulin
d'Inigo Jones (in *Jaune Bleu Blanc*); the *Enfantine* "Dolly,'"
which uses passages from "Leamington" (in which reference
is made to Hawthorne's residence there in 1853–57); "Tan
Callando," which transcribes descriptions of Birmingham, descriptions which also appear in *Barnabooth* (in the Winifred
incident). Several of the *Douze Villes et Paysages* (Chester,
Yarningdale) are also drawn from this source. Many of these
notes, fresh, lively, personal, full of a certain youthful joy of
discovery would have merited, as the editor suggests, publication during the author's lifetime. But we are well aware of how
self-critical the author was, how concerned about not publishing
too much, about "not heaping up the plate."

CHAPTER 5

The Critic:
Beauties Rather Than Blemishes

I. *Introduction*

LIKE his translations, Larbaud's criticism, which constitutes a
good third of his entire work, was deeply personal in character. He preferred to devote himself to texts which were little
known, underestimated, or neglected by the public and by professional and university critics, or written by authors with whom
he could "identify." He never attempted to present a broad, all-
inclusive estimate of writer's total production, but rather isolated
for comment and analysis one specific aspect of it which most
particularly appealed to him. For Larbaud, Walter Savage
Landor is first and foremost the author of *High and Low Life
in Italy*, a text not included in the standard editions of the collected works. But it expressed views about Italy which coincided
with Larbaud's own and therefore it was "important" for him.
Such an approach often had its positive virtues in revealing
aspects of a text which had hitherto been overlooked and in
reviving forgotten or neglected authors. However, it could also
be pointed out with some justification that Larbaud was sometimes guilty of engaging in what Aldous Huxley, in a witty
essay,[1] has called "Conxolus" tactics—"To know what everyone
else knows,— that Virgil, for example, wrote the Aeneid or that
the sum of the angles of a triangle is equal to two right angles
is rather boring and undistinguished." There is sometimes more
than a suggestion of this attitude in Larbaud, in his deliberate
rejection of accepted opinion, in his declaration that Patmore
is "greater" than Tennyson, in his fervid rehabilitation of obscure
poets such as Héroët, in "discoveries" such as Logan Pearsall

133

Smith and Digby Dolben. It appears even in the nonliterary aspects of his life. "Anyone" could winter on the Côte d'Azur; he chose Montpellier. And who but Larbaud would think of spending years in Alicante?

But personal and partial as they may be, Larbaud's critical opinions were arrived at only after long and deliberate reflection. The thoroughness of his preparation for his critical tasks is illustrated, for example, by the manuscript volumes of notes—on W. S. Landor, or Racan, among others—in the Fonds Larbaud. Françoise Lioure, in her excellent essay, "Sagesse de Larbaud,"[2] has pointed out that Larbaud, in spite of his much proclaimed "ethic of pleasure" and his constant ill health, was a tireless worker and an admirably conscientious one. He never "dashed off" a critical text as his extensive preparatory note taking reveals. His judgments, personal and nonconformist as they might be, were the fruit of considerable if often unsystematic research.

It would be misleading to attempt to separate his criticism from the ensemble of Larbaud's work. Increasingly, as he matured, in his search for new, more flexible forms, we encounter a *mélange de genres* within the same text, criticism, personal reminiscence, brief fictional *récits*, dialogue. However, although recognizing this "fluidity," this conscious effort to escape from genre distinctions, these comments on Larbaud's literary criticism will be arranged in the following categories:

(1) literary theory,
(2) English and American literature,
(3) French literature,
(4) Hispanic and Portuguese literature,
(5) Italian literature,
(6) the comparative method, and
(7) "Ces amours, si j'ose dire, philologiques...."

II *Critical and Literary Theory*

Larbaud always tended to shy away from abstract, theoretical considerations of literature—or anything else, for that matter. In his essay on James Stephens, he observes[3] that "generalizations falsify criticism...." He disliked "systems" of any sort and opposed Freud[4] since he felt that such theories imposed arbitrary limits on the diversity and the mystery of the human personality. Similarly, he was suspicious of elaborate "methodologies" that claimed to explain "scientifically" the work of art. What Maxime de Claremoris tells Barnabooth at their last meeting[5]—"Toute méthode est grossière"—could legitimately be attributed to Larbaud himself.

The nearest thing to a systematic exposé of his "critical theory" may be found in the unpublished ms. 8. S.E.:FVL. In addition, he touches on problems of literary criticism in a number of essays in the third section ("Technique") of *St. Jérôme*, particularly in "Renan, l'histoire, et la critique littéraire"[6] and in "Pour l'inauguration d'une nouvelle ligne."[7]

A. MS. #8.S.E.: *Brunetière, Ste.-Beuve, de Sanctis, Croce*

This manuscript consists of some 116 pages of hand written notes on (1) Croce's *Estetica* (pp. 17–47); (2) Brunetière (pp. 48–49); (3) de Sanctis (pp. 50–56), Sainte-Beuve (pp. 56–88); (4) quotations from de Sanctis (pp. 105–16). These notes are interspersed with Larbaud's own comments, which, naturally, form the most interesting part of the manuscript. In them, Larbaud constantly stresses that the critic's primary duty is the examination of the work itself and not of the historical factors surrounding it. This, according to Croce, whom Larbaud cites, was precisely what de Sanctis did. And for this quality, Larbaud places him amongst the very great nineteenth-century critics. De Sanctis was not only a critic. He was also an artist, "not a middle class intellectual journalist writing about literature, not a professor dissecting it from a University chair."

As we have seen, Larbaud had a strong prejudice against the academic study of literature and, in fact, against the entire French educational system. His disagreeable personal experiences in several *lycées* in Paris and Moulins may partly account for his attitude. Ferdinand Brunetière serves as a foil to De Sanctis, as the incarnation of all that Larbaud disdained in the university study of literature. He attacks especially Brunetière's theories of genres and their evolution[8] which "have infected academic manuals." In his *Balzac*, Larbaud points out, Brunetière never gets around to speak of the novels themselves, but is pre-occupied with defining the "laws" of the novel as a *"genre"* and with stating what the novel "ought" to be. Larbaud links Brunetière with Zola, another of his *bêtes noires*. Both had the illusion of being "scientific" and "modern." Larbaud imagines that there even might be a physical resemblance between them: "le lorgnon autoritaire et le front plissé." For Larbaud, Sainte-Beuve is the outstanding French critic of the nineteenth century, because under all "la masse énorme et lourde du discours" one feels "le frémissement au contact de l'oeuvre..."[9] He praises the *Notes* of Ste. Beuve as superior to the *Causeries*, since in the *Notes* he followed "the line of least resistance" and "as nearly always in art" the results are excellent.

B. *Critical Theory in* St. Jérôme

Comments on critical and literary theory are scattered through the essays of "Technique," the third section of *St. Jérôme* and are occasionally treated in part two, "L'Art et le métier." Larbaud is particularly concerned with the relations between literary history and literary criticism as in "Pour l'Inauguration d'une nouvelle ligne" and in "Renan, l'histoire, et la critique littéraire," with the problem of "sources and influences": ("Le Fait du prince"), with the fallibility of criticism ("Le Doigt dans l'oeil"). His antidogmatism makes him unwilling to endorse without reservations any one "critical method."

Much as he admired de Sanctis and Croce, he recognized that even they could "put their finger in their eye" and commit critical enormities.[10] Croce, "qui nous avait délivré de bien des préjugés entrés en nous avec l'enseignement" is nevertheless capable of labeling Paul Claudel "a decadent poet," counseling him to "leave the cafés of the Latin Quarter" and accept the responsibilities of "une vie active et virile," to travel (!) in order to know a world wider than that of Paris literary society. Croce's error may be attributed to insufficient information. But when de Sanctis hails Zola as a "universal value," "the validity of his whole system is called into question." Larbaud disliked intensely the scientific pretensions and the naturalistic surface of Zola's work.

There is no foolproof "critical method." He admits that even the kind of criticism he prefers and seeks to practice—"descriptive criticism" which judges a work "in and for itself,"[11] rejects the "literary history" of the professors and has certain filiations with the American "New Criticism" of the 1930s and 1940s—can also fall into error.

Like the New Critics, Larbaud makes a radical distinction between "literary history" as practiced by the "Lansoniens" and "literary criticism." The former is "scientific"; the latter is "an art." His accusations against the academic historians of literature are the conventional ones: historians of literature have no idea of what literature is; they don't know how to write and their style is bereft of any evidence of real literary culture.[12]

These professors, who dominated academic literary studies in France, inculcated in their students a view of literature which was "the pure and simple negation of aesthetic values,"[13] considering the work as essentially "a document." For them, there are no "geniuses," only (to use the expression of Taine) "hot-heads" ("têtes chaudes"). These "hot-heads" think they are "original" but the literary historian knows better. His research "proves" that all they have done is to "copier, démarquer, ou déformer"[14] the works of their predecessors. Their only excuse is that they lived before the "scientific" age; henceforth, such "égarements de l'esprit" will be done with.[15]

Literary manuals, which have exercised such a profound influence on students, continually reproach poets for their "contradictions," their "incoherence," present them as "minus habentes."

Larbaud urges the professors to recognize their limitations, to admit that "literary history" is not "literary criticism" and to "inaugurate a new line" "by simply printing up their cards and presenting their factual research without critical commentary." In "Renan, l'histoire, et la critique littéraire"[16] Larbaud examines one of Renan's "Notes de jeunesse," which proposes that historians of literature can and should also be critics, a view, of course, to which Larbaud takes exception, since "the same man may be an excellent critic and a lamentable literary historian.... Renan confuses these two quite different activities." Here, we would agree with the youthful Renan; good literary history implies a sense of literary criticism and valid literary criticism depends in part on a firm foundation of literary history—their relationship is inevitably complimentary.

Larbaud is on firmer ground when he deplores a certain tendency on the part of literary scholars, proud in their possession of diplomas and university chairs, to consider themselves somehow superior to the writers who are the objects of their studies—their vanity leads them to believe that since they are in possession of a "scientific method" they can pass judgment on the creators who had none.[17]

But characteristically, Larbaud is not dogmatic even in his criticism of the professors. In several entries in his *Journal*,[18] he refers to these questions and, on the occasion of the death of Lanson, praises his history of French literature in spite of its "limitations universitaires, normaliennes" and deplores Péguy's "savage attacks" against him.[19]

Some of Larbaud's most original critical observations are expressed almost *sotto voce* when talking of something else, as in his comments on the conventional novel in *Férmina Márquez*[20] or are embodied in concrete form in the increasingly subtle and complex formal experiments in non-critical writing, such as in the pieces of *Aux Couleurs de Rome*.

In "Le Fait du Prince,"[21] he raises the complex question of literary "originality," of "sources and influences"—questions extensively and simplistically treated by the professors of literature. In citing a "seizan" that he attributes to "Charles-Marie Bonsignor,"[22] he points out that "not one of its 16 lines is original" and proceeds to identify each one. Some are direct quotations from earlier poets, others are *loci communes*, topoi of the sort that E. R. Curtius (whom Larbaud knew and admired[23]) would later study in his great work, *European Literature and the Latin Middle Ages*.[24]

Larbaud, with his deeply ingrained instinct to establish cultural continuities, is constantly looking for the poet's sources. "Where did he get it?" Although convinced that all art comes from other art, he is very far indeed from the run of the mill source hunter, for he has an artist's sense of the mysteries of the creative process. In literature, "everything is autobiographical and nothing is"[25] and nothing is "original" and everything is.

He saw very clearly that what is important is not "the source," but rather the way the poet uses it, distorts it, recombines it in order to make something new and distinctively his own. In understanding this process, "so-called scientific criticism" is as yet of little help. Perhaps one day it will be able to penetrate beneath "the sources" and grapple with the ultimate problem, that of poetic creation itself, with "le fait du Prince." Larbaud will further discuss this question of "originality" in his little study in comparative literature, "Trois Belles Mendiantes."[26]

C. *The Reader-Writer Relationship*

Occasionally Larbaud touches on a problem of central interest for the contemporary critic: the relation between the reader and the text, the reader-writer collaboration. In the introductory essay of *Ce Vice impuni, la lecture (Domaine anglais)*, he notes that such an active collaboration is common among young readers, for the child is gifted with a creative energy that the adult has lost or renounced. Although the name of Jules Verne may figure on the cover, "the book the child is reading is his own work, created in collaboration with the author."[27]

D. *Beauties Rather Than Blemishes*

Larbaud's criticism emphasizes the beauties rather than the blemishes of a work. Discreet and "bien elevé," in his criticism as in his personal relations, he disliked noisy controversies and always sought to avoid them. He has no desire to follow the example of "Jules Lemaître denouncing G. Ohnet or of Léon Bloy imperially executing mediocre best sellers."[28] He often speaks elsewhere of his disdain for "literary brawlers," like Bloy, of whom Larbaud could not wholly approve in spite of—or because of—Bloy's Catholicism, so different from his own tolerant, very indulgent creed. He comments at some length on Bloy's critical style.[29] "He 'gueules' too much. But then 'gueuler' is always too much." (These entries were written directly in English). An intellectual aristocrat, who addressed himself to a small public of the truly literate, Larbaud considered that in the area of literary criticism, as elsewhere, "coarse insults are out of place."[30] He avoided literary polemics, and when, against his will, he was drawn into them, he never performed very brilliantly nor aggressively, as we can see in his controversy concerning *Ulysses,* with the Irish-American critic Ernest Boyd.[31] For him, the most legitimate role of the critic was to "hail the appearance of great works and to rediscover those which have been neglected or forgotten."[32]

III *Critical Practice*

A. *English and American Literature*

Larbaud's interest in English and American literature, spans his entire career from adolescence,[33] and with many interruptions, until his fatal illness in 1935.[34]

His most important essays in the Anglo-American field are contained in *Ce vice impuni, la lecture: (Domaine anglais)* and include studies on Coventry Patmore, Samuel Butler, Thomas Hardy, Digby Dolben, W. E. Henley, Joseph Conrad, Francis Thompson, Arnold Bennett, H. G. Wells, E. A. Poe, Walt Whitman, William Faulkner, James Stephens, and James Joyce. To reveal certain aspects of Larbaud's critical approach and to indicate its qualities and its shortcomings, the essays on Whitman and Joyce have been singled out for closer attention.

The essay on Whitman,[35] "serious," documented, even rather pedagogical, begins with a long bibliographical survey, continues with a section on "the relations of the man and the work," and concludes with an attempt to define the permanent and the perishable in Whitman's poetry. Dominique Fernandez has remarked in it a certain "school masterish" tone.[36] Rejecting views that have seen in Whitman a "prophet," a "Socialist," a "workman," Larbaud substitutes an even more dubious one—that his work was directly inspired by the philosophy of Hegel. He falls indeed into the very error that he denounces in the university critics, that of trying to force a poetic work into the strait jacket of a "system," of considering "ideas" as a source of poetry. His attempt to demonstrate that Whitman was a "thinker" scarcely holds water. Nor does his contention that *Leaves of Grass* follows a well-defined plan. Even the hastiest examination of its successive editions reveals that such "unity" never existed. Moreover, the statement that Whitman was " 'un grand fils de civilisation,' whose doctrine is German and whose masters are English," betrays fundamental lack of understanding of the nature of Whitman's achievement. For the *Oeuvres choisies* Larbaud has translated "The Sleepers," one of the most beautiful and enigmatic of Whitman's poems, a descent into the irrational domain of dreams and night, whose method of composition by free association recalls the techniques later employed by the Surrealists. But this aspect of Whitman, an aspect to which one would think Larbaud would be particularly drawn, seems to have escaped him. No formal stylistic analysis is attempted. In fact, the bulk of the essay is devoted to "information about Whitman" and very little to the poetry itself (none is quoted in the article), to "the close examination of work" which Larbaud regards as the specific task of the critic. Nor did it "reveal an unknown writer." *Leaves of Grass* had received much critical attention in Europe from the 1880s onward.[37]

It might be said, of course, that this essay is a youthful work, composed when Larbaud was still doing university studies in English literature. However, he had adequate opportunity to revise it, to make it more "critical" and less "historical," before its publication in 1918—and certainly before its inclusion in *Domaine Anglais* in 1925.

The essay on James Joyce, presented first as a lecture, was Larbaud's opening salvo in that vigorous campaign he conducted throughout the 1920s in support of the author of *Ulysses*.[38] The first French critic to proclaim the genius and the profound originality of Joyce, Larbaud had enjoyed the advantage of close personal contact with him during the months following their first meeting, presumably in Sylvia Beach's bookshop in December 1920. Joyce had explained to him the significance of the title *Ulysses* and also the Homeric scaffolding of the work. It is clear why Joyce appealed to Larbaud. He made use on a large scale and with dazzling virtuosity of the "stream of consciousness" technique towards which Larbaud's own work had been evolving. Although at the first glance, Joyce seemed revolutionary and *avant-garde*, Larbaud rightly recognized in him an artist "of the tradition," an example of that European cultural continuity that he admired. Finally, Joyce's work (in spite of its anti-clericalism) appeared to him as deeply Catholic[39] with its allusions to Thomism, its reminiscences of the liturgy, even its sexual frankness, a quality which Larbaud mistakenly considered characteristic of a "Catholic" culture. Ernest Boyd[40] bluntly set him right on this—no society could be more puritanical, more prudish about sexual matters than very Catholic Ireland—and deplores his lack of information about Ireland and Irish writing. There was also, as usual, an element of personal identification: Joyce, the linguist, the classicist, the traveler, who hated his native city, seemed in many ways a spiritual brother. After repeating a tirade on "American puritanism and hypocrisy" which had resulted in the banning of *Ulysses* in the United States, Larbaud provides "the indispensable biographical notice" in which he emphasizes Joyce's Irish and Catholic background, his expatriation, his internationalism, his social and political non-involvement.[41]

After noting the earlier works—*Chamber Music, Dubliners, A Portrait of the Artist*—he concludes with an analysis of *Ulysses.* Here Larbaud dwells especially on Joyce's technical innovations. "He makes clear how rigorously the eighteen chapters are organized following a strict Homeric pattern. And how, within this pattern, still other strict patterns are imposed."[42] And in spite of this technical complexity, he contends *Ulysses* remains "a work that is alive, moving and human."

Significantly, Larbaud did not share the view of the many critics that *Ulysses* expressed disgust with life, a blackly pessimistic view of human existence. Rather, he stressed its "humanity," since he himself was constitutionally opposed to pessimism, suffering, and despair. For him, Bloom, far from being an ineffectual nonentity, possessed a certain greatness in his unquenchable love of life. After the mid-1920s, as we shall observe,[43] Larbaud seemed less interested in Joyce, although he continued his collaboration on the French translation of *Ulysses.* He never seemed to have great enthusiasm for *Finnegans Wake* (a reservation shared, to Joyce's distress, by Pound) and, apparently considered it[44] a "divertissement philologique." Did Larbaud, more and more attracted to classical and Mediterranean "mesure," consider the *Wake* simply too "far-out"? Or, always mobile, always eager for change, was he simply desirous of devoting himself more intensely to Italian literature, in which, for a number of reasons, he became more and more interested from the mid-1920s onward?

In the essay on Faulkner's *As I Lay Dying,* prepared as the preface to Maurice Coindreau's translation,[45] Larbaud contested the opinion that Faulkner was a "brutal naturalist." He discovered rather, in the characters of *As I Lay Dying,* "A true humanity which touches us more deeply than the exoticism of their milieu."[46] He also remarks on the epic quality of the work and situates it as belonging to a long European literary tradition.[47]

The essays on English literature give particular attention to a group of nineteenth century Catholic poets—Coventry Patmore, Digby Dolben, and Francis Thompson—who played an important role in Larbaud's "going over to Rome" in 1910. He had studied them closely during the years 1908–1913, when he frequented the circle of Alice Meynell, an important center of English Catholic literary thought. The most important of these studies is devoted to Coventry Patmore and was written as the preface to Claudel's translation[48] of his selected poems. Patmore's belief that "human love is a prefiguration of divine love" appealed strongly to Larbaud but was viewed by Claudel with the sternest of reservations. Larbaud was only too willing to subscribe to it quite literally, as a further indication of Catholic "liberty" in contrast with the "repression"—sexual and social—represented by the hated "republican" and pragmatic Protestantism of Mme Veuve Larbaud.

Digby Dolben, a young English poet, dead at nineteen (in 1867), was introduced in France by Larbaud's review article (*La Phalange,* October 20, 1912). Like the Patmore essay, it is more anecdotal than critical, dwells on Dolben's passion for medieval Catholicism and for a school friend, Archie Manning. It comes rather as a surprise to find Larbaud writing about Arnold Bennett and H. G. Wells, with whom, it would seem, he had so little affinity. Nevertheless, he had translated Bennett's short story, *The Matador of the Five Towns*[49] and was often received by Bennett during his visits to England. They had met in Paris in May 1911 at the home of the painter, Cyprien Godebski. During Bennett's stay in Cannes in February 1912,

Larbaud was an almost daily visitor, sometimes bringing Gide with him.[50]

Bennett, the autodidact, admired Larbaud as the very quintessence of "sophisticated," continental culture, deferred to his judgment, respected his taste. Years later he followed Larbaud in taking up the cause of James Joyce. Larbaud's article—or rather, note—on Bennett's "Literary Taste" (first published in the August 1914 number of the N.R.F.) states it "treats the most interesting and difficult problems of style from a point of view which resembles that of Croce."[51]

The Wells article consists simply of two brief reviews, one of Tono-Bungay (originally published in La Phalange in August 1909) and of Marriage (in the N.R.F. of February 1, 1913).

One might well question the utility of gathering many of these brief pieces of literary journalism into a volume, first in 1925 (Messein) and again in 1936 (Gallimard). With a few exceptions (such as the essay on Joyce), even the more ambitious studies are literary-historical rather than critical in nature and are chiefly interesting for the light they shed on the tastes and attitudes of Larbaud himself during "the English period" (roughly 1906–1914) of his literary career. (In addition to the articles included in Domaine anglais, Larbaud wrote on a number of other British, Irish, and American writers, among them Chesterton, George Meredith, Jack London, R. L. Stevenson, Alice Meynell, J. M. Synge, William Beckford, H. K. Vielé, Eugene Field, F. Marion Crawford, Vachel Lindsay, etc.) One important essay, not included in Domaine anglais, is "Une Renaissance de la poésie américaine" (essentially a long review-article on L. Untermeyer's Modern American Poetry) first published in La Revue de France in 1921.[52]

On his return from Alicante where he had little opportunity to inform himself concerning recent developments in international literature, Larbaud became interested once again in American poetry and particularly in the "Renaissance" that had begun to be apparent around 1912. He was particularly attracted to the "Chicago poets" (Lindsay, Sandburg, E. L. Masters) whom he considered as "authentically American," and especially to Vachel Lindsay, "the most American of all," the one who conformed best to his ideas of American exoticism.[53] Of course,

Larbaud had never visited the United States. Perhaps he feared that the experience of the concrete reality might upset his preconceived ideas.[54]

Lindsay's flamboyant "local color" may have concealed for Larbaud the mediocrity of many of the "Chicago poets." The more restrained and laconic New Englanders, such as Frost, have aged better, but Larbaud, deafened apparently by the brasses of "General William Booth Enters into Heaven," paid little heed to their music. After the "Chicago School," Larbaud discusses "the New York School"—an arbitrary grouping of poets lumped together as a "school" simply because they all had been published in the *Dial*, "one of the best literary reviews of the world,"[55] edited by Marianne Moore, whose work Larbaud recommends to G. Jean-Aubry.[56]

Of this group, T. S. Eliot is singled out as the most remarkable. Larbaud notes the influence of Laforgue, of Rimbaud, and Bainville on him and comments very astutely on his early poems, with their "contrastes inattendus, des rappels de grands mythes."[57] Eliot and Larbaud had probably met at Sylvia Beach's; both were friends of Princess Caetani (then Princess di Bassiano), the founder of *Commerce*.[58] They began a correspondence in 1922[59] that continued—with very long interruptions—until 1953. Eliot invites Larbaud to write for the *Criterion*[60] and personally translates the final section of the essay on Joyce, which appeared in the first number; he considers Larbaud better qualified to speak on many aspects of English literature than "anyone else in this country." Eliot expresses his admiration for the *Poèmes d'un riche amateur*[61] and sees in the book "the parentage of what is now a very distinct frame of mind among our contemporaries" —a "frame of mind," ironic, cosmopolitan, quite characteristic of Eliot's own early poems. Larbaud (June 14, 1923), replies in English, telling Eliot "how much I value your opinion," recalling to him the articles in which he has spoken of Eliot's work[62] and concluding: "with you, poetry is entering new regions where even music does not reach." Larbaud immediately recognized the importance of *The Waste Land*, which had just appeared (1922). Although many Anglo-Saxon critics denounced it as obscure and difficult, Larbaud rightly insists that it needs only to be read with sufficient *attention* (a virtue he never tired of extolling) and everything becomes clear.[63] He also insisted that *The Waste Land,* far from being a despairing abdication of the artist before the chaos of his society, represented rather an effort to impose a form and to restore an order, finding in it, "the serenity of great poetry, of great music." And with his usual penchant for situating contemporary artists within the framework of a cultural tradition, he compares Eliot to Boileau, a comparison which left Eliot himself bemused.

"And in what school can we put Ezra Pound, this American who lives in Paris?" asks Larbaud.[64] That's all he has to say about the great mover and shaker of the Modernist movement in Anglo-Saxon poetry. His silence seems all the more surprising since he was undoubtedly aware that Eliot then considered Pound as his master and had dedicated *The Waste Land* to "il miglior fabbro." Moreover, he had known of Pound for a number of years. He had met him at the Meynells' about the time of the publication of the first volume of *Georgian Poetry.* He had hoped that Pound would "make the English more aware of the importance of Whitman," but he soon learned that Ezra was "pas de tout Whitmanien." Pound was rather interested in "de vieux poètes provençaux, la poésie italienne d'avant Dante, des curiosités extrême–orientales ou byzantines." Not a word of Pound's achievements as a poet, although, by the time the *Revue de France* piece was written, he had published a dozen or more volumes and had acquired an international reputation. A note of Larbaud addressed to Francis Jammes,[65] in which he speaks of an "odieux poète américain qui m'a accaparé chez Alice Meynell," hints at a reason for this silence. The "odious American poet" was certainly the talkative, tactless, irrepressibly exuberant Uncle Ez. Larbaud, that incarnation of well-bred discretion, could not tolerate those wild Western ways, that he admired in theory, when he encountered them in the poetry of Lindsay, but which he found intolerable in practice. There was also the question of Joyce. Both Pound and Larbaud considered him their personal discovery. Pound, of course, could claim a definite priority, since he had written to Joyce as early as December 1913, offering to try to place Joyce's writing in several of the reviews with which he was then associated—Mencken's *Smart Set* and H. Monroe's *Poetry* among them.[66]

But whatever the reasons may be, Larbaud in his comments on American poetry is eloquently silent on the subject of Pound. After Lindsay, the contemporary American poet for whom he was most enthusiastic was William Carlos Williams. He probably came to know his work through Robert McAlmon, the expatriate American publisher of "Contact Editions"[67] and writes to Adrienne Monnier on May 4, 1921, that he is busy "boning up" on the work of Williams. In his article in *La Revue de France,* he singles out Williams and M. Moore as "the only American poets" that "les lettrés," for whom Góngora, certain Précieux, Rimbaud, Mallarmé, P. Valéry, and L. P. Fargue are "*the* poets," consider with interest and curiosity. He praises, in their work, a complete renunciation of "all the facilities of emotion, sentimentality, irony." And he cites as an example, one of the "improvisations" of *Kora in Hell* (Larbaud was certainly the only Frenchman of his generation to have read this collection!) in which he discovers traces of Rimbaud and Lautréamont, but also an original and specifically American tone.

In 1923, the Three Mountains Press, Bill Bird's small *avant-garde* publishing venture on the Ile St. Louis, issued a new work of Williams, a text of 70 pages entitled, ironically, *The Great American Novel,* a "novel" about a novelist who can't write his novel. Larbaud immediately devoted an important article to it in *La Revue européene.*[68] He considered it "a profound meditation on his art, on his time, on his country, on the problems of American civilization, on the future of the U.S." and expressed the desire that he might meet Williams "at a table at the Rotonde or, still better, in Sylvia Beach's bookshop and talk all these things over." We can understand this sympathy for Williams, for Williams was precisely the type of poet that Larbaud had decided was specifically American, a poet who refused to become "Europeanized" like Henry James (whom Larbaud never mentions in spite of James's many French and English connections) or Eliot or Pound, a poet who could declare that the culture of the Old World had no meaning for *him.* Moreover, both Larbaud and Williams denounced the Puritanism of Protestant, North American civilization. Larbaud (like Williams, whose mother was of Latin origin and who spoke Spanish at home as a boy) preferred the Latin and

Catholic culture of South America to the Anglo-Saxon Calvinist
culture of the North. Williams, however, was unable to share
Larbaud's admiration for the Conquistadores. . . . Larbaud judici-
ously perceived in *The Great American Novel* a kind of love-hate
relationship between Europe and America, which has marked
the entire history of the development of American culture:
"l'appel à l'Europe et la dispute avec l'Europe." Williams evidently felt for Europe what Larbaud felt for the U.S.: a simul-
taneous attraction and repulsion.

In 1924, Williams came to Paris and Adrienne Monnier encouraged him to go and call on Larbaud in the flat on the rue
Cardinal Lemoine that Larbaud had lent to Joyce a few years
before. There they had a long conversation[69] which formed the
basis of one of the most important chapters, "Père Sebastien
Rasles" of *In the American Grain*. Williams, deliberately or not,
often misinterprets the intellectual position of his interlocutor
and Larbaud often appears simply as a "straw man" for the
demonstration of Williams's own arguments.

During the early years of Larbaud's career, he extended his
studies of Whitman to include other nineteenth century American
writers. Already in August 1901, he proposed to Karl Boes, the
editor of *La Plume*, a series of articles on four poets: Whitman,
J. G. Whittier, J. R. Lowell, and Sydney Lanier. Of these, only
the paper on Whitman ever got written. Between 1901–1910,
Larbaud also studied the works of Hawthorne and began to
translate *The Blithedale Romance, Grandfather's Chair,* and
fragments of Hawthorne's journal (later published in revised
form in *Commerce* in 1928). Some of his youthful American
enthusiasms may somewhat surprise us—Bayard Taylor, for example, whose "Quaker widow" so moved the young Barnabooth[70]
and who is mentioned in the essay on Vachel Lindsay[71] as a precursor, together with Longfellow, James Whitcomb Riley, and
Bret Harte. In 1911, he devoted an article in *La Phalange* to
The Complete Poems of Eugene Field, in which he criticized
the American's treatment of childhood, one of his own key
themes (he was then writing *Enfantines*).[72] Bédouret cites
significant passages of this text in his article on "Larbaud et
l'Amérique."[73]

In 1919, during a stay in England, Larbaud "discovered" another "American poet," Logan Pearsall Smith, of whom he speaks in articles in *La Revue de France*[74] and in the *N.R.F.*[75] Through his efforts, Smith's poems in prose, *Trivia*, were translated into French by Philippe Néel and appeared in a volume (in the collection "Les Cahiers verts") to which Larbaud contributed the preface.[76] His sponsorship of Smith had its personal reasons. Larbaud saw in the wealthy American expatriate a kindred spirit, "un riche amateur" like himself. Moreover, Smith wrote, in the preface to the English edition of *Trivia*, that he desired to express "moods, brief impressions, and modern ways of feeling for which no exactly appropriate way of expression was at hand" —something very much akin to Larbaud's own literary purposes. Larbaud, in his piece in the *N.R·F.* in 1919,[77] declared that Smith's prose-poems were the form best suited to that kind of poetry in which "le tempérament individuel est toute la substance de l'art." He compares *Trivia* to another "discovery" of his, *Greguerías* of Ramón Gómez de la Serna, as "brief notations of fugitive impressions, almost like the *greguerías....*" *Trivia*, moreover, apparently had an impact on Larbaud's own work, especially in the poems in prose *Septimania* and *Douze villes et paysages* (1925). In them, Larbaud does not attempt to give an objective description of "towns and landscapes" but rather to record his own subjective reactions in contact with them.

B. French Literature

Before 1914, most of Larbaud's published criticism, as we have seen, was in the field of Anglo-American literature, with the exception of a few, brief, scattered notes on C. L. Philippe (1910, 1911), on Saint-John Perse (1911) and Lautréamont. But during the 1920s, he devoted himself more and more to French literature, particularly in two areas: to contemporaries like Levet, Mirbeau, J. A. Nau, Morand, Arland, Dujardin, P. Valéry, L. P. Fargue, L. Chadourne, and to poets of the late sixteenth century—notably Maurice Scève—and of the early seventeenth—Antoine Héroët, Jean de Lingendes, Racan—who, he felt, had been unjustly forgotten. Many of the longer critical articles on French literature were collected in *Ce Vice impuni, la lecture (Domaine français)* published by Gallimard in 1941. It included an introduction and (in the first section) essays on Antoine Héroët, Maurice Scève, Jean de Lingendes, Racan, D'Ablancourt, and Patru. The second section is devoted to nineteenth and twentieth century writers: Prosper Merimée, Théophile Dondey de Santeny, Mirbeau, C. L. Philippe, Marguerite Audoux, Edouard Dujardin, P. Valéry, L. P. Fargue. (In the *Oeuvres complètes*, essays on "La Vie de Mélanie, Bergère de la Salette," "Conversation de L. P. Fargue et Valery Larbaud" [on Levet] and on Saint-John Perse's *Eloges* were added.)

The epigraph of *Domaine français*, a quotation from Racine's *Bajazet*—"Mais sans cesse occupé des grands noms de ma race. . .," underlines Larbaud's devotion to cultural continuity. In his "excuses pour ce livre," written evidently in the 1930s, he avows that despite his own linguistic facility (we recall that he wrote articles for *La Nación* directly in Spanish, for the *New Weekly* directly in English), he does not believe that an artist is able to express himself—that an artist even would desire to express himself—in two literary languages. For the chosen literary language is like a jealous mistress, "who demands total devotion and will brook no rivals." But "this game" of writing in a language not one's own has its compensations. His Spanish articles in *La Nación* gave Larbaud "the agreeable impression of intellectual communion with Argentine writers."

Larbaud began to read extensively in sixteenth- and seventeenth-century French poets while in Alicante.[78] He was drawn to them, especially to Scève, because of his constant effort to "rediscover" and to "rehabilitate." And coming to them after the English Metaphysicals, he desires to "place" both groups within the framework of a European literary tradition, and to find a French equivalent to the Metaphysical revival. French academic criticism had decreed that the seventeenth century was "classical" and simply paid no attention to poets who did not conform to "classical" norms. The idea that French Classicism might simply be a national variation on the international pattern of "The Baroque"—which had long been discussed in Germany, particularly after the book of Heinrich Woefflin, *Renaissance und Barock* (1888)—apparently did not occur to French literary historians. But Larbaud, with his international background, his acquaintance with Donne and Góngora, was able to detect family relationships between them and certain French poets of the period. Recent critics have recognized Larbaud's clairvoyance —Odette de Mourgues[79] and Franco Simone[80] among others. Already in 1920, Larbaud had published an essay on Vincent Voiture (1597–1648) in the *N.R.F.*

But the most significant of his "rediscoveries" is certainly Maurice Scève, author of *Délie* and *Microcosme*, of whom I. D. McFarlane[81] writes: "Eclipsed in his time by the *prince des poètes*, he stands as a kind of poetic John the Baptist, whose full genius has come to be recognized only in our time." We may accurately claim that Larbaud was a pioneer in that revival of Scève which has steadily gathered momentum ever since the War. Larbaud's first publication on Scève appeared in 1924 (in *La Nación*) and others followed in 1925 (*Commerce*), 1926, and 1928. The long piece in *Domaine français* is divided into three sections: a biographical sketch; a study of *Délie*; an analysis of *Microcosme* (1562), a poem of some 3,000 lines on the history of mankind since Adam and Eve. Larbaud begins by deploring the fact that this major poet has long been considered by the professors of literature as a curiosity, an eccentric, "en marge de la Grande-Tradition-Française." Even Sainte-Beuve was guilty of declaring (in his *Tableau de la Poésie français au 16è siècle*) that the *Délie* is "à peu près illisible"—but Larbaud points out that this judgment shows a lack of knowledge of the text. He defends Scève against the charge of "préciosité provinciale." Provincial? Of course, he is an honor for Lyons, as Montaigne is an honor for Bordeaux, but he "doesn't belong to Lyons; Lyons belongs to him." And he goes on to claim—outrageously, certainly, for the academic critics—that Scève resembles Baudelaire, but that Baudelaire is much less original. As usual, Larbaud tends to extend his comparisons too far and we accept with a certain skepticism the statement that of all nineteenth-century poets, "Poe is closest to Scève" (p. 59). He admits that Scève is "difficult" but insists that all great writers, finally, are "difficult." The section devoted to *Microcosme* consists largely of a line-by-line résumé.

In spite of Larbaud's proselytizing, the other sixteenth-seventeenth century poets he seeks to rehabilitate have not emerged from obscurity: Antoine Hèroët, author of *La Parfaite amie*

(1542); Jean de Lingendes (1580–1616), friend of d'Urfé for whom, as a "Bourbonnais" and a native of Moulins, Larbaud felt a special affection; and Honorat de Bueil, Marquis de Racan (1589–1670), remembered particularly for his adaptations of the *Psalms* (1654). In rereading their poetry, one can easily understand their eclipse. Perhaps Larbaud defended them deliberately to oppose the often distorted ideas enshrined in "standard literary manuals," to encourage the cultivation of individual taste, even when it was in conflict with the accepted taste of a period, and to assert the importance of minor poets in maintaining a literary tradition. His remarks on such larger themes constitute the most interesting passages of these essays which are weighed down with bibliographical and biographical information (much of it outdated) and which betray once again the "pedagogical" side of Larbaud's critical activity. At the end of his "Notes sur Racan," he emphasizes the *collective* character of literature, to which all poets—even minor versifiers—contribute, and claims that traces of Scève can be found in Henri J. M. Levet, of Racan in Saint-John Perse.

The second part of *Domaine français* is largely devoted (with the exception of the pieces on Dondey de Santeny [Philothée O'Neddy] and Merimée) to brief, impressionistic essays on contemporary writers, many of whom Larbaud had known personally. Especially interesting from the personal point of view are his remarks on Ch. L. Philippe,[82] P. Valéry, and Fargue.

Larbaud published, in addition, a large number of reviews, prefaces, and critical articles on French writers, many of which were never collected for publication in volume form. The "conversation" between Larbaud and L. P. Fargue which served as an introduction to Larbaud's edition of the poems of Henry J. M. Levet[83] is one of the most interesting of them,[84] for its comments on Larbaud's conception of poetry and his own evolution as a poet. John-Antoine Nau, to whom Larbaud devoted a long essay in *La Revue européene* of September 1, 1924,[85] has also been discussed in the chapter "Larbaud: Poet."

Both Levet and Nau appealed to Larbaud because of their cosmopolitanism, their irony, their gift for incorporating "the modern" into their verse, and their independence from the Paris literary establishment. Larbaud was the first critic to hail the work of the youthful Saint-John Perse [Alexis Saint-Léger-Léger] in a review of *Eloges* which appeared in *La Phalange* (December 20, 1911). He later (1926) wrote the preface for the Russian translation of *Anabase*. Well before the canonization of Lautréamont by the young Surrealists, Larbaud proclaimed the genius of Maldoror in an article (*La Phalange*, February 20, 1914), "Les Poésies d'Isidore Ducasse." He drew attention to Paul Morand (*N.R.F.*, 1923), a fellow "globe trotter"; to Marcel Arland in whom he recognized a kindred spirit and who was to show (in his preface to the *Pléiade* edition) a continuing devotion to Larbaud; to Francophone writers of Belgium like Franz Hellens; to young, unrecognized poets like Louis Chadourne and E. Lochac. But outside the Renaissance and the twentieth century, there are whole areas of French literature to which he paid little or no attention, notably the Classical age and the eighteenth century.

C. Spanish and Hispanic Literature

On his return from Alicante in 1919, Larbaud increasingly devoted himself to Spanish literature and somewhat later, because of his friendship with the Argentinian, Ricardo Güiraldes, and the Mexican, Alfonso Reyes, to Latin American writing. He had first come to know Spain in trips with his mother in 1897 and 1898. They made a deep impression on him as he recalls them on several occasions and notably in an entry (in English) in his *Journal* (Monday, February 4, 1918).[86] He had already acquired a knowledge of Spanish America during the years (1891–1894) he spent at the Catholic "collège" of Ste. Barbe-des-Champs—the St. Augustin of *Fermina Márquez*—which was frequented by many Latin Americans and where Spanish was heard as frequently as French. There he began to feel that "The Castilian world is my second country" ("le monde castillan fut notre seconde patrie") especially because of his close friendship with two Latin American brothers, La Salle, and their sister, Mercedes, later to appear as characters in *Fermina Márquez*. In November 1905, in the company of "Inga" (the dancer of *Amants, heureux amants*) he arrived in Valencia for a stay of six months. But his longest and most decisive Spanish

experience occurred during the war years when he lived in
Alicante from January 1916 until April 1920. Thereafter, he
returned only on one occasion in 1923. Characteristically, his
vision of Spain was partial and personal. His knowledge of the
country was limited to his residence in Alicante, with occasional
visits to Barcelona and Madrid.[87] He never studied Spanish
systematically. His only "professors" were the young daughters
of the family with whom he lodged in Alicante—and their grasp
of classical Spanish, it would appear, was rather defective.[88]
He never read systematically the great masters of the Golden
Age—Lope, Cervantes, Calderón, the Mystics. He concentrated
on twentieth century authors such as Ganivet, G. Miró, Ramón
Gómez de la Serna chosen, and once again, because of his
personal sense of identification with them.[89]

The essay "Rouge Jaune Rouge" presents a synthesis of his
Spanish experience, a recollection of places, of people, of books,
beginning with his trip in 1898. It well illustrates his approach
to Spain (and to other foreign countries that he loved as well).
It makes no attempt to "inform" us systematically, for Larbaud
(as he reminds us on many occasions) is not an "enquêteur,"
but rather a "jouisseur." He was not bent on "learning" or acquiring information, nor on "teaching" the reader. In "Paris
de France," he ironizes about the spirit in which the "enquêteur"
approaches a foreign culture.[90]

His Spain? A procession of random images, snapshots of scenes
that he has lovingly preserved in his memory: "Vallons de terre
rose sous les sombres couronnes des orangers . . . ballet des tram-
ways sur la Puerta del Sol . . .," and the "pretty girls" with whom
he so enjoyed flirting. His life in Alicante, in spite of bouts of ill
health, was a thoroughly pleasant one; he lived, in an idealized
Spain, the existence of "the wealthy foreigner" protected from
the harshness of daily reality. He writes, in his *Journal* (January
12, 1920, p. 219): "The delight of going about in the warm sun;
the sea; the songs everywhere, the fountains, the palm trees;
and that other delight; hearing and speaking that beautiful language. And so many small details, so Alicantine: a child swearing
in Valencian, some tremendous blasphemy, with such an innocent look. Good and kind people. . . ." Or again, on March 13,
1920 (p. 235): "O, I must remember that glorious Sunday, Feb.

15—the whole afternoon of feast and music and dear Araceli and what *she* said, and all the little incidents, so full of meaning. 'Asking of thee only/love and love and love!'/" In his journals, he constantly refers to his flirtations with young girls. On March 17, 1920 (p. 235), he admits that "... I have bursts of delirious passion and feel very happy to flirt in a quiet way with youngsters who make confidences to me and who are not slow to answer my looks and—when I am alone with them—my spoken hints ... of course, I could go much farther if I chose; but then, I am a gentleman and must not take advantage of the inexperience of these young—too young—little women."

Mathilde Pomès[91] remarks that the kindness, the "gentillesse essentielle" of Larbaud rendered him "totally impermeable" to all the harsh, dry, pitiless side of the Spanish character. She never had the heart "to tell him the truth about what people in Alicante really thought of him." Those young girls, with whom Larbaud flirted, played tennis and with whom he considered himself a great success, "made fun of him behind his back."[92] In Alicante, few were able to recognize his value, intellectual and spiritual. He was, for most of the people he met there, simply "an old Frenchman," whose health was not good, who had money, and who liked to flirt with young girls.

He approached the literary landscape in the same spirit of delighted discovery. He is not interested in understanding the "development of Spanish literature" from the Cid to Lorca. He is acquainted with the novels of Galdos, Pereda, and Valera, which he reads since they describe that provincial life which he prefers to life in the big cities. "An American," Rubén Darío, early introduced him to Spanish poetry, and soon he was reading other poets, notably Juan Ramón Jiménez. Soon afterwards he encountered the work of Angel Ganivet, "la première grande oeuvre dans laquelle notre vie espagnole rejoint notre vie européenne," and Pio Baroja and Valle-Inclán. Gradually, as he acquired mastery of the language he could liberate himself from "dreary dictionaries"[93] and the words on the page began "to glow, to take on life, to breathe."[94] He came to know Unamuno, Ortega y Gasset, Manuel Machado, Díez-Canedo.

The stars of what he called "notre belle Folie espagnole" were two writers on whom he lavished his talents as critic and translator throughout the 1920s: Gabriel Miró (1879–1930) and Ramón Gómez de la Serna (1888–1963).

Miró, born in Alicante, wrote about the city and the surrounding countryside, one reason why Larbaud (faithful amateur of the regional) was drawn to him. A minor civil servant, he published his first novel *Del vivir* in 1904; a series of others followed, many on religious themes (*Figuras de la Pasión del Señor*, 1916; *Nuestro Padre, San Daniel*, 1921). Larbaud recognized in him a kindred spirit, an artist whose major talent was for description rather than for narration. "Plot" is of little importance in his work, which, like that of Larbaud, deals essentially with impressions, memories, landscapes, and persons. Miró returns again and again to the world of childhood, a world still fresh and vivid, untarnished by the conventions of adulthood. His approach to life is sensuous, rather than intellectual, and his sensuousness goes hand in hand with melancholy and an all-pervading sense of mortality. It was in 1916 that a Catalan friend, José Junoy, lent Larbaud Miró's *Las Cerezas del Cementario* (1910); the following year, he read *El Abuelo del Rey* (1915), was "emballé"[95] and introduced, by a mutual acquaintance from Alicante, Eduardo Irles, entered into correspondence with Miró to arrange a French translation of *Las Figuras de la Pasión del Señor*.[96] Larbaud confided this translation to a young woman, Mme Klotz, who lived in the province of Alicante. She turned it out in six months, with disastrous results, and Miró refused to authorize its appearance.[97] Then, as he recounts in a little article, "Souvenir de Gabriel Miró,"[98] he sat down and began to translate it himself. Done in collaboration with Noémi Larthe, it appeared in 1925, under the title *Semaine Sainte*, with a preface by Larbaud. Before its appearance, he had already spoken about Miró in the course of his series of four lectures on the modern Spanish novel which he gave in the theater of the Vieux Colombier in February 1923.[99]

But his major Spanish revelation was the eccentric, flamboyant, theatrical Ramón Gómez de la Serna, whom Larbaud, in the course of a trip to Madrid, had encountered one Saturday evening in May 1918. Ramón, already a local celebrity, was throning it among his admirers in the literary café, El Pombo, near La Puerta del Sol. Larbaud had some acquaintance with his works;

he had read with enthusiasm *Greguerías, Senas,* and *El Circo*[100] and recognized in them something authentically original. Meeting the author only heightened his appreciation. "Je l'ai adoré," he writes to his friend Eduardo Irles on May 28, 1918. "Ramón," as he liked to be called, had an astonishing facility, which went hand in hand with a certain superficiality, and produced over a hundred volumes in the course of his career. Larbaud especially appreciated—perhaps appreciated more than they deserved—his "greguerías" (outcries), "an almost indefinable literary genre, a hybrid between the poetic metaphor and the prose aphorism."[101] Although he had never warmed to the Surrealists, the pre-Surrealist experiments of Ramón (with their echoes of Maldoror) appealed to him. These brief, sometimes outrageous, more often simply facile or vulgar "outcries" rely heavily (as the Surrealist image did) on their "shock" value.

Larbaud soon began a campaign in order to make Ramón (whom he classes imprudently, with Joyce and Proust, as "the three most important European writers of their generation") better known outside of Spain. He published a piece on him in *Littérature,*[102] followed by "Poètes espagnols et hispano-americains contemporains" in the *N.R.F.,*[103] by "La Renaissance des Lettres espagnoles" in *Les Ecrits nouveaux,*[104] by "Enchantillons par R. Gómez de la Serna interprète de l'Espagne contemporaine,"[105] by R. Gómez de la Serna et la littérature espagnole contemporaine" in *La Revue Hebdomadaire.*[106] A choice of Ramón's *greguerías,* selected and translated by Larbaud and Mathilde Pomès, under the title *Echantillons,* appeared in 1923, in the Grasset collection, *Les Cahiers Verts.* Ramón, of course, was delighted to be published in Paris, to enjoy there, even in a very small circle, a reputation that he had not yet really acquired in his own country.

When he arrived in Paris to bask in the glow of his success, he indulged in a series of Daliesque escapades, motivated as much by a desire for publicity as by personal eccentricity. He appeared, for example, in a circus on the back of an elephant.[107] Larbaud did not witness these pranks. He was busy copying in red ink, on yellow paper (the colors of the Spanish flag), the text of *Echantillons* for presentation to Ramón. Ramón, according to Mathilde Pomès, did not appreciate this touching, but somewhat child-like, gesture and promptly gave the copy away, apparently to one of his friends (Ventura García Calderón?) so this bibliographical curiosity then disappeared, never to turn up again. Among Larbaud's articles about Ramón, that which appeared in *La Revue européenne* on March 1, 1924,[108] is probably the most substantial. In it, he traces the evolution of "Le Moi," of that subjectivity which has increasingly dominated Occidental poetry since the end of the eighteenth century. Some writers, like Ramón, find themselves in the objects about them, by means of a certain "objectivisme subjectif." Larbaud also encouraged Marcelle Auclair (with whom he was in close contact at this time[109]) to translate Ramón's *Le Docteur invraisemblable* for the Editions du Sagittaire in 1925.

After the mid-twenties, his interest declined. However, he continued to keep in touch and visited Ramón when he went to Portugal in 1926. He speaks of the visit, "la belle journée passée avec Ramón" in "Lettre de Lisbonne" (*Pl.*, pp. 932–33) and indicates some of the common traits of character that had drawn them together: like all of us, Larbaud writes, he needs change, he wants to live several lives, to have several pasts behind him. He needs both solitude and the spectacle of human activity. Larbaud, the amateur, also appreciated Ramón's refusal to be a professional "man of letters" or a "professional anything" (*Pl.*, p. 948).

Ramón did not completely forget the long efforts of Larbaud to launch him as a "European" writer, even if those efforts failed to produce the desired results. From Buenos Aires, a refugee from the Franco régime, Ramón sent Larbaud, then paralyzed for more than ten years, a copy of his autobiographical *Automoribundia*, in which he nostalgically describes their first memorable meeting in the café Pombo.

Larbaud was turning more and more during the twenties to the exploration of the literature of Latin America then practically unknown in Europe. Of course, he had read Rubén Darío as a very young man, but Darío was an international phenomenon, as much European, perhaps, as American. (In 1917, Ventura García Calderón had proposed that Larbaud do translations of a selection of Darío's verse, but the project never materialized.) In the literary salon of "Femina" (Mme Bulteau) Larbaud met, in 1919, a young Argentinian writer and poet, Ricardo Güiraldes (1886–1927), who had spent several years of his youth in France and who, like so many Latin-American æsthetes, considered Paris his spiritual homeland.[110] Güiraldes was one of the outstanding Argentine writers of his generation. His most widely acclaimed work, *Don Segundo Sombra* (1926), is a modernist handling of the classical gaucho theme. Earlier books include *El cencerro de cristal* (poems) (1915), *Raucho* (1917), *Rosaura* (1922). He was also the founder of the *avant-garde* review *Proa,* which aspired to be an Argentinian *N.R.F.* Güiraldes, who already knew and admired the work of Larbaud, soon became a friend; the friendship was favored by Larbaud's feeling that he should be "of service" to Latin American literature, and in the July 1, 1920, number of the *N.R.F.*[111] he mentions Güiraldes in an article "Poètes espagnols et hispano-americains."

In 1922, Güiraldes, discouraged by the indifference of the Argentine literary establishment, returned to Paris. He transmits to Larbaud a proposition from *La Nación,* the principal daily of Buenos Aires, to do a series of articles about French literature. Larbaud accepted and in the course of the next three years contributed to the paper some twenty-three literary chronicles, written directly in Spanish. He speaks at length of this enterprise in the introductory essay ("Excuses pour ce livre") of *Domaine français.* Larbaud hails the appearance of a new book by Güiraldes, *Xaimaca,* in 1923 in an article in *La Revue euro-péene.*[112]

In the second number (Autumn 1924) of *Commerce,* Larbaud published his "Lettre à deux amis" addressed to Güiraldes and his wife, Adelina. After saluting the function that Güiraldes's review *Proa* is playing in the intellectual life of Argentina and Latin America, he returns to one of his favorite themes: the stability of the cultural world in contrast with the instability of the world of politics. He encourages Latin American writers to rediscover "their patrimony, the great Castillian classics." He expresses the hope that there may arise "An Argentinian, Chilean or Colombian writer of the stature of a Whitman and Poe." In a second "Lettre à deux amis," written after the publication of *Don Segundo Sombra* in 1926, and published many years later in 1965,[113] Larbaud congratulates Güiraldes on the success of his novel, which he hails as a "national classic," and recalls that already in 1907, in his article "La influencia francesa en las literaturas de lengua castellana" (*El Nuevo Mercurio,* no. 4, April 1907), he had indicated that the theme of the gaucho should be exploited by Argentine writers. Güiraldes died in Paris in October 1927. In the *N.R.F.* of January 1, 1928, Larbaud devotes a brief, moving article to him; in number XV of *Commerce* (pp. 90–107), he publishes his translation (accompanied by an introduction), of Güiraldes's *Poemas misticos* and *Poemas solitarios,* which express the tension between Oriental theosophy and Roman Catholicism which preoccupied the poet during the last few years of his life. The most moving testimony of Larbaud's friendship for Güiraldes is the long letter in Spanish that he gave to Güiraldes's widow in the railroad station of Genoa in April 1928, asking her to read it in a moment of calm because of its very personal nature.[114]

The encounter with Güiraldes contributed to Larbaud's interest in Latin American literature, which was to be one of his major areas of critical activity during the 1920s. His long and fruitful collaboration with *La Nación* not only reinforced his existing convictions concerning the necessity for a comparative approach to literary studies, but also made the intellectual elite of Latin America aware that there existed in Paris "a man of great talent and of great influence as well who was ready to help them."[115]

Many ties united Larbaud and Alfonso Reyes (1889–1959), the Mexican diplomat and man of letters. They shared a profound humanistic culture, which embraced several languages and literatures; a fervent internationalism; a taste for travel; and even a common passion for collecting lead soldiers. With Güiraldes, Reyes was Larbaud's closest and most faithful friend among Latin American intellectuals. Their extensive correspondence provides a rich and varied chronicle of their long relationship.[116] Larbaud first became aware of Reyes quite by chance. He notes in his *Journal* (Friday, May 25, 1917) that he happened to drop into Pastor's Bookshop in Alicante and saw there a translation of Chesterton's *Orthodoxy* by Alfonso Reyes, who, like Larbaud, was a connoisseur of English literature. "The book was so tastefully printed that I could not help buying a copy . . ." They first met personally in 1923, and when Reyes was named Mexican minister in Paris in 1924, Larbaud wrote a glowing welcome, which appeared in *La Revue de l'Amérique latine*.[117] It is quite possible that Larbaud's own critical perceptions concerning Spanish Baroque literature were broadened through conversations with Reyes, who had been instrumental in the rehabilitation of the great poets of this period. Larbaud and Reyes often met during the years 1924–1927, when Reyes was representing his country in Paris, and their letters indicate some of the numerous contacts of Larbaud in Spanish-speaking circles of the capital, with Jean Cassou, F. de Miomandre, Jules Supervielle, Ventura García Calerón, Unamuno, and others. In one of his rare "public actions," Larbaud participated in the campaign protesting against Unamuno's expulsion from Spain.[118]

Larbaud introduced Reyes to the *N.R.F.* and encouraged the translation of one of Reyes's most striking texts, *Vision de l'Ana-huac*, which appeared in 1927,[119] with an introduction by Larbaud. When Reyes was named Ambassador to the Argentine, then to Brazil, the correspondence increased in volume.

No other contemporary writer, French or Spanish, was more temperamentally attuned to Larbaud than Reyes. They were both "men of letters" in the most complete sense. Many of Reyes's essays recall the elegant, unpretentious, discreetly erudite tone of *Jaune Bleu Blanc*. Larbaud is often mentioned in them as, for example, in the essay on the Portuguese language "Adduana linguistica" (which refers to "Divertissement philologique"), in *La Experiencia literaria* (Buenos Aires, Losada, 1942). The two voices seem to conmingle—there is no question of "influence" here, but rather an instinctive *affinity*—in phrases such as these: "En rigor, no quiero concluir nada. Solo quise pasar un poco por esta frontera de las lenguas, donde, como en toda frontera, aprendemos a perdonar y a pedir perdón; es decir, a entender."[120] Reyes probably interested Larbaud in other Mexican writers, those of the past (like Sor Juana de la Cruz) and of the present as well, and encouraged him to write the preface for the translation of one of the most important novels to come out of the Mexican Revolution, *Los de abajo* by Mariano Azuela (1873–1952).[121]

In reading these articles on Hispanic literature, usually brief and often superficial, one often has the impression that Larbaud, in spite of his knowledge of the language, was not always sufficiently informed about the subject matter, which he had often picked up in a random, unsystematic fashion from Spanish and Latin American acquaintances. One is inclined to agree with Anne Poÿlo when she asserts that he wrote about Unamuno, for example, without a sufficiently broad firsthand knowledge of his work.[122]

Through Güiraldes, Larbaud came to know two other Argentine writers, Jorge Luis Borges and the novelist Manuel Gálvez. In an article in *La Revue européenne*,[123] Larbaud salutes Borges's *Inquisiciones* as "the best work of criticism that has come to us from Latin America," a book typical of Buenos Aires, "a capital more cosmopolitan than any of our great European cities, destined to give birth to an intellectual elite which will produce a form of literary criticism which is both American and European—liberal, liberated, bold—a criticism of humanists and of Catholics (in the dual sense of the word), a form of criticism which will be of primary significance to Europeans." He also did a brief piece on Manuel Gálvez in *Les Nouvelles littéraires* of March 11, 1933, in which he dutifully commends the documentary, "realistic" novels (so remote from his own ideas of fiction!) of the Argentinian who had produced books such as *La Maestra Normal* (about a "progressive" country schoolmistress at war with her narrow village environment) or *Nacha Regules* (1919), a kind of minor, Latin American *Nana*. Larbaud's last text dealing with Latin America, a review of *El Nuevo acento*, a book by the Uruguayan José J. Atuña, proclaiming the end of the New World's cultural dependence on Europe and stressing the need to use indigenous subject matter, appeared in the *N.R.F.* in 1935.[124]

Prophetically, in the light of what José Donoso has called the "contemporary boom" in Latin American literature, Larbaud envisages that in the future South American literature—both in Spanish and in Portuguese—will overshadow the contemporary literature of the mother countries, will be liberated from European models and take on a distinctive character of its own. Larbaud hints at a problem which has occupied Americans of both continents from the beginning of their history: the problem of their identity, a problem even more complicated in the South, where there were often great indigenous cultures, than in the predominately Anglo-Saxon North, which could look exclusively to Europe as its place of origin.

D. Portuguese Literature

Larbaud visited Portugal in 1926 on the invitation of Ramón Gómez de la Serna. He remained some six weeks, from January 25 until March 8, when he was recalled to Vichy by the death of his maiden aunt, Jane des Estiveaux. Most of the time he spent in Lisbon, except for a trip to Bussaco where he stayed in the Palace Hotel (from February 27 until March 8) and where he began to write his essay "200 Chambres, 200 Salles de Bain," memories of the various hotels in which he had lived from the days of his childhood onward. The Portuguese experience, brief as it was, obviously pleased him and he deals with it in three substantial pieces: "Lettre de Lisbonne,"[125] "Divertissement philologique,"[126] and "Ecrit dans une cabine du Sud-Express"[127] (published in a small volume with the Portuguese title *Caderno*[128] and later republished in *Jaune Bleu Blanc*), as well as a preface to the French translation of Eça de Queiroz's novel *A Relíquia*.[129] The trip to Portugal, projected since mid-1925, was complicated by the fact that Larbaud, even at the age of forty-four, felt that he was obliged to justify his absence because of possible objections from his mother. He writes to Henry Hoppenot, a friend in the diplomatic service, that he must find "a pretext so that my family will accept the idea of my spending six months in Portugal."[130] Proper strings were pulled at the Quai d'Orsay, and Larbaud was invited to give a lecture in Lisbon, where the distinguished Hispanist, Marcel Bataillon, was then the French cultural representative. The lecture, on Maurice Scève, was delivered in the theater São Carlos on February 20, followed (on February 22) by a banquet offered by a group of intellectuals and writers. Larbaud, in spite of his shyness and love of solitude, was obviously pleased with all the attention he was getting at these official goings on and speaks of them delightedly in "Lettre de Lisbonne."[131]

The essays in *Caderno* have very little to do, really, with literary criticism. They treat only very incidentally of writers and writing. As a matter of fact, Larbaud's acquaintance with Portuguese literature was limited to a few authors (Eça de Queiroz notably) of the late nineteenth and early twentieth century.[132] "Lettre de Lisbonne" is essentially a "travel piece," light, personal, allusive, sometimes a little arch. It dwells on small details like Eiffel's "jules vernesque" public elevator connecting the high" and the "low" town; on the masses of pineapples, hanging like "Venetian lanterns" in the market; or the animals in the Lisbon zoo, especially Larbaud's favorite, the hippopotamus, who, when instructed "abra mais," would open his cavernous maw, "to receive the offerings made to his behemothian majesty...."[133] "Lettre de Lisbonne" mentions the names of numerous Portuguese writers who attended the banquet honoring Larbaud, but he makes no attempt to discuss their works, since he was probably unfamiliar with them. "Divertissement philologique", recording his flirtation with the Portuguese language, is a charming piece of linguistic popularization. Only in "Ecrit dans une cabine du Sud-Express," does he touch at any length on literary questions, in hailing Eça de Queiroz as "a master, one of the great European novelists of the XIXth century" (*Pl.*, p. 956).

Much of the material written by Larbaud on Spanish and Portuguese literature is on the level of graceful literary journalism, and he understandably eliminated the bulk of it from his collected works. As the only outstanding French man of letters of the period who was professionally interested in Spanish and Portuguese literature, both on the Continent and in the New World, he was naturally besieged by aspiring writers who dreamed of the consecration of having their works published in Paris or having an article about them in a Paris review. Many of his notes and prefaces were evidently acts of friendship and, during the final years of his literary activity, he was something of a victim of his own generosity.[134]

E. *Italian Literature*

As the years went by, Italy became Larbaud's favorite country, the place where he felt most at home, where he traveled with greatest pleasure. Rome emerged even more strongly for him as *the* center of European civilization, as a symbol of European unity, as the point of intersection of the Pagan and Christian worlds, whose mingling marked the beginning of "modern" culture. As we have seen, his earlier studies in English literature were oriented toward those authors who loved Italy and wrote about it—notably Walter Savage Landor and Samuel Butler. And, beginning in 1926, he translated selections from a number of contemporary Italian authors for *Commerce*.[135]

Although principally interested in contemporary writers, he read Dante and around 1930 he set seriously to work on a study of the *De Monarchia*. (Ms. XLV–5, FVL, contains extensive notes for it.) It was to be entitled "Amour et Monarchie," but only a few pages (S.E. 12, FVL) were written. They render homage to Italy as the spiritual homeland of the West. This project is often discussed in Larbaud's correspondence with G. Jean-Aubry.[136]

Petrarch also interested him, as a major source of European lyricism and as one of the direct ancestors of Maurice Scève. Furthermore, he considered Petrarchism an outstanding example of the unity of European literature and discerned close connections between the *Marinisti* and his minor French "Baroque" poets. The only Italian writer of the eighteenth century whom he mentions is Alfieri. His article, "L'affaire Bertana-Alfieri," which first appeared in *France-Italie* in 1914 (no. 3; later reprinted in *Technique*),[137] deals with E. Bertana's study in which he sets out to show that Alfieri's autobiography *La Vita* is a collection of misrepresentations and of falsifications. But even admitting the "truth" of Bertana's charges, the *Vita* itself, Larbaud contends, when re-read, appears "resplendissante, non seulement d'art, mais de vérité." The truth of art is not the truth of life and autobiographies such as those of Alfieri, or Rousseau, or Chateaubriand are "true," although they may indulge in shameless or unconscious mythologizing. Larbaud sees in the study an example of that disdain of the scholar for the artist which he had already deplored in "Renan, L'Histoire et la Critique littéraire."

Larbaud's deepest admiration was reserved for Leopardi. He had read (around 1912) Chiarini's *La Vita di Leopardi* and immediately established parallels between the life of the poet in Recanati and his own in Vichy. In 1924, during a trip to

Italy, he visited Recanati and took many of the notes on which
"La Lettre d'Italie" is based. As in so many of his texts, "La
Lettre d'Italie" "beats around the bush" and is in no hurry to
get to the matter at hand. He makes observations about the
Tuscan dialect, about his most recent visit to Florence, about his
stay in Rimini and in San Marino, before settling down to speak
of Recanati and Leopardi. He is psychologically prepared for
the townspeople who, he finds, have the same disdain for the
artist as the *bonne bourgeoisie* of Vichy (*Pl.*, p. 814). He pities
Leopardi, virtually held prisoner for so many years in that provincial town, where "he continued to sing in his cage," se-
questered by an "absurd and spineless father and a savage
mother, stupidity personified." He identifies closely with Leopardi, whose parents wanted to maintain him in a state of
permanent dependence, fearing that the heir "might dilapidate
his inheritance if he were permitted to be free" (*Pl.*, p. 816).

Commenting on the divided Italy of Leopardi's time (*Pl.*,
p. 818), he wonders if this political fragmentation may not have
encouraged the poet "to dream of unity," and to hope that one
day, in his patriotic poems, he might be able to replace the
term "Italy" by "Europe." "I make such a substitution myself,"
Larbaud adds, "when I read the poets and historians of the
Risorgimento."[138] After tracing a brief portrait of Leopardi's
father, a "hen-pecked husband," he attacks the mother with an
almost personal hatred as "la Mamma cattiva," a peasant, harsh,
brutal, and illiterate in spite of her title of Marquise (*Pl.*,
p. 820). But Leopardi somehow overcame the disadvantages,
disadvantages which had contributed—as in Larbaud's case—to
his spiritual and artistic growth. He became "the literary hero
of 19th century Italy." After concluding his comments on the
poet's life and character, Larbaud begins to consider the poet's
work, which, formally at least, continues a specifically Italian
classical tradition. But his "deep pessimism" is something that
had disappeared in Italian literature since Dante. Yet even in
venturing these generalizations, he admits that Leopardi is one
of the classical authors he knows least well and excuses himself
for his "rash judgements." The "lettre" is truly as charming and
graceful and *désinvolte* as Princess Bassiano found it.[139] But
even as a very rapid critical analysis of the *work* of Leopardi,

it leaves much to be desired. Accustomed as we are to the heroic wrestlings of modern criticism with the text, it seems that Larbaud continually steps gracefully out of its way.

All during the 1920s and early 1930s, Larbaud multiplied his contacts with contemporary Italian writers. His "cultural services" brought him to the attention of the Italian government (of which he approved, since, like many of his fellow countrymen, he was much impressed by the fact that Mussolini had the trains running on time). As a "gran amico," he was received officially in Rome by Signor Bottai, the Fascist "Minister of Corporations," one of the most liberal high officials of the régime, for his contributions to "the cause of Italian literature."[140]

Although several of the authors backed by Larbaud—Alermo, Capasso, Settani—no longer figure on the international literary scene, Italo Svevo (Ettore Schmitz) has remained a truly "major" discovery. Larbaud first heard of Svevo through James Joyce, who knew him well during the Trieste years when he was a pupil of Joyce's in the Berlitz school there. Joyce immediately recognized the originality of Svevo's novels *Una Vita* and *Senilità*, but after his departure from Trieste could do little about "promoting" them. However, in 1924, Svevo published *La Coscienza di Zeno* and sent a copy to Joyce who reacted enthusiastically: "You must know that it is by far your best work." Joyce immediately suggested that copies be sent to a number of internationally influential literary figures, including Larbaud, Crémieux, Eliot, Ford. On April 1, 1924, he wrote to Svevo that Larbaud was very impressed and, after having read *Senilità* and *Una Vita* as well, Larbaud himself sent off two flattering letters to Trieste. Svevo was delighted, as his subsequent correspondence with Larbaud reveals.[141] Larbaud translated passages from *Senilità* that "he would have liked to have written himself" and tried without success to publish them in the *N.R.F.* and in *Commerce*. Finally, Adrienne Monnier accepted them for *Le Navire d'Argent* (no. II, February 1926).[142] It is a tribute to the catholicity of Larbaud's taste that he was able to appreciate the achievement of Svevo. Svevo's analysis of character is detached, unemotional, even clinical and much influenced (especially in *La Coscienza di Zeno*) by Freudian psychoanalysis, which Larbaud had long disliked.[143] Larbaud loved stylistic refinement, while Svevo wrote asyntactically, in a mixture of Italian and Triestino, with Austrian-Hungarian overtones, a manner which Larbaud may have considered as a much-needed reaction against the flamboyance of D'Annunzio.[144]

It was Svevo who brought Eugenio Montale to Larbaud's attention. Montale first wrote to Larbaud, on the suggestion of Svevo, on March 5, 1926; in this letter he speaks of his articles on Svevo and of a very short piece he had devoted to Larbaud himself.

Svevo, of course, was Larbaud's major revelation, but there were others as well. A warm friendship developed with Gianna Manzini,[145] whose work "of a simple and unpretentious genius" he had praised in "La Pierre Ponce et la Pépite."[146] Larbaud also encouraged another woman writer, Sibilla Aleramo (1871–1960), for whom he did a brief preface for the French translation of her volume of essays[147] (one of which was devoted to his work) emphasizing their poetic quality and the acuteness of their perceptions. He also wrote a preface for the French translation of a volume of poems by Aldo Capasso (1909)[148] in which he salutes him as "the best Italian critic of his generation" and praises his poetic technique as "new and personal." In a subsequent collection of essays (*Sapere distinguere*, 1934), Capasso includes a long analysis of the entire work of Larbaud. Ettore Settani came to Larbaud's attention because of Settani's skill in handling the "stream of consciousness" technique in his novel *Chi ha ucciso Gianni Randone* (1932), which Larbaud praised in his "Lettera a Ettore Settani," in the Italian literary magazine *Occidente* (October-December 1933). Subsequently, he succeeded in having the novel translated into French and he himself did the brief introduction. [149]

Among his many Italian literary friends figured the internationally oriented poet, Lionello Fiumi, Mario Puccini, Ungaretti, Corrado Alvaro, Massimo Bontempelli, Ugo Betti, G. B. Angioletti. Most of them corresponded—some, like Fiumi, extensively—with Larbaud, and their letters are preserved in the FVL. Fiumi, who organized the French section of the semiofficial review *Dante*, had Larbaud named (in 1931) an honorary member of the Dante Society and published his text "Ma Dette envers l'Italie"[150] in the society's journal. In return, Larbaud translated two of Fiumi's poems: "Ode" (*Dante,* March 1935) and "Les Pauvres petites prostituées" (*Cahiers du Sud,* April 1935). Most of these brief prefaces and articles on contemporary Italian writers are essentially acts of friendship and have few critical pretensions.

F. Conclusion

But in the midst of all this secondary activity, had the earlier creative energy lessened? Perhaps, with the passing of the years, Larbaud increasingly recognized the impossibility of that "quest for the Absolute" which had motivated Barnabooth. And, particularly after the death of his mother, he was no longer troubled by the many personal problems created by their difficult and ambiguous relationship. For the first time, he was able to "settle down," live openly with his beloved companion, and enjoy a domestic tranquility which is not always the best spur to creative activity. Did he increasingly feel that temptation of happiness, did he resign himself, with a certain relief, to encouraging others and saying pleasant things about them? The fever of *Barnabooth,* cooling, it would seem, from the time of his conversion onward, had quite abated. And during the rest of his active writing life, criticism, translation, and his allusive and Protean essaylike texts would constitute the quasi-totality of his work.

As a critic, his urbane and pleasure-oriented "amateurism" was achieved only at a certain price. Moved by curiosity and generosity, as well as by his restless mobility, he attempted perhaps to embrace too much. During the 1920s, he was dealing with English and American literature, French literature, Spanish and Latin American literature, as well as with Portuguese and Italian literature. He was spreading himself thin and often (with certain noteworthy exceptions) the results resemble cultivated literary journalism rather than in-depth literary criticism. He seemed temperamentally more interested in proclaiming his discoveries and encouraging others to share them than he was in carefully examining a text. Finally, he emerges as a superb *animateur,* as an intermediary of unusual taste, discernment, and generosity rather than as a professional critic. But, as he so often insisted, he didn't want to be a "professional" in anything.

Nevertheless, his achievement was a considerable one. He succeeded in widening the literary horizons of his countrymen, of making them aware of some of the most significant literature of their time that was being produced outside of their own borders, in defending the unity of European literature at a time when it was being increasingly threatened by forces of disruption.

IV *"Ces amours, si j'ose dire, philologiques ..."*

Larbaud was a lover of words. He delighted in tracking down their origins, in establishing their etymologies, in following their changes in meaning. His philological investigations, conducted, as always, as an "amateur," gave him never-ending pleasure.[151] He was drawn to the study of philology and linguistics partly through a disdain for "rhetorical facility," as he tells us in the essay "Honneur des hommes."[152] He had clearly read extensively in these fields as various references to Bopp, Bréal, A. Meillet, Ferdinand Brunot, W. von Wartburg, and others in his *Journal* and in *Saint Jérôme* indicate.[153] He is fascinated by the spectacle of linguistic change, of "the instability of languages." Nothing lasts and even the name of God changes in response to linguistic laws.[154] For him, language is always a living thing and in his hands the phenomena of philological mutations assume a dramatic quality. He describes the disappearance of the classical word for horse ("equus") replaced in Vulgar Latin by "caballus," a word which would have a numerous progeny in the Romance languages. "Neighing, mane tossed in the wind, nostrils dilated, the countrified 'caballus' sets off on a glorious career, leaving under the ice of the ravaged earth, the corpse of 'equus' soon to become a fossil."[155] But quite typically, as he continues to meditate on the problems of language, he modifies his initial positions and begins to "glide" toward other different and even contradictory ones. Although he condemns its excesses, he cannot but admit that literature is inevitably a matter of rhetoric and that even if linguists are principally interested in the spoken work, it is "across the sumptuous screen" of the written word that they are often obliged to study it. But linguists, he finds, are sometimes suspicious of literature, which is made of "a special language" quite different from everyday usage. Moreover, such usage ages very quickly. Larbaud instinctively puts his finger on the naturalistic error that literature can be created from "the speech of every day," literally reproduced. Literary language is inevitably "artificial" and conventional and the writer is forced to return to the rhetoric which he had wished to abjure, not to its vulgar facilities, to be sure, but rather to its difficulties, in order to be able to "weave those garlands of words to bear to the altar of the God who fills with joy the eternal youth of the soul."

Two longer essays in *Jaune Bleu Blanc*, "Divertissement philologique" (*Pl.*, pp. 934–46) and "Des prénoms féminins" (*Pl.*, pp. 884–90), also deal with questions of languages. "Divertissement philologique," as we have said, recounts his love affair with the Portuguese language. Larbaud insists that the acquisition of a new language must be a form of courtship. "I learned this language the way one wins the love of a woman." Like most of his essays, it does not lend itself to an orderly résumé. The announced subject is only a pretext for personal asides, reminiscences, impressions. The movement is instinctive rather than logical, and the reader is carried along as though he were engaged in a lively, civilized, somewhat random conversation. We can be sure that Larbaud consulted grammars, dictionaries, histories of the Portuguese language, but he rarely cites them. Here, as elsewhere, he is often somewhat coy in avoiding the slightest hint of "pedantry," even when a little documentation would be in order. Reading the Byzantine historian, Psellos, he is enchanted by the name of the Empress Zoé. "I caught myself saying: what a woman! and what a beautiful name!" And so he is led to write one of his most attractive philological "diversions": "Des prénoms féminins" (*Pl.*, pp. 884–90). He passes in review a variety of surnames: "Quintilie," "Ruth," "Otilia," "Mercedes," "Edith," chosen from several countries. The essay is also a celebration of the love of woman and concludes with a delicate tribute to the companion who shared his life for over thirty years and who cared for him so devotedly during his long illness: of all the many diminutives of Mary, the one he loves best is "le diminutif italien, Marriuccia. . . ."

V *Larbaud, Comparatist*

Larbaud, as we have seen, was always searching for connections, for continuity. He was convinced that the various national literatures of Europe, especially those of Latin Europe, of "Romania" (which also embraced certain areas of Northern Europe), could be understood only imperfectly if studied separately, since they were all related parts of a common culture, founded on the heritage of Greco-Roman antiquity and of Roman Christendom. His approach to literature, as his correspondence (in FVL) with E. R. Curtius testifies, was instinctively comparative.

CHAPTER 6

The Translator:
In the Service of Saint Jerome

I *Introduction*

LARBAUD'S criticism was closely allied with his tireless activity as a translator, for, as we have seen, many of his critical studies dealt with authors he had either translated himself or whose translation he had encouraged. Moreover, he was always very much aware that translation, fundamentally, is a form of criticism (*St. J.*, pp. 75–76). He devoted much of his life to making accessible in French those foreign works, English, American, Spanish, Portuguese, Italian, that he admired and that he often "discovered" for the literary public. He spent many years on his translations of Samuel Butler, several more in bringing out, in collaboration with Auguste Morel, Stuart Gilbert, and Joyce himself, the French version of *Ulysses*.

In addition to these major undertakings, he translated a large number of shorter texts, many of which appeared during the twenties in *Commerce*, that handsome review founded and financed by the American-born Princess Marguerite Caetani, of which he was considered somewhat as the "official translator" and the authority on foreign literatures.[1] His devotion to the art of translation dates from the very beginning of his literary career. In 1901, he published a version of "The Rime of the Ancient Mariner." Ten years later, dissatisfied with this first effort, he brought out a revised edition, "La Chanson du vieux marin," in order, as he said, "to offer his excuses to Coleridge and to himself."

II *Theoretical Problems of Translation*

Larbaud began thinking, early in his career, about the theoretical problems of translation. In an article[2] which appeared
in *L'Effort libre* (November 1913), he criticizes uninspired literal
translations and defends "personal interpretation," a view which,
as we shall see, he will considerably modify in the light of later
experience. He declares that "the desire to translate comes to
me naturally" and that it forms a necessary part of any literary
apprenticeship. It is also a journey into the unknown, a kind of
erotic experience, like "the loves of an explorer with the daughter
of a barbarian king" ("...les amours d'un explorateur avec la
fille d'un roi sauvage"). He apparently liked this phrase, which
he will use, slightly modified, in the essay, "L'Amour et la
traduction" (*St. J.*, p. 93). He praises Claudel's translations of
Coventry Patmore (for which, we recall, he did an introduction) and rebukes those critics, "including some of our most
competent Anglicists" who object that they are not sufficiently
literal. The urge to translate, he tells us, springs from a desire
to be of service; it is a humble, self-effacing exercise and Larbaud, as we know, set great store on humility.

During the war years in Alicante, when he was doing little
original work, he devoted most of his time to translating Samuel
Butler and recalls, in his *Journal,* the difficulties involved in
translating from one language into another while living among
people who are speaking a third. Back in Paris in the twenties,
he was occupied with the demanding and exasperating task of
trying to "supervise" the Morel-Gilbert version of *Ulysses,* as
well as with his translations (in collaboration) of Ramón Gómez
de la Serna and Gabriel Miró and of a great variety of shorter
texts, ranging from English classics like Sir Thomas Browne to
contemporaries like Barilli and Archibald MacLeish, which he
regularly contributed to *Commerce.* During these years, he was
certainly concerned with the problems of translation, although
never in a very theoretical or systematic fashion, since, as we
have observed in other contexts, such an approach was contrary
to his nature. He preferred doing it to talking about it.

He settled down to write specifically about such questions
only in the early thirties and especially after visits to Rome in

1929 and 1934, when he became increasingly interested in Saint Jerome, "the patron saint of translators." The book which resulted, finally published in 1946, under the title of *Sous l'invocation de Saint Jérôme*³ had long figured among his projects. In "El cuento de nunca acabar" (*St. J.*, p. 97), he notes that he had been thinking for more than fifteen years of writing about "the art and craft of the translator." However, only a relatively small portion of the book is specifically devoted to problems of translation. The first section, "Le Patron des traducteurs," is largely a biographical essay on Jerome, which stresses the importance of the Vulgate in Western civilization (*St. J.*, p. 51). He presents Jerome's text "De optimo genere interpretandi" as "the translator's breviary," whose guiding principle might be summed up in the phrase, "non verbum e verbo, sed sensum exprimere" (*St. J.*, p. 50). Translate the sense, not the words.

A series of notes and mini-essays specifically dealing with translation composes the first section, "De la traduction" (*St. J.*, pp. 59–123), of the second part of *Saint Jérôme*, "L'Art et le métier." The remaining two-thirds of this charmingly miscellaneous collection (which should not be crushed by the reputation for "great erudition" which has sometimes been attached to it), entitled "Remarques" and "Technique," covers a wide range of subjects, including linguistics, comparative literature, and literary criticism, which have been dealt with in the preceding chapter. "De la traduction" is made up of twelve very brief essays. "Vocation" (*St. J.*, pp. 59–61) lauds the "humble, meticulous task" of translation, a task which may render greater service than personal creation, in which pure vanity often plays such a large part. Indeed, he reminds us in "Joies et profits du traducteur" (*St. J.*, pp. 73–81) that translation can serve as a kind of substitute for original creation, since the translator feels that he is "entering into possession" of his text and that now, somehow, "it belongs to him." Capable and dedicated translators, he claims, stand more of a chance of winning "a small, discreet immortality" than third-rate "creative" writers. "Les Balances du traducteur" (*St. J.*, pp. 82–85), warning of the inadequacies of bilingual dictionaries, insists that the translator must always be a vigilant "weigher of words," since an author, depending on the context, may often employ a term in a sense at variance with its usual dictionary definition. The word, which he describes as "tremblingly iridescent" is a living thing, always changing, always in movement, always defying the efforts of dictionary makers to immobilize it, to embalm it once and for all. The translator is engaged in the miraculous activity of attempting to reconstitute a living text, cell by cell, in a new body, a body which he, "like a Pygmalion of verbal forms," has created. "L'Amour et la traduction" restates once again Larbaud's conviction that you must love what you are doing, if you are to do it well. Good translations are the children of a love match and nothing distresses him more than when a beautiful text, like a Christian maiden delivered to wild beasts, is martyrized in the hands of a coarse and pedantic translator (*St. J.*, p. 95).

We can perceive a modification in his approach to the craft between 1929, when he wrote the essay on Saint Jerome, and 1935, when he was composing the notes of "De la traduction," a shift from a defense of "free interpretation" to an insistence on fidelity to the text. Challenging Thomas Francklin, the eighteenth-century author of *Translation: A Poem*, who recommended that the translator should "soften each blemish and each grace improve," Larbaud holds that the main concern should be to render the text as accurately as possible. He admits that he realizes that it is not possible to produce work of the literary excellence of an Amyot or of a Florio while rigorously respecting the original. Either exactitude is sacrificed to "beauty" or "beauty" to exactitude—and he opts for exactitude.

Possibly this change of heart was prompted by the problems he had encountered in his translation of "Yerbas de Tarahumara," a poem by his friend Alfonso Reyes, the Mexican diplomat and man of letters.[4] Published in the summer 1929 issue of *Commerce* (no. XX), it was disfigured by a number of howlers, tactfully pointed out by Reyes in a letter to which Larbaud refers indirectly in his mini-essay "Gent irritable" (*St. J.*, p. 107). Moreover, certain of Larbaud's friends who knew Spanish, among them Paul Valéry, extravagantly praised the beauty of the original without ever mentioning the translation. In "Les Carnets de Samuel Butler: Avant-propos du traducteur,"[5] Larbaud again insists that the translator must renounce "the heroic passion and all the vanity of literary creation" in order to become the humble servant of his author (*St. J.*, p. 9).

III *Translations of Brief Texts*

Larbaud's briefer translations, which appeared for the most part in *Commerce, La Phalange,* and *N.R.F.,* include a wide range of English, American, Irish, Italian, and Spanish-American texts.[6] Among the English: Francis Thompson, R. L. Stevenson, Walter Savage Landor, Chesterton, Arnold Bennett, Edith Sitwell, Sir Thomas Browne. Americans include Whitman, Hawthorne, Archibald MacLeish. One Irishman: Liam O'Flaherty. The Spanish and Spanish-Americans are represented by Ramón Gómez de la Serna, Gabriel Miró, Ricardo Güiraldes, Alfonso Reyes, Eugenio d'Ors. From the mid-1920s onward, for a number of reasons, sentimental as well as literary, Italy became Larbaud's favorite country,[7] and he translates many contemporary Italians —Emilio Cecchi, Bruno Barilli, R. Bacchelli, Gianna Manzini. In addition, he was continually engaged in encouraging others to translate and publish foreign texts that he had "discovered" or with which he felt a special kinship—texts like *Trivia* of Logan Pearsall Smith or *Greguerías* of Ramón Gómez de la Serna. In fact, many of his friends like Saint-John Perse thought that he gave too generously of his time and effort.

IV *Translations of Samuel Butler*

During the war years in Spain, Larbaud worked intensively on his translations of Samuel Butler. He had first heard of Butler in Cannes, in 1912, during a meeting with Arnold Bennett, who told him that Butler was enjoying a kind of modest revival in England as a precursor of anti-Victorianism. When he first read *The Way of all Flesh,* however, he didn't particularly like it, but as he came to know Butler better, he increasingly identified with him.[8] By August 1915, he was at work on his translation of *Erewhon* and at the end of the year he had decided to undertake the long-term project of translating, not only *Erewhon,* but also *Erewhon Revisited, The Way of All Flesh,* and the *Note-*

books.[9] In a journal entry of June 11, 1917 (*Journal*, pp. 64–65),
he notes that he has been reading Butler's *Evolution Old and
New* and considers it a genuinely great book. He prefers it to
Darwin, since it proclaims the ability of man to overcome blind
biological determinism. He is surprised to find that Butler, although English, was also so "Continental and Catholic." (Of
course, he always liked those Englishmen, like Landor or Patmore or Chesterton, who were deviants from the proper British
pattern.) Butler, he declares, is truly "mon homme" and "dearer
than ever to me" (*Journal*, p. 63). He proceeds to list important
issues on which they are in agreement: the relations between
parents and children; money, and the liberty it purchases; European unity; a love for London, for Italy, and for French literature.

But Butler's antireligious bias, his hostility to the Church
disturbed Larbaud from the first. In a letter (dated June 5,
1916) to Gide, included in the G. Jean-Aubry edition of their
correspondence (Paris, La Haye: Stols, 1948), he speaks of the
Note-Books, noting that he feels qualms of conscience, because
certain pages are so stupidly irreligious and was able to bring
himself to translate them only because of his great liking for
Butler personally. Indeed his uncritical enthusiasm for certain
works of Butler may stir doubt concerning his literary judgment,
which on occasion could be swayed by an admiration for the
character of the writer. One raises an eyebrow when reading in
the *Journal* that *"Life and Habit* is one of the grandest books of
the XIXth century and indeed of the last 30 years."

Fragments of *Erewhon* appeared in the January 1, 1920,
number of the *N.R.F.*, and the entire text was published toward
the end of the year. In 1921, parts of *La Loi et la grâce* came
out in the December number of *Les Ecrits nouveaux*, and the
N.R.F. issued *Ainsi va toute chair* in two stout volumes. There
followed (in 1922) *La Vie et l'habitude (N.R.F)*, fragments from
Nouveaux voyages en Erewhon (*La Revue de France*, October
1 and 15, 1923) and the complete edition (*N.R.F.*, 1924) and
the *Note-Books* (*N.R.F.*, 1936).

During the 1920s, Larbaud also made a considerable effort to
publicize the work of Butler. His lecture, given in Adrienne
Monnier's bookshop on November 3, 1920, helped launch *Erewhon*; it was followed by numerous articles in various reviews,

including the *N.R.F.* and *La Revue de Paris*. But these efforts were largely unavailing. He did not succeed in "imposing" Butler on the French literary public any better than he succeeded with another discovery, Ramón Gómez de la Serna. The critical reaction was lukewarm. The *Revue des revues* found *Erewhon* "terribly flat." *Littérature* politely remarked that Larbaud has "patiently translated this very long volume" but added that it is not one which is read "with avidity." Jules Romains, in *L'Humanité*, speaks vaguely of "a fine job of translation." Gilbert de Voisins, reviewing *Ainsi va toute chair* in the *N.R.F.* (July 1921), cautiously compliments Larbaud for his skill in "capturing the atmosphere of the original"—with which Voisins was not acquainted. André Maurois, unique among the reviewers in having an extensive knowledge of English, praises *Nouveaux voyages en Erewhon* (*N.R.F.*, November 1, 1924) for Larbaud's "skill in reproducing the author's style." He feels, however, that certain characteristic English expressions familiar to the French reader should have been retained and strongly disagrees with the translation, "Viens, poupoule" (!) for "Home, Sweet Home." No critic even remotely shared Larbaud's enthusiasm for Butler as one of the very great writers of the nineteenth century and as a precursor of twentieth-century trends. Gallimard lost money on the undertaking and became more and more reluctant to bring out the succeeding volumes. Larbaud, in his "Les Carnets de S. Butler: l'avant-propos du traducteur" (*N.R.F.*, January 1, 1935) deplores (p. 84) "the lack of commercial success" of the translations and "the indifference of the French public" to Butler's work.

V   *The Translation of* Ulysses

Sylvia Beach introduced Larbaud to *Ulysses*. He writes to her on February 15, 1921 (FVL): "I am reading *Ulysses*. Indeed, I cannot read anything else, even think of anything else. Just the thing for me. I like it better than *A Portrait*. . . . Breaks new ground. Goes deeper." He had read both *Dubliners* and *A Portrait of the Artist* by the end of 1920.[10] *A Portrait* has a special appeal for him as a study of the resistance of the artist to a hostile environment. Stephen in Dublin joins Larbaud's gallery of misunderstood artist-heroes: Stendhal in Grenoble, Butler in Langar, Leopardi in Recanati[11]—and, of course, the young Larbaud himself, in Vichy. Just a week after his first letter, he writes again to Sylvia Beach (FVL): "I am raving mad over *Ulysses*. Since I read Whitman when I was 18, I have not been so enthusiastic about any book. I think that I should like to translate a few pages for the *N.R.F.* or, if they don't want it, for *Les Ecrits nouveaux*.... It is as great, and comprehensive, and human as Rabelais...." We can easily understand his enthusiasm. Certain aspects of the book could not fail to appeal to him, notably the Homeric superstructure which demonstrated Joyce's feeling for cultural continuity and the "stream of consciousness" technique, toward which Larbaud has been indirectly working his way for years. Thus began an intense, complicated, often strained involvement with Joyce and his work which resulted, nearly a decade later, in the publication, in 1929, of the French translation of *Ulysses* by Adrienne Monnier's "La Maison des amis des livres"; "James Joyce, *Ulysse*, traduit de l'anglais par August Morel, assisté par Stuart Gilbert. Traduction entièrement revue par Valery Larbaud, avec la collaboration de l'auteur...."

Both Adrienne Monnier[12] and Sylvia Beach[13] have given their versions of the history of this enormous undertaking, which dragged on for years and strained, almost to the breaking point, the nerves of all concerned. Too many cooks were stirring the broth. Sylvia Beach describes the first meeting of Joyce and Larbaud: "I arranged a meeting between the two writers at Shakespeare and Company on Christmas Eve, 1920. They immediately became great friends. Perhaps I realize more than anyone what the friendship of Valery Larbaud meant to Joyce. Such generosity and unselfishness towards a fellow-writer as Larbaud showed to Joyce is indeed rare." During the summer and early fall of 1921, Larbaud lent Joyce and his family his apartment on the rue Cardinal Lemoine. Joyce writes about it to his Italian correspondent, Alessandro Francini Bruni (in Italian) telling him about his good luck. The flat is "unbelievable." It is located "ten minutes from the Luxembourg" in a "kind of little park, with access through two barred gates, absolute silence, great trees, birds ... like being a hundred kilometers from Paris...."[14] During this first year of their friendship, Joyce and Larbaud spent many evenings together, sometimes in the company of Robert McAlmon, husband of Bryher and publisher of "Contact Editions."[15] Joyce, in a letter to Larbaud thanking him for dedicating the *nouvelle* "Amants, heureux amants" to him (November 6, 1921, FVL), writes: "I recognized in the story many points we discussed during our *notti bianche*."

Joyce wanted Larbaud himself to undertake the herculean task of putting *Ulysses* into French, a project that Sylvia Beach and Adrienne Monnier had been considering since 1922. Larbaud, quite understandably, in spite of his immense admiration for Joyce, was unwilling to commit himself to such a long, difficult, and time-consuming enterprise. He did, however, agree to "supervise" the translation and recommended a young Anglicist, Auguste Morel, who had sought his advice on some translations of English poetry, as a suitable person for the job. The translation, after many delays, finally got under way in the spring of 1924 and Larbaud, in a letter of March 26 to Sylvia Beach (FVL) notes: "I saw Morel the other day and he told me that he would be able to begin his translation of *Ulysses* early in May." Stuart Gilbert, a former British civil servant in Burma, arrived in Paris in 1927 to pursue a literary career. He visited Sylvia Beach's bookshop; she showed him some of the Morel translations, in which he discovered errors. He then offered to be of assistance in the preparation of the French translation and Joyce accepted the offer, to the displeasure of Morel, who was not flattered that someone should be supervising his work. Larbaud's role, apparently, was to supervise the supervisor. The long affair dragged on. Larbaud writes to Sylvia Beach on September 18, 1927 (FVL): "We have finished 'Penelope' and are about to begin the final revision of 'The Lastrygonians.'" At one point, in the early stages, the help of Léon-Paul Fargue was solicited, for Joyce admired Fargue's gift for word play. But Fargue, as usual, seldom showed up for appointments and was soon out of the picture.

As in the case of Butler, Larbaud made a considerable effort to introduce Joyce to the literary public. On December 7, 1921, he gave a lecture on him in Adrienne Monnier's bookshop. It was a great success. The audience was a distinguished one and did not conceal its enthusiasm. "Joyce himself," writes Richard Ellmann,[16] "was hidden behind a screen, but was obliged, much against his will, to come forward afterwards in response to enthusiastic applause. Larbaud fervently embraced him, and Joyce blushed with confusion...." The text was published in the *N.R.F.* in the April 1, 1922, number and was subsequently reprinted in *Ce Vice impuni, la lecture: Domaine anglais.*[17] An English translation of the concluding section of the talk (done by T. S. Eliot) appeared in the first number of *The Criterion.* Fragments of *Ulysses* were featured in the first number of *Commerce* (summer 1924) with an introduction by Larbaud. Other articles by Larbaud came out in the *N.R.F.* in the numbers of January 1 and March 1, 1925. Additional fragments of *Ulysses,* translated by Larbaud and Morel, were published in the June 1927 numbers of *Les Feuilles libres.*

Close personal contacts between Larbaud and Joyce declined after the intimacy of 1921–1922. Larbaud, characteristically, was developing new interests, was drawn more and more to contemporary Italian writing. But he was still uncomfortably aware that he had promised to revise the translation. Although Morel's version was nearly completed, Larbaud proceeded very slowly and meticulously and made little progress in his revisions. Adrienne Monnier was furious about what she considered his "dilatoriness" and "irresponsibility" and after the translation appeared, Larbaud definitely broke with her. He managed to settle down to work seriously during the summer of 1926, in the seclusion of Valbois, and continued his efforts until the end of the year, in the midst of sharp exchanges between translators and publisher and among the translators themselves. Joyce, on the sidelines, seemed to enjoy observing all the fuss. In a letter of March 28, 1928, to Larbaud,[18] he assures him that "on my return to Paris, I shall put matters right with Miss Monnier." He recounts the intrigues going on in a letter to Miss Weaver, on April 8, 1928: "... But as you were, luckily for me, present at one heated scene, I want you to know that it's quite as warm as ever in Paris. I have, I think, smoothed over matters between Larbaud and Her (A. Monnier), but there remains to be rubbed down S.G. [S. Gilbert] and A.M. [A. Morel], the two translators who dislike each other and V.L. and are heartily disliked by him in return. Fortunately [???] they all like ME."[19] By the spring of 1928, Larbaud had not yet finished his work, claiming that he had been ill. In May, fleeing the wrath of Miss Monnier, he retired to Italy, where he completed his labors by the end of August. But it was not simply "dilatoriness" that had held things up. Larbaud, with his scrupulous concern for accuracy and "rightness" of tone, was constantly questioning the version of Morel. As we can see from samples of his revisions which he submitted to Joyce,[20] he performed a valuable function in toning down Morel's often unnecessarily coarse and violent language, of giving finish and polish to the style, and in insisting on the precise rather than the approximate word.

Joyce's reply, of October 1928 (FVL), to Larbaud's long letter of June 14, 1928, suggesting numerous revisions, acknowledges the corrections: ". . . I passed on all your corrections with my suggestions to Miss Monnier. Morel I have not seen for a long time but I shall write to him if and when I feel a little stronger. He has misunderstood here and there but it would be unfair to lay too much stress upon that in a work of such length and difficulty. . . ." In a letter to his protectress, Miss Weaver, on September 20, 1928,[21] he speaks out more frankly:

. . . The French translation of *Ulysses* is now finished. V. L. sent me a list of difficulties which I solved for him and informed me that he would celebrate his birthday, twenty-ninth of August, by going off his diet of milk and rusks in favor of some wine of the country in my honour and to celebrate both events. His work is now at an end. A. Morel, the translator, has taken a great deal of license here and there, sometimes incorporating whole sentences of his own manufacture. These were struck out. The translation is really his and has been done with great care and devotion, but like many other people by dint of brooding on it he sees one aspect to the exclusion of another. In his case, it is the coarseness which excludes the others, or perhaps I should say the violence. I said to A. Monnier, the publisher, about these bits, "A little too much Madagascar here." He is in fact a French colonial born. Perhaps this explains it. I hope the three patch up their differences when the work is out. S.G.'s [Stuart Gilbert's] work was very useful, but it was absolutely necessary to have V.L.'s final revision, as he is very accurate, slow, fastidious, and rather timid . . . She [A. Monnier] becomes more and more superstitious, thinks that V.L. is being bewitched by L.P.F. [Fargue] and I wish she could find out who is bewizarding me. . . .

Not one of the estranged and exasperated translators attended the lunch given on June 27, 1929, by Adrienne Monnier at the Hôtel Léopold in Les Vaux-de-Cernay near Versailles, to celebrate the publication of the translation. Larbaud, moreover, seems to have destroyed all the letters he received from Monnier, Beach, and Morel concerning the project.

Joyce and Larbaud remained faithful friends until the departure of Joyce for Zurich in 1940. The Joyces, fleeing the Occupied Zone, spent nearly a year with the Jolases at Saint-Gérand-le-Puy near Vichy in 1939–1940, and were in touch with Larbaud and Mme Nebbia. Larbaud, always ready to be of service, cashed a check for Joyce's former secretary, Samuel Beckett, when the latter was stranded in Vichy without funds.[22]

VI   *With the Blessings of Saint Jerome*

Larbaud, as we have seen, was deeply committed to translation as a necessary literary apprenticeship, as an activity which inculcated humility and conscientious workmanship and which promoted an understanding of the unity of European literature. However, his comments on the technique of translation (contained largely in unpublished sections of the journal, especially during the period 1917–1919 and in one part of *Saint Jérôme*), although sensitive, subtle, and perspicacious, are not particularly profound or "scientific."

Was Larbaud "a great translator"? French critics usually praise him as such, but, in general, without making any close comparison of the translation with the original, since, in the majority of cases, they were linguistically unqualified to do so. He was the first to admit that he was not infallible. In his charming and rather rueful letter to Alfonso Reyes, dated August 21, 1929,[23] in reply to the latter's comments on Larbaud's version of his poem "Yerba de Tarahumaras," he offers his apologies for misinterpreting the term "bravos," adding that all translators occasionally make slips and ascribes them to "a little devil" who is always trying to lead them astray. He mentions this "little devil" again in several passages of *Saint Jérôme*: in "Gent irritable" (*St. J.*, p. 109) where he speaks of "les diablotins idiotisme et modisme" and in "Jhon, le Toréador" (*St. J.*, p. 220), of "le très actif petit démon."

Larbaud was always critical, indeed overcritical, of his own abilities as a translator. In an English entry in his journal for December 8, 1918 (*Journal*, FVL), he comments on the work of Auguste Jean-Baptiste Defaucompret, the tireless French translator of Cooper, noting that he is more scrupulous and painstaking than Defaucompret, but that his very scrupulousness may sometimes prevent him from writing naturally in French. He continues, in the English entry for December 11 (*Journal*, FVL) that he desires first and foremost to be faithful to the text even though such fidelity may demand the sacrifice of literary elegance. He was scrupulous, too, in the efforts he made to inform himself thoroughly concerning the subject matter of works he was translating. During the period 1917–1918, he was continually reading books in English and French in order to master the technical vocabulary he needed for Butler's *Life and Habit.*

No French writer of his generation, certainly no French writer of his reputation and achievements as an original artist, devoted himself more lovingly, more conscientiously to the translator's craft, strove more successfully to make of it an art, wrote more penetratingly, more winningly of its problems, of its joys, and of its frustrations. And none certainly did more to introduce significant and often neglected foreign writers to the French literary elite, a group which often tended to ignore literatures other than their own.

CHAPTER 7

Conclusion:
The Cosmopolitan Man of Letters

LARBAUD, a painstaking craftsman, always reluctant to publish any text that had not been "aged" and scrupulously revised, had little patience with colleagues who were proud to bring out a book every year. His friends, indeed, sometimes chided him for not producing more. However, each of his major works, although not numerous, marks a new departure, often established new trends.

The *Poèmes d'un riche amateur* introduced—before Cendrars, before Morand—a "new cosmopolitanism" in French literature and in European literature as well. Alain Bosquet finds "a direct influence" of these poems on the Imagists in England and America, on Mayakovsky and Esenin in Russia. The originality of their tone, a fusion of tenderness and irony, of lyricism and cynicism, was immediately apparent to contemporaries like Gide and C. L. Philippe. *Le Journal intime de A. O. Barnabooth,* with its emphasis on the quest for identity, which has increasingly occupied the twentieth-century artist, revitalized the traditional concept of the *Bildungsroman. Enfantines,* so admired by Proust, demonstrated a fresh way of writing about children, not from the outside but from the inside, and expressed that nostalgia for "le vert Paradis des amours enfantines," which has become a dominant note in modern Western literature. Later French writers have often echoed the accents of Larbaud; and even outside of France, the young heroines of Carson McCullers would recognize their kinship with "Milou" and with "Rose Lourdin." *Fermina Márquez* proposes comparable innovations in the novel of adolescence, which, in the wake of Larbaud, became a flourishing subgenre, illustrated, for example, by Alain-Fournier's *Le*

Grand Meaulnes and Cocteau's *Les Enfants Terribles.* The texts of
Amants, heureux amants ... experimented brilliantly with various
forms of the stream of consciousness technique, advanced even
further towards that "inwardness" which, in reaction against
naturalistic fiction, has characterized the major lines of development of the modern novel. All of these works, disregarding conventional genre distinctions, broke down the frontiers between
poetry and prose, between fiction and nonfiction. In the essays
of the latter part of his career, Larbaud goes even further in his
effort to make French prose more supple and more fluid, to
liberate it from formal constraints, from Cartesian logic, from
the strait-jacket of "la dissertation." As Roger Nimier puts it, he
writes "un français sans corset." And, indeed, his French needs
no corset, for its natural shape is so svelte and comely. This
liberation of language, the invention of new forms of expression
capable of capturing the ceaseless "oscillation" which marked
his own sensibility, may well be one of Larbaud's essential
achievements.

But there are others, more exterior, perhaps, more obviously
apparent. No writer of his time, as a critic and as a translator,
revealed a wider range of interests, a surer instinct for significant
contemporary work. He explored not only French literature but
Anglo-American, Italian, Spanish, Portuguese, and Latin-American literature as well. His "discoveries" included moderns like
Joyce and Svevo and Borges—but also great and forgotten figures
of the past like Maurice Scève. It is typical of him that his
intuition of the "modern" went hand in hand with a commitment
to the past. Curtius, with reason, hailed him as "the European
representative of French literature." We might add that he was
equally the French representative of European and Latin American literature. T. S. Eliot, recalling the early days of *The
Criterion,* includes Larbaud among those "great European
writers"—Gide, Hofmannstahl, Ortega y Gasset—whom he re-
vered, since "no ideological differences poisoned our discourse,
no political oppression limited freedom of communication." Larbaud was the friend and often the intimate (as the thousands
of letters in the FVL reveal) of some of the most distinguished
of his contemporaries: Joyce, Gide, Claudel, Valéry, T. S. Eliot,
all of whom had the highest esteem for the man and his gifts.

His gifts, of course, were not those of a Promethean—of a Whitman, a Dostoyevsky, a Balzac. His was a deliberately small-scale world, a world of Mediterranean *mesure*, a world of inwardness and of privilege far removed from social struggles and political strife, a world which may easily strike us, in the midst of our contemporary tumult, as a remote, even anachronistic one. He was quite aware of these limitations and willingly chose to work within them. Yet Benjamin Crémieux (among others) was ready to wager (in *XXe Siècle*) that Larbaud was one of the writers of his time who had the surest chances of survival and situated him among the major "minors" (or, if you like, the minor "majors"), in the company of Maurice Scève, Théophile, G. de Nerval, a situation, certainly, not without honor.

Crémieux might have also added Laurence Sterne, for in reading Larbaud one is often reminded of the wayward author of *A Sentimental Journey*. Many of the qualities which Virginia Woolf, in her preface to the Oxford "World's Classics" edition (1928) of this work, found attractive in him could be easily ascribed to Larbaud.

No realist could be more brilliantly successful in rendering the impression of the moment.

The flight of this erractic mind is zigzag like a dragonfly's, but one cannot deny that this dragonfly has method in his flight. . . .

He leads us to the brink of the precipice; we snatch one short glance into its depths; next moment, we are whisked around to look at the green pastures glowing on the other side. . . .

And one of the final episodes of *A Sentimental Journey* could not have failed to delight Larbaud, especially since it takes place in his beloved Bourbonnais, "the sweetest part of France." After supping with a family of peasants, the narrator watches them as they dance happily together and imagined that he beheld "Religion mixing in the dance."

In the introduction to *Ce Vice impuni, la lecture* (*Domaine anglais*), Larbaud, after speaking of Antoine de Nerveze, a contemporary of Honoré d'Urfé, "a minimus among the minors," who has sunk into complete obscurity, goes on to add: "And when, in my turn, after having been a little-known author, I shall have become a completely unknown one, when my books shall share the fate of all the vain and perishable things of this world, perhaps some scholar (one, I hope who really loves literature) may mention my name along with yours." For Nervèze, he reminds us, was nevertheless one of the countless small links in the long chain connecting Rabelais and Racine and "without him French literature would not be precisely what it has become."

In our time of verbal inflation, when the slightest novel is ballyhooed as "a revelation," when every writer is hailed as "major," the modesty of Larbaud, a modesty tempered with wit and irony, cannot fail to be salutary. Yet this modesty should not deceive us. He was well aware of his own value. He was convinced that his place, a minor place if you wish but one distinctively his own, would be secure when most of the best sellers, most of the Prix Goncourt of his time would have been long forgotten. And we realize more and more that he was not mistaken.

Notes and References

(Place of publication is Paris, unless otherwise noted)

Chapter One

1. These anecdotes figure in the article by M. Constantin-Weyer, Larbaud's cousin, "Dans l'intimité de Valery Larbaud," *Hommage*, pp. 421–28.
2. Dated January 3, 1912. Omitted from Alajouanine's edition of the Fargue-Larbaud correspondence, it is cited by Jean Charpentier, *Cahiers* 8 (November 1971): 31.
3. Constantin-Weyer, "Dans l'intimité de Valery Larbaud," *Hommage*, p. 425: "Je crois que Mme Larbaud le (Fargue) détestait, l'accusant de corrompre son fils." Mme Larbaud (according to Robert Mallet, "Valery Larbaud, le grand enfant," *Hommage*, p. 443) disapproved of her son's literary friendships: "Il n'a pas les fréquentations de fils de millionaire."
4. *Aubry*, pp. 225–26.
5. *Journal*, p. 33.
6. Letter to Adrienne Monnier, dated "mercredi" September 1922, FVL.
7. Postcard to Mme Larbaud, dated February 20, 1926, FVL.
8. Letter dated May 3, 1907. Cited by Patrick McCarthy, "The Valery Larbaud-Marcel Ray Correspondence, 1899–1908," *Revue de littérature comparée* 42 (1968): 438.
9. Jean-Claude Corger, "Quelques considérations sur le glissement chez Valery Larbaud," *Colloque, '72*, p. 90. See also Robert Champigny, "Spatial Anxiety in the Poems of Barnabooth." *Modern Language Quarterly* 16 (1955): 78–84.
10. August Anglès, "Le Compagnon de route des fondateurs de la *Nouvelle Revue Française*," *Cahiers* 4 (1969): 11–15. See also Anglès, *André Gide et le premier groupe de la Nouvelle Revue Française* (Gallimard, 1978), pp. 255–58.
11. L. P. Fargue-Valery Larbaud, *Correspondence, 1910–1946*. Texte établi . . . par Th. Alajouanine (Gallimard, 1971), p. 81.
12. Shakespeare, *Les Sonnets*. trad. d'Emile Le Brun. Intro. de Valery Larbaud (J. Schriffrin, 1927). See also the letters of Le Brun

(February 2, 1927) and of C. du Bos (February 10, 1927) to Larbaud, FVL.

13. Claude Roy, *Hommage*, p. 466.

14. *Aubry*, p. 185.

15. For a study of the relations between Claudel and Larbaud, see Françoise Lioure, "Paul Claudel-Valery Larbaud: Contacts et Circonstances," *Bulletin de la Société Paul Claudel* 65 (1er trimestre, 1977): 6–20. Her conclusion: "Une rencontre spirituelle manquée. . . ."

16. Dominque Fernández, "Le Souterrain de Larbaud," *Hommage*, p. 482.

17. "J'ai assez avec l'Occident et Rome," cited by P. Mahillon, "Valery Larbaud et le Protestantisme," *Hommage*, p. 430.

18. Patrick McCarthy, "V. Larbaud-M. Ray Correspondence," p. 437.

19. McCarthy, p. 437.

20. Letter to Francis Jammes, August 4, 1914, *Aubry*, p. 241.

21. V. Larbaud, "Une Crise de l'humanisme," *Anglo-French Review* 9 (October 1920): 231.

22. First published in the June 1, 1925, number of Adrienne Monnier's *Le Navire d'argent* and reprinted in *Jaune Bleu Blanc*.

23. J. P. Segonds, "Procès à Larbaud: un pamphlet de Georges Friedman," *Colloque, '72*, p. 257.

24. Cited by Segonds, p. 259.

25. Françoise Lioure, "Sagesse de Larbaud," *Cahiers* 3 (1968): 15.

26. Roger Martin du Gard, "Rencontres," part 2, "Une Journée de travail," *Hommage*, pp. 453–55.

27. François Jourdain, "Remarques," *Hommage*, p. 415.

28. Anne Poÿlo, "Güiraldes and Larbaud," *Cahiers* 11 (August 1973): 18–19.

Chapter Two

1. Marcel Ray to V.L., September 17, 1921, FVL.

2. *Journal*, p. 296.

3. Ibid.

4. E. R. Curtius, "Valery Larbaud," *Revue nouvelle*, June 15, 1926, p. 19.

5. After *Barnabooth*, his only poetry appearing in volume form was published clandestinely in the Hague, during the Occupation, by A. A. M. Stols. See note 18, below.

6. *Pl.*, p. 1152.

7. *Aubry*, pp. 122–23.

8. John K. Simon, "Larbaud et le journal intime," *Cahiers de l'Association internationale des études françaises* 17 (1965): 157.

9. A. Gide, *Journal*, Ed. Pléiade p. 269.

10. F. E. G. Quintanilha, *Fernando Pessoa: 60 Portuguese Poems* (Cardiff: University of Wales Press, 1971), p. 89.

11. *N.R.F.*, February 1, 1909, p. 103.

12. Larbaud wrote an article on Nau (1860–1918) which first appeared (in Spanish) in *La Nación* (Buenos Aires) and then in *La Revue européene* of September 1, 1924. He cites "Lily Dale" in his review of the poems of Eugene Field in *La Phalange* of June 20, 1911. *Cahiers* devoted an entire number, 12 (May 1974), to Levet (1874–1906).

13. Henry Jean-Marie Levet, *Poèmes, précédés d'une conversation de MM Léon-Paul Fargue et Valery Larbaud* (La Maison des amis des livres), 1921. The *Conversation* was re-edited by Gallimard in 1943.

14. Delvaille, p. 18.

15. *St. J.*, pp. 185–89.

16. *St. J.*, p. 186.

17. See Yves-Alain Favre, "Nuance et rhythmes dans la poésie de Larbaud," *Colloque, '72*, pp. 96–108.

18. These poems appeared in a volume (a bibliographical rarity) purportedly published clandestinely in Copenhagen by "Jens Skovgaard" "pour les amis danois de Maxime Claremoris" as a homage to Larbaud on his sixtieth birthday. The full title: *Les Poésies de A. O. Barnabooth, Dévotions particulières, Poésies diverses*. The text of *Les Poésies d'A. O. Barnabooth* is reproduced from the Gallimard edition of 1923. In reality, it was brought out in the Hague, probably later than 1941, although during the Occupation, by Larbaud's friend and frequent publisher, A. A. M. Stols.

19. Letter of Larbaud to E. R. Curtius, January 21, 1935, FVL.

20. *Cahiers* 13 (May 1975): 20–22. This letter was included among those of Philippe to Larbaud published by G. Jean-Aubry in the *N.R.F.*, August 1, 1939, pp. 278–85.

21. *N.R.F.*, February 1, 1909, pp. 101–103.

22. *Pan*, November-December 1908, pp. 340-42; *La Phalange*, October 15, 1908, pp. 356–58.

Chapter Three

1. On the relations between Larbaud and Philippe, see number 13 (May 1975) of *Cahiers*.

2. *Gaston Ercoule* (Editions Vrille, 1952). The text and Mallet's

introduction are included in the Pléiade edition. Mallet believes the judgment of Philippe was too severe.

3. John K. Simon, "Larbaud, Barnabooth et le journal intime," *Cahiers de l'Association internationale des études françaises* 17 (1965): 158.

4. *Pl.*, p. 98: "... Je me suis élancé à l'assaut de l'absolu." See also *Pl.*, pp. 84, 90, 227.

5. Jean Charpentier, untitled article, *Colloque*, '72, p. 62.

6. Simon, p. 154.

7. Ibid., p. 160.

8. Gilbert Nigay, "Valery Larbaud et Charles-Louis Philippe," *Colloque, '72*, pp. 172–84.

9. Th. Alajouanine, "Valery Larbaud religieux: un aspect méconnu de Valery Larbaud" in *Valery Larbaud sous divers visages* (Gallimard, 1973), 46–51.

10. *Pl.*, p. 128: Cartuyvels, his administrator, reprimands Barnabooth: "... Mais la petite épargne a dû à votre caprice des journées bien mauvaises."

11. *Pl.*, p. 130: "Je songe à sa saleté morale."

12. Among others: "L'Eterna Voluttà"; "Aspirations"; "Envoi à tous les hommes de lettres et artistes."

13. Anne Chevalier, "L'Amateur de la hiérarchie des trois ordres," *Colloque, '72*, p. 66ff.

14. *Pl.*, p. 94: 'Chez moi, elle (mon image) n'est pas encore formée."

15. *Pl.*, p. 94: "Inattentif à bien des choses parce qu'il se donne tout entier à une seule, qu'il appelle le Culte de Beauté...."

16. Maurice Saillet, "Valery Larbaud et M. Ménard, artiste lyrique," *Cahiers* 9 (May 1972): 14.

17. Jean Charpentier, *Colloque, '72*, p. 59.

18. *Journal*, pp. 265–69.

19. *Pl.*, pp. 1161–62.

20. E. R. Curtius, "Valery Larbaud," *La Revue nouvelle*, May 15, 1925, p. 4.

21. Claude Roy, "Je voudrais remercier Valery Larbaud," *Hommage*, p. 46.

22. J. C. Conger, "Quelques considérations sur le 'glissement' chez Valery Larbaud," *Colloque, '72*, p. 81.

23. The Larbaud-Dujardin correspondence, edited with notes by Frida Weissman, has been published in *Cahiers* 14 (March 1976): 1–45.

24. *Colloque, '72*, pp. 281–89. See also Melvin Friedman, *Stream*

of Consciousness: A Study in Literary Method (New Haven: Yale University Press, 1955).

25. Jacques Nathan has produced in his critical edition "avec des pages inédites, une étude littéraire, des notes" of *Beauté, mon beau souci* (Nizet, 1968), a valuable instrument for understanding Larbaud's methods of composition and revision.

26. There are numerous references to the moralists in the published journals, especially for the period 1931–1935. He also wrote an unpublished essay on La Rochefoucauld, ms. XVIII, FVL (fol. 151–63).

27. Patrick McCarthy, *Valery Larbaud, Critic of English Literature* (Doctoral thesis submitted to the Faculty of Medieval and Modern Languages at the University of Oxford), 1968, p. 242.

28. Friedman, *Stream of Consciousness* (p. 175), compares this passage (why not?) to "a fugue," noting that "the analogy with music, whether intended or not, is a convention of the craft."

29. Published in *Pl.*, 716–19, as an appendix to *Amants, heureux amants. . . .*

30. Valery Larbaud, *Le coeur de l'Angleterre suivi de Luis Losada*, textes établis, présentés et annotés par Frida Weissman (Gallimard, 1971).

Chapter Four

1. Laurence Sterne, *A Sentimental Journey through France and Italy*, Introduction by Virginia Woolf (London: Oxford University Press, 1928), p. viii.

2. Robert Tournaud, review of *Allen*, N.R.F., 193 (October 1, 1929): 558. "Combien un écrit semble à la fois étranger et intime à celui qui l'écrit. . . ."

3. Delvaille, p. 131.

4. *Paris de France* (Maastricht: Stols, 1926); *Lettre d'Italie* (Liège: "A la Lampe d'Aladin," 1926).

5. See Chapter 5.

6. He reviewed this pious saint's life in, of all places, the *N.R.F.*, April 1, 1912. But after the success of *Fermina Márquez*, the far from pious editorial board apparently felt obliged to humor "le petit père Larbaud."

7. *St. J.*, p. 139.

8. Maurice Saillet has described the passion of Larbaud and his friends, especially Fargue and Adrienne Monnier, for the *caf' conc'*, in a witty and immensely informed article in *Cahiers* IX (May 1972):

1–32, "Valery Larbaud and Monsieur Ménard, Artiste lyrique." Ménard's stage name was "Dranem," and all the "potassons" around Adrienne Monnier knew his songs by heart. Sallet claims that "il y aurait beaucoup à dire quant à l'influence de Dranem" (as the practitioner of a kind of "Dadisme populaire") "sur le dernière génération symboliste."

9. Valery Larbaud, *Le Coeur de l'Angleterre suivi de Luis Losada,* textes établis, présentés et annotés par Frida Weissman (Gallimard, 1971).

Chapter Five

1. Aldous Huxley, "Conxolus," *Essays Old and New* (New York: Doran, 1927), p. 228.

2. *Cahiers* 3 (1969): 11.

3. *D.A.,* p. 226.

4. Valery Larbaud, "Freud et la littérature," *Disque vert* (Bruxelles), special number on Freud, 1924.

5. *Pl.,* p. 288.

6. *St. J.,* pp. 264–74.

7. Ibid., pp. 248–63.

8. Ferdinand Brunetière, *L'Evolution des genres dans l'histoire de la littérature française* (1890).

9. Ms. no. 8 S.E. FVL., p. 55.

10. *St. J.,* pp. 130–33.

11. Ibid., p. 133.

12. Ibid., p. 251.

13. Ibid., p. 252.

14. Ibid., p. 254.

15. Ibid., p. 255.

16. Ibid., pp. 264–74.

17. Ibid., p. 274.

18. *Journal,* pp. 337, 338, 339.

19. Ibid., p. 339.

20. *Pl.,* p. 381.

21. *St. J.,* pp. 185–89.

22. Bonsignor reappears as the protagonist of "Le Vaisseau de Thésée" in *Aux Couleurs de Rome.*

23. Curtius devoted an essay to Larbaud in *Französicher Geist in neuen Europa* (1925) and maintained an extensive correspondence with him, preserved in the FVL.

24. E. R. Curtius, *Europäische Literatur und lateinisches Mittelalter* (Berne: A. Francke, 1948).

25. Valery Larbaud, "Ramón Gómez de la Serna," cited by Delvaille, p. 91. "En art, tout est autobiographie et rien ne l'est."

26. *St. J.*, pp. 285–300.

27. *D.A.*, p. 13.

28. Ibid., p. 25.

29. *Journal*, p. 89.

30. *St. J.*, p. 202.

31. Valery Larbaud, "A propos de James Joyce et de '*Ulysse*': Réponse à M. Ernest Boyd," *N.R.F.*, January 1, 1925.

32. *D.A.*, p. 25.

33. At eighteen, at Louis-le-Grand, he "discovered" Whitman, his great enthusiasm during the period 1900–1910.

34. His interest in Anglo-American literature has been extensively studied, notably by Vincent Milligan, "Valery Larbaud, Anglicist," Diss., Columbia 1954; Patrick McCarthy, "Valery Larbaud, Critic of English Literature," Diss., Oxford 1968; and John L. Brown, "Valery Larbaud, amateur de la littérature américaine," *Colloque*, '72, pp. 39–46.

35. *D.A.*, pp. 185–217.

36. Dominique Fernández, "Le Souterrain de Larbaud," *Hommage*. p. 480.

37. Gay Wilson Allen, ed., *Walt Whitman Abroad* (Syracuse: Syracuse University Press, 1955), pp. 56–109.

38. See Chapter 6, pp. 181–82.

39. *D.A.*, p. 239.

40. Ernest Boyd, *The Irish Literary Renaissance*, 2nd ed. (New York: John Lane, 1922), p. 116.

41. *D.A.*, p. 233.

42. Ibid., p. 250.

43. See Chapter 6, p. 182.

44. *Journal*, pp. 362, 363, 364.

45. William Faulkner, *Tandis que j'agonise*, trans. M. Coindreau (Gallimard, 1934).

46. *D.A.*, p. 219.

47. Ibid.

48. Coventry Patmore, *Poèmes*, trad. de Paul Claudel précédé d'une étude de Valery Larbaud (Editions de la *N.R.F.*, 1912). Larbaud's study had previously appeared in the September 1 and October 1, 1911, numbers of the *N.R.F.*

49. Arnold Bennett, *Le Matador des Cinq Villes*, trad. V. Larbaud (*N.R.F.*, August 1, 1912).

50. Arnold Bennett, *Journal* (New York: The Literary Guild, 1933), p. 457. "Larbaud who calls to see me almost every day."

51. *D.A.*, p. 167.

52. Valery Larbaud, "La Renaissance de la poésie américaine," *La Revue de France* 1 (September 1 and 15, 1921). The text is reproduced in Delvaille, pp. 175–92.

53. Delvaille, p. 174.

54. One might question the validity of Larbaud's reputation as a tireless "globe-trotter." In spite of his long professional interest in the literatures of North and South America, he never visited the New World.

55. Delvaille, p. 179.

56. Valery Larbaud–G. Jean-Aubry, *Correspondance, 1920–1935,* ed. F. Weissman (Gallimard, 1971), p. 13.

57. Delvaille, p. 186.

58. John L. Brown, "Guiding the Commerce of Ideas: Marguerite Caetani," *Books Abroad* 47 (Spring 1973): 307–11.

59. T. S. Eliot to V. Larbaud, March 2, 1922, FVL.

60. Eliot to Larbaud, March 22, 1922, FVL.

61. Eliot to Larbaud, May 16, 1923, FVL.

62. In addition to the article in *Revue de France,* Larbaud speaks of Eliot in his "Réponse à John Rodker," *La Revue européenne* 1 (March 1, 1923): 81–84.

63. *La Revue européenne* 1 (March 1, 1923): 82.

64. Delvaille, p. 179.

65. Larbaud to F. Jammes, November 17, 1911. F. Jammes et V. Larbaud, *Lettres inédites,* intro. G. Jean-Aubry (Paris–La Hague: A. A. M. Stols, 1947), p. 23.

66. Richard Ellmann, *James Joyce* (New York: Oxford University Press, 1959), p. 360.

67. Robert McAlmon, *McAlmon and the Lost Generation: A Self-Portrait,* ed. Robert E. Knoll (Lincoln: University of Nebraska Press, 1962), p. 243.

68. Valery Larbaud, "The Great American Novel par W. C. Williams," *La Revue européenne* 8 (November 1, 1923): 65–70. A partial French translation, evidently suggested by Larbaud, appeared in A. Monnier's review *Le Navire d'argent* 10 (pp. 125–35). See also Serge Fauchereau, "Valery Larbaud et William Carlos Williams," *Critique* 240 (1971): 627–31.

69. Letter to Marianne Moore, February 21, 1924, in W. C. Williams, *Selected Letters* (New York: McDowell, Obolensky, 1957), p. 60.

70. *Pl.*, p. 1170.

71. Delvaille, p. 78.

72. "Eugene Field ne peut être un grand poète de l'enfance . . .

l'enfance qu'il chante est ... cette espèce de gâtisme gai que, sous le nom de l'enfance, V. Hugo et Mme. Tastu ont célébré."

73. *Hommage,* p. 565.

74. Valery Larbaud, "Lettres anglaises: jeunes poètes et jeunes revues," *N.R.F.* 7e année, no. 75, nouv. série (December 1, 1919): 1110.

75. Valery Larbaud, "Trivia de L. P. Smith," *N.R.F.* 9e année, no. 104, nouv. série (May 1, 1922): 624–25.

76. Grasset, 1921.

77. "Lettres anglaises...," *N.R.F.,* December 1, 1919, p. 1110.

78. *Journal,* pp. 151–53.

79. Odette de Mourgues, *Metaphysical, Baroque et Précieux Poetry* (New York: Oxford University Press, 1953), pp. 11, 141.

80. Franco Simone, "La critica francesa e il Barocco." *Umanesimo, Rinascimento, Barocco in Francia* (Milan: Mursia, 1968), pp. 333–35.

81. I. D. McFarlane, *A Literary History of France: Renaissance France 1470–1589* (London: Benn, 1974), p. 161.

82. On Larbaud's relations with Philippe, see Françoise Lioure, "Témoignages sur une amitié...," *Cahiers* 13 (May 1975): 3–18; with Fargue, their correspondence, edited by Th. Alajouanine (Gallimard, 1971).

83. Henry J. M. Levet, *Poèmes,* précédés d'une conversation de MM. L. P. Fargue et Valery Larbaud (Gallimard, 1943), the reprint of the original edition which had appeared in 1921 under the imprint of A. Monnier's "A la Maison des amis des livres."

84. It was subsequently included in vol. VII of the Jean-Aubry-Mallet edition of *Les Oeuvres complètes.*

85. Delvaille, pp. 188–203.

86. *Journal,* p. 109ff. This entry furnished material for the essay "Rouge jaune rouge" later included in *Jaune Bleu Blanc, Pl.* pp. 911–17.

87. Anne Poylo, "Valery Larbaud, amateur comparatiste de l'Espagne," *Colloque,* '72, p. 227. "Le destin de l'Espagne, en effet, ne pèse pas lourd sur les épaules de Larbaud. Pourquoi? Parce que son expédience espagnole est finalement restreinte."

88. Mathilde Pomès, "Valery Larbaud, Hispaniste," *Cahiers* 2 (1967): unpaginated.

89. Anne Poylo, p. 220: "Tard venu aux lettres espagnoles, il les découvre sans méthode." Larbaud willingly admits his own deficiencies in various entries in his journal. *Journal,* p. 141 (entry in English): "Besides, I don't know anything about contemporary (and less about older) Spanish literature...."

90. *Pl.,* p. 787.

91. Mathilde Pomès, "Valery Larbaud et l'Espagne," *Hommage*, p. 530. "Je ne lui ai jamais dit le souvenir que l'on avait gardé de lui à Alicante, ni les rires cruels des jeunes filles qui s'y étaient si fort amusées de leur flirt avec 'le vieux Français.'"

92. *Ibid.*, p. 531.

93. *Pl.*, p. 916.

94. *Ibid.*

95. *Journal*, p. 45.

96. Poylo, P. 220.

97. Letter of G. Miró to V. Larbaud, February 10, 1918, FVL.

98. Written in Alicante "on the feast of Saint Gabriel," it was published only years later first, in 1950, in *La Revue Suisse romande*, subsequently in the *Nouvelle N.R.F.*, March 1, 1957.

99. Jean-Aubry, p. 309, note 2.

100. *Ibid.*, p. 265.

101. M. Newmark, *Dictionary of Spanish Literature* (Paterson: Littlefield Adams, 1963), p. 141.

102. Valery Larbaud, "Ramón Gómez de la Serna," *Littérature*, September 7, 1919.

103. *N.R.F.*, July 1, 1920.

104. *Les Ecrits nouveaux* 7 (March 1921).

105. *Les Nouvelles littéraires* 12 (January 6, 1923).

106. *La Revue hebdomadaire* 13 (January 20, 1923).

107. Pomès, *Hommage*, p. 530.

108. This article, slightly revised, appeared as the preface to R. Gómez de la Serna, *La Veuve blanche et noire*, trans. J. Cassou (S. Kra, 1924).

109. "Fragments de lettres de Valery Larbaud à Marcelle Auclair," *Cahiers* 2 (1967): unpaginated.

110. Alberto-Oscar Blasi, *Güiraldes y Larbaud: una amistad creadora* (Buenos Aires: Biblioteca Arte y Ciencia de expresión, 1970). Reviewed by Anne Poylo, "Güiraldes et Larbaud," *Cahiers* 11 (1973): 1–34.

111. *N.R.F.*, Tome XV, pp. 141–47.

112. *La Revue européenne*, 27 (May 1, 1925).

113. Poylo, p. 10.

114. *Ibid.*, p. 17. Mme Güiraldes later published the letter in *La Nación*, March 24, 1957.

115. Letter of R. Güiraldes.

116. Valery Larbaud-Alfonso Reyes, *Correspondance*, *1923–1952*. Avant propos de Marcel Bataillon. Introduction et notes de Paulette Patout (Didier, 1972).

117. Valery Larbaud, "Alfonso Reyes," *Revue de l'Amérique latine* 9 (February 1, 1925): 106–108.

118. "Au nom des écrivains français, V. Larbaud proteste contre l'exil du grand écrivain Miguel de Unamuno," *Les Nouvelles littéraires*, March 1, 1924. See also Valery Larbaud, "Unamuno," *La Revue européenne*, April 1925. This article served as the basis of Larbaud's preface to the translation by J. Cassou and M. Pomès of Unamuno's *Trois nouvelles exemplaires et un prologue* (Editions du Sagittaire, 1925).

119. Alfonso Reyes, *Vision de l'Anahuac*, trad. par J. Guérandel avec une introduction de V. Larbaud (Editions de la *N.R.F.*, 1927).

120. Alfonso Reyes, *La Experiencia literaria* (Buenos Aires: Losada, 1942), p. 147.

121. Mariano Azuela, *Ceux d'en bas*, trad. par J. et J. Maurin avec une préface de V. Larbaud (J. O. Fourcade, 1930).

122. Poylo, p. 222.

123. Valery Larbaud, "Lettres argentines et uruguayennes, un critique argentin, un poète uruguayen, une revue," *La Revue européenne*, December 1, 1925.

124. Valery Larbaud, "Notre Amérique," *N.R.F.* 259, (April 1, 1935): 606–15.

125. Valery Larbaud, "Lettre de Lisbonne," *Le Navire d'argent* 11 (April 1, 1926): 333–36.

126. Valery Larbaud, "Divertissement philologique," *N.R.F.* 156 (June 1, 1926): 684–92.

127. Valery Larbaud, "Ecrit dans une cabine du Sud-Express," *Commerce* 7 (Spring 1926): 25–37.

128. Valery Larbaud, *Caderno* (Au Sans Pareil, 1927).

129. J. M. de Eça de Queiroz, *La Relique*, traduit du portugais par Georges Raeders. Préface de Valery Larbaud (Sorlot, 1941).

130. Letter to Henri Hoppenot, June 16, 1925, FVL.

131. *Pl.*, pp. 929–31. The prose has a distinct "cultural relations" flavor. "The banquet was a memorable expression of the prestige that French literature enjoys in Portugal."

132. Rainier Hess, "Valery Larbaud au Portugal," *Revue de Littérature comparée* 40 (1966): 271–88.

133. *Pl.*, p. 921. A photo of Larbaud of this period shows him feeding the beast. It is reproduced on the cover of the catalogue of the exposition "Valery Larbaud" held at the Gulbenkian Foundation in Lisbon (December 17, 1973–January 6, 1974).

134. Saint-John Perse wrote in the copy of T. S. Eliot's translation of *Anabase* which he inscribed to Larbaud: "A vous, Larbaud,

honneur des lettres françaises qui avez trop souvent délaissé votre
oeuvre admirable pour parler de vos amis en terre étranger...."

135. Larbaud's relations with Italy have been extensively studied:
Ortensia Ruggiero, *Valery Larbaud et l'Italie* (Nizet, 1963), presented
for the doctorate at the University of Paris, with a "Thèse complé-
mentaire," consisting of an edition of Larbaud's "Corrispondenza
inedita con gli amici d'Italia: L. Fiumi, M. Puccini, E. Settani." In
addition, Italian "tesi di laurea" have been written on various aspects
of Larbaud in Italy by M. Landoni (1956), Adriana Batignani (1958),
R. Bruzzone (1968), M. L. Zoppi (1969). The catalogue of the
exposition "Valery Larbaud et l'Italie," organized by Mlle Monique
Küntz, Director of the Municipal Library of Vichy, is a mine of
information.

136. V. Larbaud to G. Jean-Aubry, August 27, 1933. Valery Larbaud–G. Jean-Aubry, *Correspondance, 1920–1935*. Introduction et
notes de Frida Weissman (Gallimard, 1971), pp. 139–40.

137. *St. J.*, pp. 275–84.

138. Although Larbaud is usually represented as an "unpolitical
man," he appeared to be deeply interested in the history of the
Risorgimento, as "la préfiguration d'un autre Risorgimento" which
would create a genuine European unity (*Pl.*, p. 819).

139. Letter to Larbaud, "mercredi" 1924, FVL (B37).

140. *Journal*, p. 263.

141. "Lettres inédites à Italo Svevo," editées par O. Ruggiero,
Revue des Etudes italiennes 1 (January 1962).

142. Svevo was delighted. He writes to Larbaud: "Come suona
bene il mio pensiero nella sua bella lingua," cited in the catalogue
of the exposition "Valery Larbaud et l'Italie," p. 54.

143. Valery Larbaud, "Freud et la littérature." *Disque vert*
(Bruxelles), 2nd year, 3rd series. Special Freud number, 1924.

144. *Journal*, p. 205.

145. Gianna Manzini, "La Femme du sourd," trad. par Henri
Marchand et Valery Larbaud, *N.R.F.*, July 1, 1934.

146. *St. J.*, pp. 169–70.

147. Sibilla Aleramo, *Joies d'occasion*, trad. par Yvonne Lenoir.
Préface de Valery Larbaud (Nouvelles Editions Latines, 1933).

148. Aldo Capasso, *A la nuit et autres poèmes*, trad. par Armand
Guibert. Préface de Valery Larbaud (Tunis: Editions de Mirages,
1935).

149. Ettore Settani, *Les Hommes gris*, trad. de l'italien par A. A.
Auscher. Préface de Valery Larbaud (Rieder, 1933).

150. Valery Larbaud, "Ma Dette envers l'Italie," *Dante* 6 (September-October 1932).

151. *St. J.*, p. 163.
152. Ibid., pp. 116–23.
153. Ibid., p. 118; *Journal*, p. 339.
154. *St. J.*, p. 119.
155. Ibid., p. 120.

Chapter Six

1. John L. Brown, "Guiding the Commerce of Ideas," *Books Abroad* 48 (Spring 1973): 307–12.
2. Paulette Patout, "L'Evolution des idées de Valery Larbaud sur la traduction," *Colloque, '72*, p. 196. See also *Aubry*, p. 232.
3. The first part of the volume, "Le Patron des traducteurs" (pp. 7–57), has been translated by William Arrowsmith under the title, "The Translator's Patron," in *Arion*, NS, vol. 2, no. 3, pp. 314–57.
4. *Valery Larbaud–Alfonso Reyes, Correspondance (1923–1952)*. Avant-propos de Marcel Bataillon. Introduction et notes de Paulette Patout (Didier, 1973). See also Patout, *Colloque, '72*. p. 197ff.
5. *N.R.F.* 256 (1er janvier 1935): 89.
6. These briefer translations, listed chronologically, include F. Thompson (*La Phalange*, 1909); R. L. Stevenson (verse) (*La Phalange*, 1909); W. S. Landor (*N.R.F.*, 1911 and *La Phalange*, 1911); Chesterton (*La Phalange*, 1911); Arnold Bennett (*N.R.F.*, 1912); Walt Whitman (Ed. de la *N.R.F.*, 1918); Samuel Butler (*N.R.F.*, 1920); Archibald MacLeish (*Commerce*, 1925 and 1927); Edith Sitwell (*Commerce*, 1926); Emilio Cecchi (*Commerce*, 1926); B. Barilli (*Commerce*, 1926 and 1929); R. Bachelli (*Commerce*, 1927); Liam O'Flaherty (*Commerce*, 1928); N. Hawthorne (*Commerce*, 1928); A. Reyes (*Commerce*, 1929); Sir Thomas Browne (*Commerce*, 1929); G. Mazzini (*N.R.F.*, 1934); Lionello Fiumi (*Cahiers du Sud*, 1935).
7. *Journal*, p. 256.
8. Patrick McCarthy, "Valery Larbaud, Critic of English Literature" (Unpublished diss. submitted to the Faculty of Medieval and Modern Languages at the University of Oxford, 1968), p. 195.
9. Anna-Maria d'Aldaz, "Valery Larbaud as Translator of Samuel Butler," *DAI*, 31:1256A (Oregon) and Alison Connell, "Forgotten Masterpieces of Literary Translation: Valery Larbaud's Butlers," *Canadian Review of Comparative Literature* 1, pp. 167–90.
10. P. McCarthy, "Valery Larbaud, Critic of English Literature." p. 226.
11. Larbaud sent Joyce a postcard from Recanati on August 11, 1924, FVL.

12. Adrienne Monnier, "La Traduction d'Ulysse," *rue de l'Odéon* (Albin Michel, 1960), pp. 161–70.

13. Sylvia Beach, *Shakespeare and Company* (New York: Harcourt Brace, 1959), pp. 54–60.

14. James Joyce, *Letters of James Joyce,* vol. III, ed. Richard Ellmann (New York: Viking Press, 1966), p. 45.

15. Robert McAlmon, *McAlmon and the Lost Generation: A Self-Portrait,* ed. with commentary by Robert E. Knoll (Lincoln: University of Nebraska Press, 1962), pp. 163, 169.

16. Richard Ellmann, *James Joyce* (New York: Oxford University Press, 1959), p. 537.

17. *D.A.,* pp. 230–52.

18. James Joyce, *Letters,* III, p. 175.

19. Ibid., pp. 175, 176.

20. R. Ellmann, *James Joyce,* p. 614.

21. Ibid., p. 616.

22. Ibid., p. 745.

23. P. Patout, *Colloque,* '72, pp. 203–204.

Selected Bibliography

(Place of publication is Paris, unless otherwise noted.)

PRIMARY SOURCES

1. Major Works

Oeuvres Complètes, édités par G. Jean-Aubry, Robert Mallet, et Vincent Milligan. 10 volumes. Gallimard, 1950–1955.

Oeuvres. Bibliothèque de la Pléiade. Gallimard, 1957. This volume does not include *Ce Vice impuni, la lecture* (*Domaine anglais*), *Ce Vice impuni, la lecture* (*Domaine français*), *Sours l'Invocation de Saint-Jérôme*, or the journals. It contains two texts not found in the *Oeuvres complètes*, *Gaston d'Ercoule* and the 1908 version of *Barnabooth*. This is the most accessible edition of the selected works of Larbaud and citations from the fiction, the poetry, and the essays are made from it. Works not included in it are cited from individual editions, since the *Oeuvres complètes*, originally issued in an edition of 1,500 copies, are now completely out of print and difficult of access.

Ce Vice impuni, la lecture: Domaine anglais. Gallimard, 1936. A shorter version had appeared under the imprint of Messein in 1925.

Ce Vice impuni, la lecture: Domaine français. Gallimard, 1941.

Sous l'Invocation de Saint-Jérôme. Gallimard, 1946. This volume includes titles such as *Sous l'Invocation de Saint Jérôme* and *Technique*, which had been published previously in reviews and by Gallimard.

Journal 1912–1935. Introduction de Robert Mallet. Gallimard, 1955. This edition is less complete than the two volumes devoted to selections from the journals in the *Oeuvres complètes*. It is rather indiscriminately edited. A more complete edition of Larbaud's surviving journals remains to be done.

2. Correspondence

Larbaud maintained tireless correspondence with many of the leading literary men of his time—French, European, Latin American—as the thousands of letters in FVL reveal. They are now being edited and published.

LARBAUD, VALERY–JAMMES, FRANCIS. *Lettres inédites.* Introduction et notes de G. Jean-Aubry. The Hague: A. A. M. Stols, 1947.

LARBAUD, VALERY. *Lettres à André Gide.* The Hague: A. A. M. Stols, 1948.

LARBAUD, VALERY–FARGUE, LÉON-PAUL. *Correspondance 1910–1946.* Texte établi, présenté, et annoté par Th. Alajouanine. Gallimard, 1972.

LARBAUD, VALERY–JEAN-AUBRY, G. *Correspondance 1920–1935.* Introduction et notes de Frida Weissman. Gallimard, 1971.

LARBAUD, VALERY–REYES, ALFONSO. *Correspondance 1923–1952.* Avant-propos de M. Bataillon. Introduction et notes de Paulette Patout. Didier, 1972.

LARBAUD, VALERY–RAY, MARCEL. *Correspondance, 1899–1937.* Texte établi, présenté et annoté par Françoise Lioure. 2 vols. Gallimard, 1979, 1980. The first two volumes cover the period 1899–1920. A third is announced.

3. Bibliography

FAMERIE, JACQUELINE. *Valery Larbaud Essai de bibliographie.* Coll. Bibliographia Belgica, vol. 35. Bruxelles: Commission Belge de Bibliographie, 1958. A thoroughly competent job, which includes many items not found in the bibliographies of the *Oeuvres complètes.* It has been republished, with the omission of descriptive material, in the Pléiade edition.

4. Translations

CANAAN, GILBERT, trans. *A. O. Barnabooth, His Diary.* By Valery Larbaud. London: Dent, 1924.

SMITH, WILLIAM JAY, trans. *Poems of a Multimillionaire.* By Valery Larbaud. New York (?): Bonacio and Saul, 1955.

ARROWSMITH, WILLIAM, trans. "The Translator's Patron." By Valery Larbaud. *Arion* NS 1 (no. 3): 314–57.

SECONDARY SOURCES

1. The *Cahiers des Amis de Valery Larbaud,* published annually since 1967, are edited by Mlle. Monique Küntz, director of the Municipal Library of Vichy, Fonds Larbaud. The series, containing articles by leading Larbaud scholars in France and abroad, is a rich source of material concerning Larbaud and his friends. In addition, Mlle. Küntz has organized a number of expositions including "Valery Larbaud and Italy" (Florence, Institut français, March 15–April 15, 1973), "Valery Larbaud" (Lisbon, Calouste Gulbenkian Foundation, December 17, 1973–January 6, 1974), "Valery Larbaud: XXᵉ An-

niversaire de sa mort" (Vichy, Centre Culturel Valery Larbaud, June 19–July 10, 1977), "Valery Larbaud" (Brussels, the Royal Library, January 14–February 25, 1978). An important exposition, commemorating the centenary of Larbaud's birth, is planned for 1981, by the Bibliothèque nationale, Paris. The detailed catalogues of these expositions are rich mines of information. In addition, a number of literary reviews have devoted special numbers to Larbaud, which often contain material not available elsewhere. These include

1922—*Intentions* (November). Contributions by B. Crémieux, C. du Bos, L.-P. Fargue, Jean Giraudoux, Paul Morand, Saint-John Perse.

1943—*Echo des Etudiants* (Montpellier, November 13–20). Contributions by R. M. Albérès, J. Giraudoux, M. Martin du Gard, Claude Roy, and others.

1945—*Confluences* (December-January, nos. 37–38). Articles by Jean Grenier, Marcel Arland, Jean Cassou, Jean Prévost, and others.

1951—*Les Nouvelles littéraires* (August 16, no. 1250). Contributions from M. Arland, J. Cocteau, J. Paulhan, A. Maurois, J. Romains, and others.

1951—*La Fiera Letteraria* (Rome, September 9). Articles by E. Henriot, Saint-John Perse, G. B. Angioletti, G. Antonini, and others.

1957—*Les Cahiers Bourbonnais* (2nd trimestre). Contributions from M. Constantin-Weyer, Th. Alajouanine, F. Talva, and others.

1957—*La Nouvelle Revue Française* (September 1, no. 57). Numerous articles including those of Saint-John Perse, J. Cocteau, M. Arland, C. Roy, R. Nimier, R. Lalou, and others.

1958—*Revue de Belles Lettres* (July-August, no. 3). Articles by M. Arland, R. Mallet, P-O Walzer, A. Wild, and others.

1972—*Matulu* (July-August, no. 16). Contributions from M. Déon, J. de Bourbon-Busset, J. P. Segonds, R. Levesque.

2. Books

ALAJOUANINE, TH. *Valery Larbaud sous divers visages*. Gallimard, 1973. Larbaud's personal physician, a distinguished neurologist with literary interests, devotes chapters to Larbaud's Catholicism, his criticism, his use of the stream of consciousness technique, and his fatal illness.

BLASI, ALBERTO-OSCAR. *Güiraldes y Larbaud, Una amistad creadora*. Buenos Aires: Nova, 1970. Blasi's account of Larbaud's friendship with Güiraldes reveals his wide-ranging interest in Latin-American literature.

CONTRERAS, FRANCISCO. *Valery Larbaud, son oeuvre*. La Nouvelle Critique, 1930. This brief, unpretentious essay by a Latin-American critic living in Paris was the first book-length critical study devoted to Larbaud.

Colloque Valery Larbaud, tenu à Vichy du 71 au 20 juillet, 1972. Nizet, 1975. Some twenty papers on the theme "Valery Larbaud, amateur" by French and foreign scholars, edited by Mlle. Monique Küntz.

Colloque Valery Larbaud, tenu à Vichy du 17 au 19 juin, 1977. C. Klincksieck, 1978. Twenty-four papers on the theme "Valery Larbaud et la littérature de son temps," edited by Mlle. Monique Küntz.

DELVAILLE, BERNARD. *Essai sur Valery Larbaud*. Collection Poètes d'aujourd'hui. Seghers, 1963. Delvaille concentrates on Larbaud's poetry, dwells on its cosmopolitan background, includes a number of uncollected texts of Larbaud, among them "Une Renaissance de la Poésie américaine."

JEAN-AUBRY, GEORGES. *Valery Larbaud, sa vie et son oeuvre d'après des documents inédits: La jeunesse (1881–1920)*. Monaco: Editions du Rocher, 1949. This is the most accurate and detailed account we possess of the first forty years of Larbaud's life. Its emphasis is almost exclusively biographical; there is little critical evaluation of the work, although Jean-Aubry, one of Larbaud's most intimate friends, was admirably acquainted with it.

KATZ, SHIRLEY. "The Theme of Solitude in the Fictional Works of Valery Larbaud." Diss., Harvard 1969.

McCARTHY, PATRICK. "Valery Larbaud, Critic of English Literature." Diss., Oxford 1968.

MILLIGAN, VINCENT. "Valery Larbaud, Anglicist." Diss., Columbia 1954.

ORNSTEIN, M. B. "Les Trois Visages de Valery Larbaud." Diss., Wisconsin 1971.

PASTUREAU, JEAN. *Enfance et adolescence dans l'oeuvre de Valery Larbaud*. Aix-en-Provence: La Pensée universitaire, 1964. Perceptive attempt to relate Larbaud's psychological problems as a child and an adolescent with *Enfantines* and *Fermina Márquez*.

RUGGIERO, ORTENSIA. *Valery Larbaud et l'Italie*. Nizet, 1963. A conscientious catalogue of Larbaud's Italian contacts, with few critical perceptions.

SEGONDS, JEAN-PHILIPPE. *L'Enfance Bourbonnaise de Valery Larbaud*. Moulins: Editions des Cahiers Bourbonnais. Well researched, strictly biographical account of Larbaud's early years, with little attempt to interpret their connection with his work.

WEISSMAN, FRIDA. *L'Exotisme de Valery Larbaud*. Préface de P. Jourda. Nizet, 1966. Conscientious but pedestrian account of Larbaud's travels, impressions in England, Italy, Spain, Portugal, Scandinavia and the use he made of them in his work.

YORK, RUTH BEATRICE. *Valery Larbaud's Works of the Imagination*. Diss., Columbia 1974. Sound critical analysis of *Barnabooth*, *Enfantines*, *Fermina Márquez*, *Amants, heureux amants*. . . .

ZOPPI, MARIA LUISA. *Valery Larbaud Traduttore d'all' Inglese*. Studi e ricerche, N.S. XXII. Universitá degli studi di Bologna, Facoltá di Lettere e Filosofia. Bologna: Zanichelli, 1969. Painstakingly researched. Little attention to translation theory or to Larbaud's qualities and defects as a translator.

3. Articles in Books and Periodicals

BRODIN, PIERRE. *Présences contemporaines*, vol. II. Nouvelles éditions Debresse, 1955, pp. 245–59. Readable general introduction.

CHAMPIGNY, ROBERT. "Spatial Anxiety in the Poems of Barnabooth." *Modern Language Quarterly* 16 (1955): 78–84. Sees Larbaud's poetry as "a transition between Symbolism and Surrealism."

CURTIUS, ERNST-ROBERT. *Französischer Geist in neuen Europa*. Stuttgart: Metzler (?), 1925, pp. 185–216. This excellent early study was translated into French and appeared in the May 15, 1925, number of *La Revue Nouvelle*. Curtius subsequently became a friend and correspondent of Larbaud.

CRÉMIEUX, BENJAMIN. *XXᵉ Siècle*. Gallimard, 1924. Crémieux predicts that Larbaud will be among the dozen or so French writers of his time who will survive.

FAUCHEREAU, SERGE. "Valery Larbaud et William Carlos Williams." *Critique* 290 (July 1971): 626–34. Although concentrating chiefly on Larbaud's relations with Williams, the article throws light on other contacts among American poets of the 1920s.

FAVRE, YVES-ALAIN. "Valery Larbaud: Structure et Signification de 'Jaune Bleu Blanc.'" *R.H.L.F.* 77 (September-October 1977): 812–21. *Jaune Bleau Blanc*: a "rhapsody of happiness" which, beneath its apparent diversity, is "cohérent et un."

FRIEDMAN, M. J. "The Creative Writer as Polyglot: Valery Larbaud and Samuel Beckett." *Transactions of the Wisconsin Academy of Sciences: Arts and Letters* 49 (1969): 229–36. The problems posed by multilingualism for the creative writer.

————. "Valery Larbaud: The Two Traditions of Eros." *Yale French Studies* 11 (number devoted to "Eros, Variations on an Old Theme"): 91–100. Contends that Larbaud in his life was torn "between a mild mysticism and an erotic impulse" while in his work he evolved in the direction of the latter.

JEUNE, SIMON. *De F. T. Grandorge à A. O. Barnabooth.* Didier, 1963, pp. 391–97. Traces the history of "American types" in the French novel and the French theater from 1861–1917. Lucid analysis of the character of Barnabooth.

LOBET, MARCEL. "La Confession par procuration: Le *Barnabooth* de Valery Larbaud," in *La Ceinture de feuillage.* Bruxelles, La Renaissance du Livre, 1966, pp. 171–84. "Larbaud examines his characters with such intensity that they become part of him—Barnabooth, finally, is Larbaud himself."

MACKWORTH, CECILY. *English Interludes: Mallarmé, Verlaine, Valery Larbaud in England.* London: Routledge, 1974. Sensitive analysis of the role of England in Larbaud's life and work.

MAY, GEORGES. "Valery Larbaud, Translator and Scholar." *Yale French Studies* 6 ("France and World Literature"): 81–90.

MORAND, PAUL. *Mon plaisir en littérature.* Gallimard, 1967, pp. 227–35. Charming evocation of a "globetrotter" by an equally famous one.

O'BRIEN, JUSTIN. *The Novel of Adolescence in France. The Study of a Literary Theme.* New York: Columbia University Press, 1937, pp. 142–45. *Fermína Márquez* seen as a new departure in the novel of adolescence.

————. "Larbaud, Complete Man of Letters," in *The French Literary Horizon.* New Brunswick, N.J.: Rutgers University Press, 1967, pp. 193–208. This essay, the earliest and one of the best general treatments of Larbaud in English first appeared in the July 1932 number of the *Symposium.*

————. "Lafcadio and Barnabooth: A Supposition," in *Contemporary French Literature.* New Brunswick, N.J.: Rutgers University Press, 1971, pp. 233–45. Establishes interesting connections between Gide and Larbaud.

ROY, CLAUDE. *Le Verbe aimer et autres essais.* Gallimard, 1969, 67–99. Insightful evocation of Larbaud's friendship with C. L. Philippe.

SIMON, J. K. "View from the Train: Butor, Gide, Larbaud." *French Review* 36 (December 1962): 161–66. The poetry of trains—and Laubaud's links with *le nouveau roman.*

————. "Larbaud, Barnabooth, et le Journal intime," *Cahiers de l'Association internationale des études françaises* 17 (1965): 151–68. Emphasizes that for Larbaud self-confession was always subordinated to the idea of literary creation and the journal of Barnabooth should not be interpreted as a transcription of his own.

————. "Valery Larbaud's *Fermina*," *Modern Language Notes* 83 (1968): 543–64. *Fermina*, "a poised little chef d'oeuvre," the precursor of many books on adolescence continues "to raise important problems of form and style."

THIÉBAUT, MARCEL. "Valery Larbaud." *Revue de Paris* 39th year, no. 24 (December 15, 1932): 822–58. This excellent general survey of Larbaud's work was reprinted in *Evasions littéraires* (1935): 50–103.

Index